D1291456

CHURCH, STATE
AND
PUBLIC JUSTICE

FIVE VIEWS

EDITED BY P. C. Kemeny

IVP Academic
An imprint of InterVarsity Press
Downers Grove, Illinois

InterVarsity Press
P.O. Box 1400, Downers Grove, IL 60515-1426
World Wide Web: www.ivpress.com
E-mail: email@ivpress.com

InterVarsity Press® is the book-publishing division of InterVarsity Christian Fellowship/USA®, a student movement active on campus at hundreds of universities, colleges and schools of nursing in the United States of America, and a member movement of the International Fellowship of Evangelical Students. For information about local and regional activities, write Public Relations Dept., InterVarsity Christian Fellowship/USA, 6400 Schroeder Rd., P.O. Box 7895, Madison, WI 53707-7895, or visit the IVCF website at <www.intervarsity.org>.

Scripture quotations, unless otherwise noted, are from the New Revised Standard Version of the Bible, copyright 1989 by the Division of Christian Education of the National Council of Churches of Christ in the USA. Used by permission. All rights reserved.

Design: Cindy Kiple

Images: church: MedioImages/Getty Images
scales: Sara Robinson/iStockphoto
Capitol building: Radius Images/Punchstock.com

ISBN 978-0-8308-2796-1

Printed in the United States of America ∞

Library of Congress Cataloging-in-Publication Data

Church, state and public justice: five views / edited by P. C.
Kemeny.
    p. cm.
Includes bibliographical references and index.
ISBN 978-0-8308-2796-1 (pbk.: alk. paper)
1. Church and state—United States. 2. Christianity and
justice—United States. I. Kemeny, Paul Charles.
  BR516.C497 2007
  261.70973—dc22

                                                              2007011613

| P | 20 | 19 | 18 | 17 | 16 | 15 | 14 | 13 | 12 | 11 | 10 | 9 | 8 | 7 | 6 | 5 | 4 | 3 | 2 | 1 |
| Y | 24 | 23 | 22 | 21 | 20 | 19 | 18 | 17 | 16 | 15 | 14 | 13 | 12 | 11 | 10 | 09 | 08 | 07 |

To my parents,

William A. Kemeny (1923-1994)

and Bessie Buckingham Kemeny

Contents

Acknowledgments 9

INTRODUCTION
P. C. Kemeny 11

1 LIFE ON THE BORDER: A CATHOLIC PERSPECTIVE
Clarke E. Cochran 39

    Classical Separation Response 67

    Principled Pluralist Response. 72

    Anabaptist Response 74

    Social Justice Response 76

2 THE CLASSICAL SEPARATION PERSPECTIVE
Derek H. Davis 81

    Catholic Response 114

    Principled Pluralist Response. 117

    Anabaptist Response 121

    Social Justice Response 123

3 THE PRINCIPLED PLURALIST PERSPECTIVE
Corwin Smidt 127

    Catholic Response 154

    Classical Separation Response 157

    Anabaptist Response 162

    Social Justice Response 164

4   THE ANABAPTIST PERSPECTIVE
Ronald J. Sider   169

     Catholic Response   198

     Classical Separation Response   202

     Principled Pluralist Response.   207

     Social Justice Response   210

5   THE SOCIAL JUSTICE PERSPECTIVE
J. Philip Wogaman   215

     Catholic Response   238

     Classical Separation Response   241

     Principled Pluralist Response.   245

     Anabaptist Response   248

Contributors   249

Index of Names.   253

Acknowledgments

Perhaps even more gratifying than finally seeing this book in print is the opportunity to thank publicly those involved in the project as well as several friends and colleagues. I want to thank Clarke Cochran, Derek Davis, Corwin Smidt, Ron Sider and Phil Wogaman for their grace and patience throughout this project. I am also thankful for Gary Deddo's advice at key junctures in the life of this work as well as his patience throughout the publication process.

Matt Beatty, Bill Birmingham, Mike Coulter, Gil Harp, Gary Scott Smith and Garey Spradley read my introductory essay carefully and offered invaluable constructive criticisms of it. I am fortunate to have them as colleagues and blessed to call them friends. Rick Downs, Amy Good and Lorraine Krall likewise provided very helpful suggestions and revisions at different stages in the project. My student assistants, Lindsay Karr and Ben Wetzel, proofread the chapters several times and offered numerous helpful suggestions. I also want to express my gratitude to the students who took my Humanities 201 course, "Civilization and the Speculative Mind," in the spring of 2006. They not only read the introductory chapter carefully but also provided me with lots of constructive feedback.

I owe the most to my wife, Betsy, and our children, Helen and Will. Finally, I want to express my eternal gratitude to my late father, William A. Kemeny, and my mother, Bessie Buckingham Kemeny. It is to them that I dedicate this book.

Introduction

More than twenty years ago Richard John Neuhaus lamented that American civic life eliminated religious voices. "The naked public square," he wrote, "is the result of political doctrine and practice that would exclude religion and religiously grounded values from the conduct of public business."[1] In the past twenty years, the "naked public square" has been transformed into a rather noisy place. Controversies over the role of religion in American public life rack civil discourse. The debate over President George W. Bush's 2001 faith-based initiative is a case in point. Slightly more than a week after he took office, Bush signed two executive orders, one creating the White House Office of Faith-Based and Community Initiatives, and the other establishing ancillary offices inside several government departments.[2] Bush's faith-based initiative is a significant expansion of the Charitable Choice amendment that President William J. Clinton had signed into law with the Personal Responsibility and Work Opportunity Reconciliation Act in 1996. This 1996 provision made it easier for churches and other faith-based social service organizations to receive government funds. Federal support for religiously oriented social service agencies was nothing new: the government often worked with religious agencies to provide social services to the needy.[3] Bush's faith-based initiative enlarged the op-

---

[1]Richard John Neuhaus, *The Naked Public Square: Religion and Democracy in America,* 2nd ed. (Grand Rapids: Eerdmans, 1984), p. ix.

[2]White House Office of Faith-Based and Community Initiatives, "Executive Order 13199," January 29, 2001, <www.whitehouse.gov/news/releases/2001/01/20010129-2.html> (accessed April 3, 2006); "Executive Order 13198," January 29, 2001 <www.whitehouse.gov/news/releases/2001/01/20010129-3.html> (accessed April 3, 2006). A version of Bush's faith-based initiative passed the House of Representatives in July 2001. In the Senate, another version of the faith-based initiative, the Charity, Aid, Recovery, and Empowerment Act of 2002 (or the CARE Act), died. In December 2002 President Bush implemented many of the controversial provisions of the CARE Act. In April 2003 the Senate passed a version of the CARE Act, but as of March 2005 the House has yet to act.

[3]For example, in the fiscal year before President Clinton's welfare reform bill went into effect, Catholic Charities U.S.A. received $1.3 billion (or 64 percent) of its income from various government agencies (Amy Black, Douglas L. Koopman and David K. Ryden, *Of Little Faith: The Politics of George W. Bush's Faith-Based Initiatives* [Washington, D.C.: Georgetown University Press, 2004], p. 21).

portunity for federal funding by potentially providing as much as eight billion dollars in funding and forging even closer partnerships between government and service agencies, including religious ones. In March of 2001, John DiIulio Jr., director of the White House Faith-Based and Community Initiatives, said, "Compassionate conservatism warmly welcomes godly people back into the public square while respecting and upholding, without fail, our wise, benevolent constitutional traditions governing church, state, and civic pluralism."[4]

Not everyone, however, welcomes the return of religion to the public square. Critics fear that the faith-based initiative will undermine religious liberty, sanction federally funded religious discrimination in hiring, and ultimately subvert the First Amendment. Congressman Robert C. Scott (D-VA) complained that Bush's plan "represents a fundamental assault on our civil rights."[5] To Barry Lynn, executive director of Americans United for Separation of Church and State, the faith-based initiative is "a serious assault on the wall of separation between church and state."[6] Its advocates, however, refute the charges that the faith-based initiative sanctions religious discrimination or violates the First Amendment. In fact, they contend that the faith-based initiative eliminates unjust discrimination against religious organizations. James Skillen, executive director of the Center for Public Justice, argues that opponents want

> to check everyone at the entrance gate to make sure that they put their distinctive faiths in a private bag and agree to participate in any publicly funded program only on a so-called "secular" basis. Only after this most egregious form of civic discrimination has been exercised do Barry Lynn and Representative Scott want to uphold equal treatment and nondiscrimination of all "secular" citizens.

A level public playing field, Skillen insists, is not one "open only to those with a 'secular' identification badge and surrounded by a fence behind which self-professed religious citizens are permitted only to watch the game."[7] Amy

---

[4]John J. DiIulio Jr., "Compassion 'In Truth and Action': How Sacred and Secular Places Serve Civil Purposes, and What Washington Should—and Should Not—Do to Help," March 7, 2001 <www.whitehouse.gov/news/releases/2001/03/20010307-11.html> (accessed April 3, 2006).

[5]Robert C. Scott, "Bush's Faith-Based Action Plan Contains Civil Rights Poison Pill" <www.house.gov/scott/legislative/charitable_choice/rcs_op_ed_01_30_01.html> (accessed April 3, 2006).

[6]Barry W. Lynn, "Pro: Is Bush Violating the Separation of Church and State?" *The Wichita Eagle,* January 7, 2003 <www.kansas.com/mld/eagle/news/editorial/4886899.htm> (accessed February 5, 2005).

[7]James Skillen, quoted in "The Growing Impact of Government Partnerships with Faith-Based Organizations: Research Findings from the States" (a press conference cosponsored by the Hudson Institute and the Center for Public Justice at the National Press Club), April 24, 2002, p. 26.

Sherman, senior fellow at the Hudson Institute, contends that some "strict church-state separationists act as though religion is somehow more toxic to poor, vulnerable people than drugs or bullets."[8] The debate over the proper role of religion in American public life has made the public square very noisy.

The origins of the debate among Americans regarding the faith-based initiative and other controversies, such as abortion, physician-assisted suicide, same-sex marriages and embryonic stem-cell research, can be traced back to four interrelated issues. The debate centers around the mission of the church (and other faith communities), the purpose of the state, the proper relationship between the two and whether the church or the state should play the primary role in redressing social ills. Such complex issues do not easily lend themselves to being solved by bumper stickers, sound bites or op-ed pieces.

One purpose of this volume is simply to lay out a taxonomy of positions that different Christian traditions hold about the relationship between church and state and public justice. Given the prevalence of ignorance and misunderstanding, this is a worthwhile goal in and of itself. This book, however, also seeks to encourage a constructive dialogue among at least some of the major Christian traditions in America about a topic that more often divides than unites thoughtful Christians.

As the title suggests, this volume consists of essays by representatives of five major Christian traditions on the question of the church, state and public justice. Each contributor is a distinguished scholar who has written extensively on this subject. J. Philip Wogaman, former professor of Christian ethics and dean at Wesley Theological Seminary in Washington, D.C., and retired pastor of the Foundry United Methodist Church in D.C., represents the traditional mainline Protestant social justice perspective. Derek H. Davis, former director of the J. M. Dawson Center of Church-State Studies at Baylor University and now dean of the college of humanities at the University of Mary Hardin-Baylor, presents the classical separationist position held by many Baptists. Corwin Smidt, the director of the Paul Henry Institute at Calvin College, outlines the principled pluralist position of the neo-Kuyperian tradition. Ronald J. Sider, president of Evangelicals for Social Action and professor at Palmer Theological Seminary, represents the evangelical Anabaptist perspective. Clarke E. Cochran, professor of political science at Texas Tech University, articulates the American Catholic position.

---

[8]Amy Sherman, "Integrating Religious Faith in Public Life Without Trivializing It," *Philanthropy* (November-December 2002) <www.hudson.org/index.cfm?fuseaction=publication_details&id=2121> (accessed April 3, 2006).

Each of the authors addresses several questions: What is the mission of the church? What is the purpose of the state? What is the proper relationship between the two? How should the church and state seek to resolve social injustice? Since each contributor explains his tradition's answers to these questions, the biblical witness to these topics will not be discussed in this introduction. Each chapter is followed by brief responses from the other four authors. While succinctly summarizing areas of agreement, each response concentrates on its significant points of disagreement. This focus on areas of disagreement should not obscure their major points of agreement.

Although these five perspectives share a number of areas of agreement, readers should be alert to subtle and sometimes significant areas of disagreement. To be sure, each contributor draws on biblical, theological and historical sources. But readers should pay attention to the starting point of each argument as well as the different ways each perspective draws on the Bible, theology and history to configure its particular arguments. For instance, the principled pluralist perspective stresses the cultural mandate in a way that is more pronounced than the classical separationist position. Commitments to certain key principles, such as the separation of church and state, are advocated by each author. Yet the exact meanings of those key ideas often get amplified in ways that are very different. While brief, the essays provide a substantive summary of each tradition's perspective on the topic. The footnotes not only provide ample documentation but also direction for interested readers to pursue particular observations in each discussion.

Several other qualifications are in order. First, Professor Cochran has a very daunting challenge because he is speaking for a tradition that includes a very wide range of convictions on the topic of social justice. American Catholicism is not a monolith. In fact, American Catholicism may hold as widely divergent positions on this topic as its Protestant counterpart. Accordingly, he articulates something of a mainstream Catholic position, while recognizing the diversity of Catholic positions.

Second, a number of Christian traditions, such as the Lutherans, who have well-articulated views on social justice, are not included in this work.[9] Their absence should not be understood to suggest that the overlooked traditions are marginal or unimportant. They are not. The unfortunate reality of space limitations simply precludes their participation in this work.

Finally, the term *social justice* is used today in a number of different ways. In its

---

[9]For a Lutheran perspective, see John R. Stumme and Robert W. Tuttle, eds., *Church and State: Lutheran Perspectives* (Minneapolis: Fortress, 2003).

broadest form it refers to the creation of a civil and fair social order. Yet the term can have more specific connotations that have to do with both distributive justice (or a just distribution of the benefits and burdens of society), which ensures that people are treated equitably in the distribution of benefits, and regulative justice, which protects the natural rights of citizens.[10] While the introduction uses the term in its looser form, the individual authors define the term for themselves.

The remainder of the introduction will attempt to set the larger historical context for the essays that follow. Today, many Christians are engaged in a variety of different forms of social activism, ranging from collecting canned goods at church for a local food pantry to campaigning for a candidate for U.S. Senate. Christians often draw inspiration from American history to bolster their efforts to reform some troubling aspect of American society. The abolitionist movement may be the most frequently cited example of a successful social reform movement inspired by Christian convictions. Although the abolitionist crusade certainly achieved its principle goal—the abolition of slavery—the movement divided Christians in many ways. The history of the abolitionist movement should not only encourage Christians but also give them reason to pause and reflect upon why it was so controversial. The introduction will briefly review the history of the abolitionist movement and show that Christians have often disagreed over the mission of the church, the purpose of the state and the proper role of each in working toward greater justice in American public life. Contemporary discussions about church, state and public justice, moreover, do not take place in a historical vacuum even if participants in the discussion are oblivious to the historical record and how it shapes contemporary realities. Americans often suffer from a case of historical amnesia. If that is true, many contemporary Christians, especially evangelicals, may have an acute case. In order to help readers better understand the different perspectives that Christians take on these issues, the introduction will attempt to situate them within the larger history of Christianity in American culture. Finally, the introduction will attempt to place the discussion over church, state and public justice in its contemporary context. Discussions today take place in a radically different context than they did 60 or 160 years ago. Today, the very possibility of a public religion is being questioned in a way that is fundamentally different than in the past. Failure to recognize the changes in the contemporary American religious landscape can undermine constructive

---

[10]For an excellent introduction to this discussion, see the essay "Christianity and Social Justice" by Nicholas Wolterstorff and responses by Ronald Nash, Ralph McInerny and Stanley Hauerwas in *Christian Scholar's Review* 37 (1987): 211-48.

discussions. Ignoring these contemporary realities probably explains why debates over church, state and public justice frequently generate more heat than light.

The Nineteenth-Century Abolitionist Movement: A Case Study in the History of Christian Social Reform

Political theorist Michael Walzer notes that the English Puritans believed that "the saints were responsible for the world—as medieval men were not—and responsible above all for its continual reformation. Their enthusiastic and purposive activity were part of their religious life, not something distinct and separate."[11] For nearly four centuries, many American Christians have assumed that the Christian faith has practical implications for reforming society. Christian social activism of the nineteenth century provides an excellent case study. According to the historian Robert T. Handy, throughout the nineteenth century Christians aspired to create a "Christian society" by evangelism, moral persuasion and, when necessary, legal coercion.[12] Political commitments, to be sure, also played a significant role in the Protestant rationale for social reform. Unlike the Jeffersonian tradition that more fully separated religion and public life, the Whig-Republican tradition of the nineteenth century stressed self-discipline, rational order and social responsibility in a way that dovetailed nicely with revivalistic Protestantism.[13] "Otherworldly convictions," the historian Timothy L. Smith observes, "imparted a sacred potency" to evangelical Protestant crusades "to sanctify the national culture and convert the world to Christian principles."[14]

An excellent historical example of Protestant efforts to "Christianize" America, as Handy puts it, is the nineteenth-century abolitionist movement. In 1787 the Presbyterian Church passed overtures condemning slavery and recommending that all churches "do every thing in their power consistent with the rights of civil Society to promote the abolition of Slavery."[15] The 1818

---

[11]Michael Walzer, *The Revolution of the Saints: A Study in the Origins of Radical Politics* (Cambridge, Mass.: Harvard University Press, 1965), p. 12.

[12]Robert T. Handy, *A Christian America: Protestant Hopes and Historical Realities*, 2nd ed. (New York: Oxford University Press, 2002), pp. 24-56.

[13]D. G. Hart, "Mainstream Protestantism, 'Conservative' Religion, and Civic Society," *Religion Returns to the Public Square: Faith and Policy in America*, ed. Hugh Heclo and Wilfred M. McClay (Baltimore: Woodrow Wilson Center and Johns Hopkins University Press, 2003), pp. 199-203.

[14]Timothy L. Smith, *Revivalism and Social Reform: American Protestantism on the Eve of the Civil War* (1957; reprint, Baltimore: Johns Hopkins University Press, 1980), p. 44.

[15]*Minutes of the Presbyterian Church in America, 1706-1788,* ed. Guy S. Klett (Philadelphia: Presbyterian Historical Society, 1976), p. 627.

General Assembly of the Presbyterian Church passed a more pointed resolution declaring that

> the voluntary enslaving of one part of the human race by another, as a gross violation of the most precious and sacred rights of human nature. . . . [I]t is manifestly the duty of all Christians who enjoy the light of the present day, . . . to correct the errors of former times, and as speedily as possible to efface this blot on our holy religion, and to obtain the complete abolition of slavery throughout Christendom, and if possible throughout the world.[16]

Leonard Bacon, antislavery activist and pastor of the prestigious First (Congregationalist) Church in New Haven, echoed this sentiment almost thirty years later when he wrote, "If that form of government, that system of social order is not wrong—if those laws of the southern states, by virtue of which slavery exists there and is what it is, are not wrong—nothing is wrong."[17] By modeling themselves on the biblical prophets, one historian of the antislavery movement observed, "abolitionists began a campaign to save the churches from divine retribution by rousing them from their toleration of the 'sum of all villainies.' "[18]

Although abolition was the most successful, and also the most violent, reform movement of the nineteenth century, Christians engaged in many others. Through moral persuasion, financial assistance and legislation, they attempted to preserve the sanctity of the sabbath, curb the spread of licentious literature, stop the ill-treatment of Native Americans, protect women and especially children from harsh working conditions, alleviate poverty, build playgrounds for urban children, secure the right of women to vote in national elections, and stamp out intemperance.

The "Golden Age" Fallacy

Although social activism often emerged from Christian belief, there was no "golden age" when enlightened and benevolent Christians worked together harmoniously to resolve social ills. In fact, each of these efforts to reform nineteenth-century American society was hotly contested. The abolitionist

---

[16]Presbyterian Church, United States of America, *Extracts from the Minutes of the General Assembly, of the Presbyterian Church, in the United States of America, 1818* (Philadelphia: Thomas and William Bradford, 1818), pp. 28-29.

[17]Leonard Bacon, *Slavery Discussed in Occasional Essays from 1833 to 1846* (New York: Baker & Scribner, 1846), p. x.

[18]John R. McKivigan, *The War Against Proslavery Religion: Abolitionism and the Northern Churches, 1830-1865* (Ithaca, N.Y.: Cornell University Press, 1984), p. 14. See also Douglas M. Strong, *Perfectionist Politics: Abolitionism and the Religious Tensions of American Democracy* (Syracuse, N.Y.: Syracuse University Press, 1999).

movement again provides a case study. While he adamantly opposed slavery, Bacon favored colonization and spent as much energy combating the radical abolitionists and their demands for immediate emancipation as he spent combating proslavery Southerners and anti-reform Northerners.[19] Although Presbyterians unequivocally condemned slavery in 1818, over the next four decades they openly debated whether or not the Bible actually condemned slavery and whether the church could legitimately address the issue. Slavery played a critical role in the 1837-1838 schism between pro-revivalist New School Presbyterians and their more confessionalist Old School opponents, with the former typically supporting immediate abolition and the latter either defending slavery or gradual emancipation. By 1861 the Old School and New School Presbyterians had divided along sectional lines. The Presbyterian Church that had existed as one denomination in 1836 had become four separate ones. Controversial New School Presbyterian minister Albert Barnes declared in 1857 that the "principles of the New Testament" would "abolish slavery." Its continued existence, he concluded, "presents one of the most formidable obstacles to the extension of pure Christianity in our land."[20] Many Old School Presbyterians, such as Princeton's Charles Hodge, who had once argued that "slavery is not a sin," were driven toward abolition by Southerners' increasingly vehement defense of slavery.[21] According to James Henley Thornwell, the leading Old School Southern Presbyterian theologian, slavery was neither a sin nor a concern of the church. After Southerners withdrew from the Presbyterian Church in 1861, he wrote that

> in our ecclesiastical capacity, we are neither the friends nor the foes of slavery, . . . we have no commission either to propagate it or abolish it. The policy of its existence or non-existence is a question which exclusively belongs to the State. We have no right, as a Church, to enjoy it as a duty, or to condemn it as a sin.[22]

---

[19]Hugh Davis, *Leonard Bacon: New England Reformer and Antislavery Moderate* (Baton Rouge: Louisiana State University Press, 1998), pp. 42-91.

[20]Albert Barnes, *The Church and Slavery* (Philadelphia: Parry & McMillan, 1857), pp. 42, 185.

[21]Charles Hodge, "Slavery," *Princeton Review* 7 (1836): 277. On Hodge's changing views of slavery, see Mark A. Noll, *America's God: From Jonathan Edwards to Abraham Lincoln* (New York: Oxford University Press, 2002), pp. 386-401, 417-21; Allen C. Guelzo, "Charles Hodge's Antislavery Movement," *Charles Hodge Revisited: A Critical Appraisal of His Life and Work*, ed. John W. Stewart and James H. Moorhead (Grand Rapids: Eerdmans, 2002), pp. 299-325.

[22]James Henley Thornwell, "Address of the General Assembly of the Presbyterian Church in the Confederate States of America to All the Churches of Jesus Christ Throughout the Earth" (Augusta, Ga.: General Assembly, 1861), p. 10. Writing shortly after the Civil War, one prominent Northern Old School Presbyterian minister described Thornwell's position as a "new and startling doctrine, contrary to the whole current of Presbyterian usage and tradition" (Samuel Miller, "Historical Review of the Church (Old School Branch)," *Presbyterian Reunion: A Memorial Volume, 1837-1871* [New York: De Witt C. Lent, 1870], p. 28).

Like Presbyterians, the nation's two largest Protestant denominations, Methodists and Baptists, divided over slavery in 1844 and 1845, respectively.

Even though both North and South "read the same Bible," as Abraham Lincoln observed in his Second Inaugural Address, and "read it in the same way," as the historian Mark A. Noll later noted, American Christians responded to the problem of the Bible and slavery in four different ways. Some argued that because the Bible sanctioned slavery, Christians should accept it out of respect for the Bible's authority. At the other extreme, some agreed that the Bible sanctioned slavery but concluded that they should abandon the Bible (and the Christian faith) in order to attack slavery. A third position held that the Bible permitted a certain form of slavery, but it did not justify the existence of slavery that was practiced in the United States. The final response differentiated between the letter of the Bible, which seemed to allow slavery, and the spirit of the Bible, which condemned the practice.[23] Given this divergence of opinion, Christians, not surprisingly, responded to the "peculiar institution" in several different ways. Radical abolitionists demanded its immediate end. Others defended the practice of slavery. Variations, moreover, existed within each of these positions. Some radical abolitionists, for instance, approved of the overthrow of slavery through military conflict, while other radicals denounced violence and hoped to liberate slaves through pacifist means. In addition to their widely varying attitudes regarding slavery during the nineteenth century, Christians took opposing positions on Sunday mail delivery, temperance, the treatment of native Americans, and American colonization.[24] In short, Christians have often disagreed about what constitutes genuine social injustice. Even when they agreed that certain practices, such as intemperance, were morally wrong, they were divided over whether or not it was the responsibility of the Christian community, the state or both to reform American society.

---

[23]Mark A. Noll, "The Bible and Slavery," *Religion and the American Civil War*, ed. Randall M. Miller, Harry S. Stout and Charles Reagan Wilson (New York: Oxford University Press, 1998), pp. 43-73. On the biblical justification for slavery, see Stephen R. Haynes, *Noah's Curse: The Biblical Justification of American Slavery* (New York: Oxford University Press, 2002).

[24]The literature on these topics include K. Austin Kerr, *Organized for Prohibition: A New History of the Anti-Saloon League* (New Haven, Conn.: Yale University Press, 1985); Alison M. Parker, *Purifying America: Women, Cultural Reform, and Pro-Censorship Activism, 1873-1933* (Urbana: University of Illinois Press, 1997); Gaines M. Foster, *Moral Reconstruction: Christian Lobbyists and the Federal Legislation of Morality, 1865-1920* (Chapel Hill: University of North Carolina Press, 2002); Wayne E. Fuller, *Morality and the Mail in Nineteenth-Century America* (Urbana: University of Illinois Press, 2003); Handy, *Christian America*, pp. 24-158.

The New Historical Context

While debates among Christians over what is a legitimate social justice concern of the church and the state are clearly not novel, what is new is the context in which contemporary debates are taking place. One cannot make complete sense of the heated controversies that abortion, same-sex marriages or physician-assisted suicide typically generate without situating them within their larger historical framework. Although each of the contributors represents a different Christian tradition's understanding of the church's role in American culture, they all share to some degree this common Christian heritage. Students of religion and American culture, moreover, might find it helpful to have some historical background knowledge. In sum, a brief historical overview of the changing role of Christianity in American public life can shed light on the dramatic changes in the contemporary context in which these debates currently are taking place. Religion in American culture has passed through three stages: from Protestantism as the established church of most colonies to Protestantism as the de facto national religion to a pluralistic, post-Protestant America.[25]

Protestantism as the Established Religion

From the time the first Europeans established permanent settlements in the New World until the First Amendment went into effect in 1791, Protestant Christianity was the established religion in several of the American colonies (and later, states). This arrangement had been the accepted pattern of church-state relations in the West for more than a millennium. From Congregationalism in New England to Anglicanism in the South, Protestant Christianity served as the official religion in the colonies. Rhode Island and Pennsylvania were the only exceptions. During the seventeenth century several colonies supported ministers with "church taxes." A number of colonies also required citizens to affirm religious oaths to hold public office. Those colonies with established churches, moreover, attempted to curb religious competition. Several factors converged that made the path to the First Amendment very appealing to many orthodox Christians, free-thinkers and deists. In addition to the impact of the 1689 Act of Toleration passed by Parliament, which guaranteed religious freedom to trinitarian Protestant dissenters, increasing immigration by individuals who were not Congregationalists or Anglicans chal-

---

[25]For a general overview of Protestantism's relationship to American culture, see William R. Hutchison, *Religious Pluralism in America: The Contentious History of a Founding Ideal* (New Haven, Conn.: Yale University Press, 2003); and Handy, *Christian America*.

lenged the dominance of the established church in certain colonies. Moreover, certain Enlightenment ideas about religious toleration and the nature of the state made the rationale supporting the established churches less tenable. Finally, and perhaps most importantly, the First Great Awakening of the 1740s helped to weaken the dominance of Congregationalists in New England and Anglicans in the South. As a result, the framers of the Constitution and Bill of Rights recognized that religious freedom and the separation of church and state were necessary. The First Amendment stipulated that "Congress shall make no law respecting an establishment of religion, or prohibiting the free exercise thereof," guaranteeing that the federal government would not be entangled with the institutions of religion by establishing a national church. Not everyone eagerly embraced disestablishment. In certain New England states, conventional patterns of church-state relations continued to persist well into the nineteenth century. Not until 1833 did Massachusetts become the final state to abolish the last traces of establishment when it agreed not to collect taxes on behalf of Congregationalist churches.[26]

Protestantism as the De Facto National Religion

While the First Amendment guaranteed religious freedom and prohibited the establishment of a national church, Protestant Christianity functioned as the de facto national religion from 1791 well into the twentieth century. The Second Great Awakening of the 1830s and 1840s not only converted thousands to evangelical Christianity but also inspired efforts to "Christianize" American society. The postmillennial eschatology of most revivalists, moreover, heightened expectations that social reform could hasten the arrival of the thousand-year kingdom of God on earth. As Handy puts it, "The Christian character of

---

[26]Maryland was originally chartered as an English Catholic colony in 1632, but after the Glorious Revolution of 1688, Parliament made Anglicanism the colony's established church. On the role of religion at the nation's founding, the First Amendment and the history of its interpretation, see Derek H. Davis, *Religion and the Continental Congress, 1774-1789* (New York: Oxford University Press, 2000); Thomas J. Curry, *The First Freedoms: Church and State in America to the Passage of the First Amendment* (New York: Oxford University Press, 1986); Mark A. Noll, Nathan O. Hatch and George M. Marsden, *The Search for Christian America,* rev. ed. (Colorado Springs: Helmers & Howard, 1989), pp. 1-124; John M. Murrin, "Religion and Politics in America from the First Settlements to the Civil War," in *Religion and American Politics,* ed. Mark A. Noll (New York: Oxford University Press, 1986), pp. 19-43; Daniel L. Dreisbach, *Thomas Jefferson and the Wall of Separation Between Church and State* (New York: New York University Press, 2002); Philip Hamburger, *Separation of Church and State* (Cambridge, Mass.: Harvard University Press, 2002); and John C. West Jr., *The Politics of Revelation and Reason: Religion and Civil Life in the New Nation* (Lawrence: University Press of Kansas, 1996).

the nation was to be maintained by voluntary means since the patterns of establishment had proved to be unacceptable and inadequate."[27] In a free society, evangelicals turned to voluntary societies to extend the influence of Protestant Christianity throughout the nation. Hundreds of national and thousands of local voluntary organizations, such as the American Bible Society, Women's Christian Temperance Union, the New York Society for the Suppression of Vice, and Hull House, attempted to alleviate a particular social ill, such as biblical illiteracy, intemperance, obscene literature and poverty. While immigration more than doubled the number of Catholics in America during the 1850s, Protestants not only formed a clear majority but more importantly dominated the key culture-shaping institutions of nineteenth-century American society, such as higher education.[28] Protestant ideals provided a unifying framework and common moral discourse for American public life. As historian Winthrop Hudson described America in 1865, "The ideals, convictions, the language, the customs, the institutions of society were so shot through with Christian presuppositions that the culture itself nurtured and nourished the Christian faith."[29]

The "Second Disestablishment"

This informal Protestant dominance of American public life experienced a "second disestablishment" in the middle of the twentieth century.[30] Evidence of the collapse of Protestant cultural hegemony began in the 1920s and climaxed in the 1960s with the election of the first Roman Catholic president, John F. Kennedy, which symbolically signaled the end of Protestantism's informal dominance over American culture. The origins of the collapse reside in the late nineteenth century. External forces—a dramatic increase in non-Protestant immigrants, especially from non–English-speaking, predominately Roman Catholic countries, and the maturation of American Judaism and Eastern Orthodox traditions—impinged upon Protestant dominance. At the same time

---

[27]Handy, *Christian America*, p. 27.

[28]Roger Finke and Rodney Stark, *The Churching of America, 1776-1990: Winners and Losers in Our Religious Economy* (New Brunswick, N.J.: Rutgers University Press, 1997), pp. 110-15; George M. Marsden, *The Soul of the University: From Protestant Establishment to Established Nonbelief* (New York: Oxford University Press, 1994), pp. 29-96.

[29]Winthrop Hudson, *The Great Tradition of the American Churches* (New York: Harper & Brothers, 1953), p. 108.

[30]Robert T. Handy, *Undermined Establishment: Church-State Relations in America, 1880-1920* (Princeton, N.J.: Princeton University Press, 1991). On the mainline Protestant establishment during the mid-twentieth century, see William R. Hutchison, ed., *Between the Times: The Travail of the Protestant Establishment in America, 1900-1960* (Cambridge: Cambridge University Press, 1989).

the fundamentalist-modernist theological controversies, the growth of Pente-costal and Holiness churches and the divisions over how best to respond to the complexities of urban-industrial life fractured the mainline Protestant estab-lishment from within. In the face of late-nineteenth-century secular challenges to the meaning and authority of the Bible, liberal Protestants insisted that tra-ditional theological ideas conform to modernity; stressed divine immanence, especially God's involvement in the inexorable progress of history; and ex-pressed a deep faith in humanity's ability to create a society that would repli-cate the kingdom of God.[31] By contrast, fundamentalists militantly opposed modernity in both the church and culture.[32] As the early twentieth century be-gan, fissures appeared in the partnership between evangelism and social ac-tion as many liberal Protestants focused attention on efforts to reform Ameri-can society while more conservative Protestants began to concentrate solely on evangelism. While most early nineteenth-century Protestants, especially in the North, had considered evangelism and social action partners in the effort to "Christianize" America, by the second decade of the twentieth century a "great divorce" had occurred.[33] In their efforts to articulate a more modern ver-sion of Christianity, some liberal Protestants began to espouse ideas about so-cial reform that would develop into a distinct Social Gospel in the early twen-tieth century.[34] Likewise, some late-nineteenth-century conservatives, in accordance with their premillennial eschatology, tended to trivialize social re-form. By the second decade of the twentieth century these different propensi-ties had developed into two distinct understandings of Christianity. Social Gospelers chastised fundamentalists for neglecting social reform. As Walter Rauschenbusch, the leading proponent of the Social Gospel, put it in 1917:

> The individualistic gospel has taught us to see the sinfulness of every human heart and has inspired us with faith in the willingness and power of God to save every human soul that comes to him. But it has not given us an adequate under-

---

[31]William R. Hutchison, *The Modernist Impulse in American Protestantism* (Cambridge, Mass.: Harvard University Press, 1976).

[32]George M. Marsden, *Fundamentalism and American Culture: The Shaping of Twentieth Century Evangelicalism, 1870-1925* (New York: Oxford University Press, 1980).

[33]Gary Scott Smith, *The Search for Social Salvation and America, 1880-1925* (Lanham, Md.: Lex-ington Books, 2000); Norris Magnuson, *Salvation in the Slums: Evangelical Social Work, 1865-1920* (Grand Rapids: Baker, 1977); Donald W. Dayton, *Discovering an Evangelical Heritage* (New York: Harper & Row, 1976).

[34]On the rise of the Social Gospel, see Ronald C. White Jr. and C. Howard Hopkins, *The Social Gospel: Religion and Reform in Changing America* (Philadelphia: Temple University Press, 1976); and Charles Howard Hopkins, *The Rise of the Social Gospel in American Protestantism, 1865-1915* (New Haven, Conn.: Yale University Press, 1940).

standing of the sinfulness of the social order and its share in the sins of all individuals within it.[35]

William Bell Riley, a leader of the fundamentalist movement, complained that
liberals had reduced the gospel to a form of "social service Christianity."[36]
With one very notable exception, prohibition, fundamentalists abandoned social reform in reaction to the modernist impulse in liberal Protestantism. While
fissures had begun to appear between conservative and liberal Protestants in
the late nineteenth century, it would be a mistake to read the fundamentalist-
modernist controversies of the 1910s and 1920s back into the nineteenth
century. Although significant theological differences existed between conservatives and liberals in the final decades of the nineteenth century, these disagreements had not led to ecclesiastical schism. Moreover, when it came to
issues of evangelism and social reform, the conservative-liberal disagreements
over theology did not fall out neatly along pro-evangelism or pro-social reform
lines. Not all late-nineteenth-century liberals or, for that matter, twentieth-
century modernists ignored evangelism and advocated the Social Gospel.
Likewise, not all nineteenth-century conservatives disregarded social reform.
By the early twentieth century, however, a great divorce had occurred. Fundamentalists continued to evangelize, but they withdrew from active engagement in American public life for much of the twentieth century.

While fundamentalists retreated, mainline Protestant mores, which fundamentalists shared despite their theological differences, continued to dominate
American public life during the first five decades of the twentieth century. Important changes, however, were taking place in American culture that would
quickly displace Protestant cultural hegemony during the 1960s. Perhaps the
most significant developments before the 1960s were the important Supreme
Court decisions that helped codify the "second disestablishment." In its 1940
decision *Cantwell v. Connecticut,* the Supreme Court explicitly applied the free-
exercise clause of the First Amendment to the states when it determined that a
Jehovah's Witness had the right to distribute religious literature for donations
without a permit granted from the state of Connecticut. Seven years later in
Everson v. Board of Education of Ewing Township, the Court applied the dis-

---

[35]Walter Rauschenbusch, *A Theology for the Social Gospel* (1917; reprint, Nashville: Abingdon
  1978), p. 5. On Rauschenbusch, see Christopher H. Evans, *The Kingdom Is Always Coming: A
  Life of Walter Rauschenbusch* (Grand Rapids: Eerdmans, 2004).
[36]William Bell Riley, "The Great Commission," in *God Hath Spoken* (Philadelphia: Bible Conference Committee, 1919), quoted in Robert D. Linder, "The Resurgence of Evangelical Social Concern," in *The Evangelicals: What They Believe, Who They Are, Where They Are Changing,*
  ed. David Wells and John Woodbridge (New York: Abingdon, 1975), p. 198.

establishment clause to the states when it concluded that the state of New Jersey could provide transportation to students attending parochial schools because, the justices reasoned, the state could not exclude children from receiving the benefits of public welfare legislation because of their faith. Nevertheless, Supreme Court justice Hugo Black, writing on behalf of the slim majority of five, supported this decision by invoking Thomas Jefferson's famous metaphor regarding the separation of church and state. Black wrote, "The First Amendment has erected a wall between church and state. That wall must be kept high and impregnable. We could not approve the slightest breach."[37] The trend toward a more strictly separatist interpretation of the First Amendment produced two critical decisions that helped institutionalize the "second disestablishment" in public education. In *Engel v. Vitale* the court rejected as unconstitutional a 1962 prayer written by the New York State Board of Regents for use in schools because it violated the establishment clause. The following year in *Abington Township School District v. Schempp* the court invalidated a Pennsylvania law requiring Bible reading because it also violated the establishment clause.[38]

The End of the Protestant Establishment in the 1960s

These critical Supreme Court decisions came at a time when new forces were dramatically changing the face of religion in American culture. The Hart-Celler Immigration Law of 1965 reopened the nation's doors to people from Asia and other non-European nations who had been excluded by the 1924 immigration law. The 1965 law, historian Peter W. Williams observes, "had one of the most profound impacts on the religious makeup of the United States of any federal legislation in this century."[39] Between 1960 and 1990 more than fifteen million immigrants came to America. The percentage of foreign-born Americans is higher today than it was even during the peak of immigration one hundred years ago.[40] Immigrants, naturally, brought their religions with them. Although precisely determining the population of Buddhists, Hindus, Sikhs, Muslims and people of other faiths is difficult, their numbers have dramatically increased over the last forty years. While Muslims from Syria started emigrating to the United States in the last quarter of the nineteenth century, the Muslim community remained rather small. In 1960

---

[37]*Everson v. Board of Education*, 330 U.S. 15-16 (1947).
[38]John F. Wilson and Donald L. Drakeman, eds., *Church and State in American History,* 2nd ed. (Boston: Beacon Press, 1987), pp. 195-96, 223-33.
[39]Peter W. Williams, *America's Religions: From Their Origins to the Twenty-First Century* (Urbana: University of Illinois Press, 2002), p. 457.
[40]Diana L. Eck, *A New Religious America: How a "Christian Country" Has Become the World's Most Religiously Diverse Nation* (San Francisco: Harper, 2001), pp. 28, 2.

there were about 100,000 American Muslims. Between 1966 and 1980, 165,472 immigrants from predominantly Muslim countries came to America. There are an estimated 2.5 to 4.4 million Muslims in America today.[41] Furthermore, Islam, like the other great religions of the world, is hardly a monolith but encompasses a remarkably wide range of beliefs and traditions. The growth in the number of Muslims, Buddhists, Hindus and Hispanic Catholics helped to diminish the Protestant majority's market share and further weaken its already waning dominance over America's culture-shaping institutions. Meanwhile, the turmoil surrounding the Civil Rights movement, the war on poverty and the Vietnam War deeply divided mainline Protestant churches. Instead of seeing Christianity as part of the solution to these national and international problems, many American youths deemed mainline Protestantism part of the problem, and many left the denominations of their youth, never to return.[42] Moreover, new religious movements began to flourish in greater number in the 1960s and 1970s. New religious movements have always been part of American religion, as evidenced by the Shakers in the late eighteenth century and Mormons in the mid-nineteenth. As a result of the Immigration and Nationality Act of 1965, however, increased numbers of Asians moved to the United States, including a number of spiritual teachers, such as Swami A. C. Bhaktivedanta, who established the International Society for Krishna Consciousness. Not all new religious movements came from overseas, as illustrated by the Jesus Movement, Jim Jones and the New Age movement. Determining the actual number of new religious movements is even more difficult than finding the actual number of Muslims in America. J. Gordon Melton estimates that there are 2,300 active religious organizations in America, but this figure includes mainstream groups and overlooks the thousands of independent Bible churches and mom-and-pop storefront cults. Timothy Miller, a religion professor at the University of Kansas, suggests that if one counted all of the groups with only a few dozen members, there may be tens of thousands of alternative religious groups.[43] As a result of the confluence of these dramatic developments, Protestant domination of American public life dissipated. "The United States has become," observes Diana L. Eck, "the most religiously diverse nation on earth."[44]

---

[41]Mohamed Nimer, *The North American Muslim Resource Guide: Muslim Community Life in the United States and Canada* (New York: Routledge, 2002), pp. 21-27.

[42]Wade Clark Roof, *Spiritual Marketplace: Baby Boomers and the Remaking of American Religion* (Princeton, N.J.: Princeton University Press, 1999).

[43]J. Gordon Melton, *Encyclopedia of American Religion,* 6th ed. (Detroit: Gale Research, 1999), p. xiii; Timothy Miller, "Religious Movements in the United States: An Informal Introduction," The Religious Movements Homepage Project <http://religiousmovements.lib.virginia.edu/essays/miller2003.htm#many> (accessed April 3, 2006).

[44]Eck, *New Religious America,* p. 4.

The Complicated Contemporary Context

In the past, debates over church, state and public justice took place in the context of Protestant-dominated American public life. Today, the Protestant establishment does not provide a unifying center to American public life. No common Protestant framework of moral discourse unites all pertinent voices. Consequently, reaching a constructive public consensus on any issue involving church, state and public justice may be even more challenging today than it was in the past. Two important contemporary developments—the resurgence of the "religious right" and the debate over public religion—further complicate constructive conversations about issues related to the church, state and public justice. If a family plans to drive from western Pennsylvania to the Outer Banks of North Carolina on summer vacation, it would want to make sure that it has a complete and up-to-date map. However, many Christians and non-Christians operate today with a partial or an outdated map of America's religious landscape. It is important to recognize the impact of these two contemporary developments in order to understand why Christians and non-Christians alike are often so deeply divided about the role of religion in American public life. Moreover, understanding the impact that these developments have had on the contemporary American religious situation can enable both Christians and non-Christians to locate their place within these debates and can also assist them in constructively participating in conversations about social justice and the proper roles of the church and state in achieving it.

The Resurgence of the Religious Right

By the time the mainline Protestant establishment's dominance over the key culture-shaping institutions of American culture had come to an end, the religious right had surged onto the scene.[45] Perhaps the most prominent manifestation of the religious right appeared in 1979 when the fundamentalist Baptist Jerry Falwell founded the Moral Majority. Falwell's organization played a significant role in politics during the 1980s by giving voice to many Christian conservatives' opposition to a number of public policy issues, most notably the Equal Rights Amendment and abortion rights. Fundamentalists, however,

---

[45]William Martin, *With God on Our Side: The Rise of the Religious Right in America* (New York: Broadway Books, 1996); Robert Booth Fowler, *A New Engagement: Christian Evangelical Political Thought, 1966-1976* (Grand Rapids: Eerdmans, 1982); Michael Lienesch, *Redeeming America: Piety & Politics in the New Christian Right* (Chapel Hill: University of North Carolina Press, 1993); John C. Green, Mark J. Rozell, and Clyde Wilcox, eds., *The Christian Right in American Politics: Marching to the Millennium* (Washington, D.C.: Georgetown University Press, 2003).

were not the only conservative Christians who regained interest in American public life. By the 1980s, many evangelicals had reunited evangelism and social reform. The intellectual roots of this reunification can be traced back to Carl F. H. Henry's seminal 1947 work, *The Uneasy Conscience of Fundamentalism*, in which he complained that for "the first protracted period in its history," fundamentalism stood "divorced from the great social reform movements."[46] It took more than twenty years for sizable numbers of evangelicals to be goaded back into public life. Although fundamentalists, evangelicals and mainline Protestants differed over a number of key theological points, they shared similar views of the evils of communism and pornography, the sanctity of marriage and family, human sexuality and other issues. Because mainline Protestantism continued to dominate American public life for the first few decades of the twentieth century, evangelicals and fundamentalists could remain in their subcultures. They did not need to address public issues since the mainline Protestant cultural hegemony was upholding values they approved.[47] By the early 1970s, however, evangelicals had already begun rethinking their role in American public life. In 1973, for instance, some fifty evangelical leaders, representing a wide variety of conservative traditions, produced the Chicago Declaration of Evangelical Social Concern. Signed by Henry, Jim Wallis, Vernon Grounds and Ron Sider, among others, the statement affirmed "that God lays total claim upon the lives of his people. We cannot, therefore, separate our lives in Christ from the situation in which God has placed us in the United States and the world. We confess that we have not acknowledged that complete claim of God on our lives." They lamented that evangelicals had "not demonstrated the love of God to those suffering social abuses" nor "demonstrated his justice to an unjust American society."[48] While evangelical leaders had been reassessing conservative Christianity's relationship to society, the 1973 *Roe v. Wade* Supreme Court decision outraged many evangelicals and fundamentalists alike, driving many out of their quietism. In 1976 Jimmy Carter ran for president as a professing evangelical Christian. *Newsweek* magazine described 1976 as "the year of the evangelicals."[49] Although Falwell's

---

[46]Carl F. H. Henry, *The Uneasy Conscience of Fundamentalism* (Grand Rapids: Eerdmans, 1947), p. 36.

[47]Hart, "Mainstream Protestantism," pp. 201-3.

[48]Ronald J. Sider, ed., *The Chicago Declaration* (Carol Stream, Ill.: Creation House, 1974), p. 1. See also Michael L. Cromartie, "The Evangelical Kaleidoscope: A Survey of Recent Evangelical Political Engagement," *Christians and Politics Beyond the Culture Wars: An Agenda for Engagement*, ed. David P. Gushee (Grand Rapids: Baker, 2000), p. 21.

[49]Kenneth L. Woodward, "Born Again! The Year of the Evangelicals," *Newsweek*, October 25, 1976, p. 68.

organization dissolved in 1989, Pentecostal televangelist Pat Robertson established the Christian Coalition, a political action and lobbying organization, that same year. Conservative Christians had reentered the public square and had begun to speak loudly about social issues.

The Restructuring of American Religion and the Culture War

The religious right signaled more than the renewed interest of conservative Christians in American public life; it helped to spark a culture war. Robert Wuthnow, a sociologist at Princeton University, argues that since World War II a major restructuring of American religion has taken place. Denominational distinctives, which mattered so deeply in the past, no longer have the same relevance. Instead, Wuthnow observes, today's division is "between self-styled religious 'conservatives' and self-styled religious 'liberals,' both of whom acknowledged a considerable tension with the other side."[50] James Davison Hunter extended Wuthnow's analysis in *Culture Wars: The Struggle to Define America*. Unlike previous conflicts, such as the nineteenth-century battle between Protestants and Catholics over the use of the King James Bible in public schools, Hunter contends, the new conflict is between two polarizing impulses, orthodoxy and progressivism, which are rooted in two "different and opposing bases of moral authority and the world views that derive from them." Although neither view is always grounded on a cogent and fully articulated worldview, the orthodox tend to espouse an "external, definable, and transcendent authority," while the progressives define moral authority "by the spirit of the modern age, a spirit of rationalism and subjectivism."[51] These conflicting impulses cut across the old divide between Protestants, Catholics and Jews by joining together liberals and conservatives from each tradition in opposition to co-religionists with the antithetical view. The emergence of the religious right helped to organize the conservative religious perspective that was set in opposition to liberal beliefs. Hunter contends that every aspect of American public life, including education, law, entertainment, media and politics, has consequently been dramatically affected by the culture war.

Yet some scholars have questioned whether a culture war is raging to the magnitude that Hunter describes. Significant sociological evidence, they note, suggests that Hunter's all-encompassing bipolar ideological axis is overly sim-

---

[50]Robert Wuthnow, *The Restructuring of American Religion: Society and Faith Since World War II* (Princeton, N.J.: Princeton University Press, 1988), p. 133.
[51]James Davison Hunter, *Culture Wars: The Struggle to Define America* (New York: Basic Books, 1991), pp. 43-44.

plistic and masks a middle ground occupied by most Americans. While elites on both sides of the divide are locked in a *Kulturkampf,* studies suggest that most Americans may not be as ideologically partisan.[52] Sociologist Christian Smith's extensive study of rank-and-file American evangelicals' beliefs and lifestyles also demonstrates that evangelicals are more divided than united over the proper role of religion in American public life. In other words, the views of the leadership of the religious right do not exactly represent the beliefs of most self-identifying evangelicals or fundamentalists.[53] Some also suggest that the culture war is in certain respects an unfortunate misunderstanding.[54]

Amid the rancor and acrimony so often displayed by religious and secular elites in the popular media, it is easy to overlook the discomfort of many conservative Christians with this culture war mentality. Some conservative Christians have declared themselves "conscientious objectors" to the culture war, while other Christians from across the theological spectrum advocate civility and offer plans for a more constructive form of civic engagement in American political life.[55] Still others have announced defeat, abandoned public life and

---

[52]Rhys H. Williams, ed., *Culture Wars in American Politics: Critical Reviews of a Popular Myth* (New York: Aldine De Gruyter, 1997).

[53]Christian Smith, *Christian America? What Evangelicals Really Want* (Berkeley: University of California Press, 2000).

[54]David A. Hoekema, "Introduction: Christianity and Culture in the Crossfire," *Christianity and Culture in the Crossfire,* ed. David A. Hoekema and Bobby Fong (Grand Rapids: Eerdmans, 1997), pp. 1-11.

[55]Gregory Wolfe, "Editorial Statement: Why I Am a Conscientious Objector in the Culture Wars," *Image* 6 (1994): 3-4. For other expressions of evangelical resistance to the culture war rhetoric and agenda, see Lawrence E. Adams, *Going Public: Christian Responsibility in a Divided America* (Grand Rapids: Brazos, 2002); John Bolt, "The 'Culture War' in Perspective: Lessons from the Career of Abraham Kuyper," Witherspoon Lecture (Washington, D.C.: Family Research Council, 2001); John Fischer, "Demagnetizing Christianity," *Relevant*, July-August 2005, p. 38; Editorial, "Worship as Higher Politics," *Christianity Today,* June 23, 2005, <www.christianitytoday.com/ct/2005/007/16.22.html> (accessed April 3, 2006); Paul Marshall, *God and the Constitution: Christianity and American Politics* (Lanham, Md.: Rowman & Littlefield, 2002); Richard J. Mouw, *Uncommon Decency: Christian Civility in an Uncivil World* (Downers Grove, Ill.: InterVarsity Press, 1992); Timothy R. Sherratt and Ronald P. Mahurin, *Saints as Citizens: A Guide to Public Responsibilities for Christians* (Grand Rapids: Baker, 1995); Tom Sine, *Cease Fire: Searching for Sanity in America's Culture Wars* (Grand Rapids: Eerdmans, 1995). A number of nonevangelical Protestants have also proposed alternatives to the culture war militancy. See, for example, Azizah Y. Al-Hibri, Jean Bethke Elshtain and Charles C. Haynes, *Religion in American Public Life: Living with Our Deepest Differences* (New York: Norton, 2001); Jackson Caroll and Wade Clark Roof, eds., *Beyond Establishment: Protestant Identity in a Post-Protestant Age* (Louisville, Ky.: Westminster John Knox Press, 1993); Stephen L. Carter, *God's Name in Vain: The Wrongs and Rights of Religion in Politics* (New York: Basic Books, 2000); Parker J. Palmer, *The Company of Strangers: Christians and the Renewal of America's Public Life* (New York: Crossroads, 2001); Oliver O'Donovan and Joan Lockwood O'Donovan, *Bonds of Imperfection: Christian Politics, Past and Present* (Grand Rapids: Eerd-

returned to their fundamentalist subculture. In 1999, for instance, Paul Weyrich, president of Free Congress Foundation and cofounder with Jerry Falwell of the Moral Majority in 1979, declared that it was time for Christians to get out of politics. "I believe," Weyrich lamented, "that we probably have lost the culture war." It was time, he concluded, "to separate ourselves from the institutions that have been captured by the ideology of Political Correctness, or by other enemies of our traditional culture."[56] In *Blinded by Might: Can the Religious Right Save America?* two other former leaders of the Moral Majority, journalist Cal Thomas and pastor Ed Dobson, have rejected pursuing purely political solutions to social problems. They urge the religious right to refocus its efforts on evangelism rather than abandon secular culture.[57] Others dismiss such reassessments as "nonsense" and "baffling" and exhort conservative Christians that it is time to take their gloves off in their fight to "reclaim America for Christ."[58] There is even a small movement of self-identifying "Christian Reconstructionists" who aspire to create a theocracy in America. Most leaders of the religious right, however, harbor no such ambitions.[59] While the reality of a culture war may be somewhat exaggerated, the popular perception of it certainly is not. The simplistic division of the Union into red states and blue states, as if each state voted unanimously for one candidate or the other, and the media's startling discovery of the importance of "moral values" to many voters in the 2004 presidential election only heighten the perception that the nation is locked in an acrimonious division pitting two equal forces against each other. Moreover, leaders in the culture war show little hesitation about engaging in histrionics. Following Bush's reelection in November 2004, Jerry Falwell announced the organization of the Faith and Values Coalition. "Our nation," he insisted, "simply cannot continue as we know it if we allow out-of-control lawmakers and radical judges—working at the whims of society—to alter the moral foundations of America."[60] Not all shared Falwell's enthusiasm "to reclaim America

---

mans, 2004); Ronald F. Thiemann, *Religion in Public Life: A Dilemma for Democracy* (Washington, D.C.: Georgetown University Press, 1996).

[56]Paul Weyrich, "The Moral Minority," *Christianity Today*, September 6, 1999, p. 44.

[57]Cal Thomas and Ed Dobson, *Blinded by Might: Can the Religious Right Save America?* (Grand Rapids: Zondervan, 1999).

[58]Tom Minnery, *Why You Can't Stay Silent: A Biblical Mandate to Shape Our Culture* (Wheaton, Ill.: Tyndale House, 2001), pp. 97-106.

[59]A good introduction to theonomy can be found in Greg Bahnsen, *Theonomy in Christian Ethics*, 2nd ed. (Phillipsburg, N.J.: Presbyterian & Reformed, 1984). For a useful critique, see William S. Barker and W. Robert Godfrey, eds., *Theonomy: A Reformed Critique* (Grand Rapids: Zondervan, 1990). Pat Robertson, for example, repudiates any theonomic designs on America (Thomas and Dobson, *Blinded by Might*, pp. 252-53).

[60]Jerry Falwell, "What We Are All About" <www.faithandvalues.us> (accessed February 5, 2005).

for God." The day after Bush's reelection, Garry Wills published an editorial in the *New York Times* describing the events of the previous day as "The Day the Enlightenment Went Out." "Jihads," he warned, "are scary things."[61]

The resurgence of the religious right and, more importantly, the ensuing culture war complicate contemporary conversations about church, state and public justice in one important way. The renewed interest in the social implications of Christianity is not the problem per se, though of course it might be for those who advocate a purely secular public square. This contemporary religious development in American culture is significant because it makes constructive conversations among Christians, indeed all citizens, much more difficult. The propensity of many on the front lines of the culture war to demonize their ideological enemies makes civility, not to mention Christian humility, a liability because it is seen as a compromise of one's convictions.[62] Furthermore, toleration of other religious viewpoints is often misinterpreted as relativism. The growth of religious diversity in America over the last generations has created a great deal of confusion. This diversity has left many unable to differentiate between the use of the term *diversity* in its descriptive and normative senses.[63] The bitter polarization raises questions about the very possibility of finding common ground among people of various religious faiths or no faith at all.

The "Deprivatization" of Religion

During the 1980s "it was hard to find any serious political conflict anywhere in the world that did not show behind it the not-so-hidden hand of religion," observes the sociologist José Casanova. "We are witnessing the 'deprivatization' of religion in the modern world."[64] In other words, the deprivatization of religion has cast grave doubts on conventional wisdom among sociologists of

---

[61]Garry Wills, "The Day the Enlightenment Went Out," *New York Times*, November 4, 2004, p. A25.

[62]On toleration, see Daniel Taylor, "Deconstructing the Gospel of Tolerance," *Christianity Today*, January 11, 1999, pp. 43-52; Brad Stetson and Joseph G. Conti, *The Truth About Tolerance: Pluralism, Diversity and the Culture Wars* (Downers Grove, Ill.: InterVarsity Press, 2005); J. Budziszewski, *True Tolerance: Liberalism and the Necessity of Judgment* (New Brunswick, N.J.: Transaction, 1992); S. D. Gaede, *When Tolerance Is No Virtue* (Downers Grove, Ill.: InterVarsity Press, 1993).

[63]See, for example, Joel Belz, "Tolerance vs. Pluralism," *World Magazine*, October 27, 2001 <www.worldmag.com/displayarticle.cfm?id=5470> (accessed April 3, 2006).

[64]José Casanova, *Public Religions in the Modern World* (Chicago: University of Chicago Press, 1994), pp. 3, 5. Casanova defines *deprivatization* as "the process whereby religion abandons its assigned place in the private sphere and enters the undifferentiated public sphere of civil society" (ibid., pp. 65-66). See also Peter L. Berger, ed., *The Desecularization of the World: Resurgent Religion and World Politics* (Grand Rapids: Eerdmans, 1999).

religion about the inevitable secularization of Western culture. As one prominent sociologist, for instance, once claimed, the "evolutionary future of religion is extinction." Furthermore, the resurgence of the religious right and the
ensuing culture war has raised a second, larger complication, one that is perhaps even more challenging for contemporary discussions of church, state and
public justice.[65] To pose the question in its broadest terms, one could ask if it is
even proper for the church to speak to matters of social justice in a democratic
and religiously pluralistic nation with no established church and a constitutional guarantee of religious freedom. To put it another way, should concerned
Christians and denominations lobby Congress; create parachurch organizations that function as their representatives, just as other special-interest groups
have in Washington and state capitals; or elect only politicians who are guided
by explicitly Christian convictions? More narrowly, one can ask if it is appropriate for Christians to base public policy on distinctly Christian values. For
example, if a fundamentalist offers a biblical warrant for curbing stem-cell research, why should a non-Christian find it a compelling basis for informing
public policy? Would an evangelical find a Mormon's proof texts from the *Book
of Mormon* compelling evidence to support Charitable Choice, or would a fundamentalist find a Sunni Muslim's invocation of the Koran a legitimate warrant for supporting school vouchers? As Neuhaus put it in his 1984 warning
that American public life was hostile to religion: "Public decisions must be
made by arguments that are public in character. . . . Fundamentalist morality,
which is derived from beliefs that cannot be submitted to examination by public reason, is essentially a private morality."[66]

The Possibility of Public Religion? Three Responses

While the effort to push religion to the margin of public life, to enforce what
Casanova calls "an incapacitating 'gag rule' " on religious citizens, has failed,
as the culture war so dramatically illustrates, the very possibility of a public
religion is now an open question. Although this collection of essays does not
focus on the question of public religion per se, it is important to recognize the
larger context in which this conversation is taking place. There is a remarkable
diversity of opinions today on the matter. Michael J. Perry, a law professor at
Emory University, provides a useful typology for understanding the range of

---

[65]Anthony Wallace, *Religion* (New York: Random House, 1966), p. 265. For a constructive alternative theory of secularization that takes into account deprivatization, see Christian
Smith, "Introduction," in *The Secular Revolution: Power, Interests, and Conflict in the Secularization of American Public Life* (Berkeley: University of California Press, 2003), pp. 1-96.
[66]Neuhaus, *Naked Public Square*, pp. 36-37.

responses to this question. According to Perry, people are agnostics, exclusivists or inclusivists when it comes to the question of religion's role in public life. The agnostics in Perry's typology "have no firm convictions about the proper role of religion in politics." One can believe or not believe in the existence of God and be uncertain about the proper role of religion in politics. By contrast, exclusivists and inclusivists have firm convictions about the proper role of religion. Exclusivists, as the name suggests, believe that religious faith should be excluded as much as possible from the public life of the nation, while inclusivists affirm that religion may be included in public life.[67] Both religious believers and religious nonbelievers can be found in each category. Since agnostics do not play a major role in discussions over the propriety of public religion, the following analysis is limited to exclusivists and inclusivists.

Exclusivists: Religion Is a "Conversation Stopper"

"The main reason religion needs to be privatized is that, in political discussion with those outside the relevant community," says the postmodern philosopher Richard Rorty, "it is a conversation stopper." According to the exclusivist view, a believer who says, for example, that her Christian commitment requires her to oppose abortion is equivalent to someone else saying, "Reading pornography is the only pleasure I get out of life these days." Rorty insists that both people would provoke the same response in the public sphere: "So what? We weren't talking about your private life."[68] Religious beliefs, argues John Rawls—a Harvard philosopher and self-identifying atheist—can be so divisive in a pluralistic culture that they subvert the stability of a society. Consequently, Rawls insists, the state should only make value judgments based on "public reason." "The point of the ideal of public reason," Rawls explains, "is that citizens are to conduct their fundamental discussions within the framework of what each regards as a political conception of justice based on values that the others can reasonably be expected to endorse and each is, in good faith, prepared to defend that conception so understood."[69] Since religion is based on private values, it has no place in "public reason." The Christian philosopher Robert Audi agrees that religiously informed reasons for public pol-

---

[67]Michael J. Perry, *Under God? Religious Faith and Liberal Democracy* (Cambridge: Cambridge University Press, 2003), pp. ix-x.

[68]Richard Rorty, "Religion as Conversation-Stopper," *Common Knowledge* 3 (1994): 3. Rorty has tempered his militant exclusivism. See Richard Rorty, "Religion in the Public Square: A Reconsideration," *Journal of Religious Ethics* 31 (2003): 141-49.

[69]John Rawls, *Political Liberalism* (New York: Columbia University Press, 1993), p. 226. See also his *A Theory of Justice*, rev. ed. (Cambridge, Mass.: Belknap Press, 1999).

icy have no place in American public life. Religious people, he contends, can be motivated by religious reasons. But when it comes to public policy, religious people should have "at least one set of evidentially adequate secular reasons." Audi does not argue that Christians do not have the right to express their religious convictions in civic discussions. But when it comes to issues involving laws and public policies that restrict human conduct, he contends, Christians must base their rationales in secular terms so that they can be shared with people outside of their religious community. The religious person "has a prima facie obligation not to advocate or support any law or public policy that restricts human conduct, unless one has, and is willing to offer adequate secular reason" for these laws or policies.[70]

Inclusivists: "Let a Thousand Flowers Bloom"

While exclusivists insist that religious people refrain from invoking religious rationales in order to participate in a liberal democracy, inclusivists find such calls for silence philosophically unwarranted and ultimately undemocratic. Keeping religion to oneself, asserts Jean Bethke Elshtain, a University of Chicago political philosopher, is "precisely what a devout person cannot do for religious faith isn't a private matter; it is constitutive of membership in a particular body."[71] Stephen Carter, a Yale Law School professor, makes a similar point in *The Culture of Disbelief*:

> Rather than envisioning a public square in which all are welcome, the contemporary liberal philosophers insist on finding a set of conversational rules that require the individual whose religious tradition makes demands on his or her moral conscience to reformulate that conscience—to destroy a vital aspect of the self—in order to gain the right to participate in the dialogue alongside other citizens.

Carter further argues that "what is needed is not a requirement that the religiously devout choose a form of dialogue that liberalism accepts, but that liberalism accepts whatever form of dialogue a member of the public offers." He concludes, "Epistemic diversity, like diversity of other kinds, should be cherished, not ignored, and certainly not abolished."[72] Like Carter, Nicholas Wolterstorff, professor of philosophical theology emeritus at Yale University,

---

[70]Robert Audi, "Liberal Democracy and the Place of Religion in Politics," *Religion in the Public Square* (Lanham, Md.: Rowman & Littlefield, 1997), pp. 138, 25. Kent Greenawalt argues that religious reasons should be translated into publicly accessible reasons (Kent Greenawalt, *Private Consciences and Public Reasons* [New York: Oxford University Press, 1995]).

[71]Jean Bethke Elshtain, "The Bright Line: Liberalism and Religion," *New Criterion* 17 (1999): 10.

[72]Stephen Carter, *The Culture of Disbelief: How American Law and Politics Trivialize Religion* (New York: Anchor, 1996), pp. 229-30.

argues that the restriction that exclusivists like Rawls and Audi place on religious reasons in a liberal democracy actually subverts the political goal of creating a stable and enduring society by privatizing religion and creating resentment that results in a confrontational and polarizing approach to politics. According to Wolterstorff, the exclusivists misinterpret the First Amendment to entail the separation of religion and public life when instead it should be understood to mean that the state should practice impartiality toward religion. This separatist interpretation places epistemological restraints on religious believers by making them hold their political views for reasons derived from nonreligious sources. To require religious believers to "not base their decisions and discussions concerning political issues on their religion is to infringe, inequitably, on the free exercise of their religion." While Christians might find biblical warrants for particular public policies compelling, inclusivists observe, they should not be surprised when people who do not share their basic faith commitments might find these reasons rather superfluous. Consequently, inclusivists suggest that believers consider providing rationales for particular laws or policies based on natural theology or general revelation. In the end, inclusivists like Wolterstorff advocate a more open approach to public life. So long as people participate in the public square with civility, Wolterstorff invites everyone to offer whatever reasons motivate them and justify their political choices. "Let citizens use whatever reasons they find appropriate—including, then, religious reasons."[73]

A House Divided: A Lack of Consensus on Public Religion

The deprivatization of religion has raised critical questions about the possibility of a public religion. To be sure, this is not the first time in American history that the question has been raised. Even if Christians in previous genera-

---

[73]Nicholas Wolterstorff, "The Role of Religion in Political Issues," *Religion in the Public Square*, pp. 105, 112. For similar views, see Michael J. Perry, *Morality, Politics, and Law: A Bicentennial Essay* (New York: Oxford University Press, 1988), and *Under God? Religious Faith and Liberal Democracy* (Cambridge: Cambridge University Press, 2003); Michael W. McConnell, *Accommodation of Religion: An Update and a Response to the Critics*, 60 George Washington Law Review 685 (1992). In America's increasingly multireligious culture, as Diana L. Eck observes, advocates of the inclusion of religion in the public square often beg an important question: whose religion? Although many proponents of inclusion, such as Wolterstorff, encourage all to participate in American public life, Eck contends, other advocates of inclusion use *religion* euphemistically when they are really talking about conservative Christianity. Still others, like Neuhaus and Carter, speak only of adherents of the Judeo-Christian tradition but ignore believers from other traditions already in the public square (Diana L. Eck, "The Multireligious Public Square," in *One Nation Under God? Religion and American Culture*, ed. Marjorie Garber and Rebecca L. Walkowitz [New York: Routledge, 1999], pp. 3-20).

tions were deeply divided over what constituted a legitimate public justice issue and if or how the church or state should address the issue, as the previous historical review suggests, the overwhelming response decidedly favored the propriety of Christians speaking as Christians on matters of social justice. For contemporary discussions over matters of church and state and public justice, it is crucial to recognize that they are now taking place in a context where the very possibility of Christians speaking and acting as Christians (or believers in other religions) is now being debated. As this summary suggests, there is no unifying consensus on the role of religion in American public life, and Christians can be found on many sides of the debate. While the contributors to this book do not focus exclusively on the question of public religion, they represent a variety of different inclusivist perspectives. In fact, this symposium demonstrates that it is possible to have a constructive conversation about these weighty matters without polarizing histrionics. Perhaps one of the greatest challenges facing Christians in America today is learning how to be faithful Christians and responsible citizens in an increasingly pluralistic nation with a Constitution that guarantees religious freedom and forbids an established church.

Life on the Border

A CATHOLIC PERSPECTIVE

Clarke E. Cochran

W e've all seen variations of the cartoon in which a main character becomes more and more frustrated over the antics of another character. Think Elmer Fudd and Bugs Bunny. As the tension, anger and frustration build, Elmer's complexion becomes redder and redder; steam begins to rise from his forehead. Finally, he explodes.

That's one picture of tension. Here's another.

The frame of a tennis racket holds the strings in tension against one another, creating the tautness essential to the sport. Too little or too much tension, and the ball will not rebound properly.

At its best, Catholic teaching on the role of the church in society, on relations with the state and on public justice are like the second picture.[1] Church and state exist in tension. The pursuit of social justice is not linear but must be balanced against the mission of charity, evangelization and human freedom. As befits a church that (despite some outward appearances) is sprawling and tangled, with nooks and crannies of doctrines and institutions, Catholic teaching likewise sprawls across ecclesiastical and social issues, in the process creating lots of untidiness, seeming or real tensions between different ethical principles, and plenty of room for debate. Catholic social teaching works in this chaotic space.

Elsewhere I have described religion and politics relations as a borderland dotted with checkpoints and hidden paths for both legitimate and illegitimate commerce.[2] The present introduction to Catholic social teaching (CST) and its applications to church and state, public justice and public policy employs this metaphor in describing both the core, settled areas of that teaching as well as

---

[1]Thanks to David Carroll Cochran and Paul C. Kemeny for comments and suggestions that much improved this chapter.

[2]Clarke E. Cochran, "Catholic Healthcare in the Public Square: Tension on the Frontier," in *Handbook of Bioethics and Religion*, ed. David Guinn (New York: Oxford University Press, 2006); and Clarke E. Cocharn, *Religion in Public and Private Life* (New York: Routledge, 1990).

legitimate diversity within the Catholic social tradition.[3] This task is complicated by the breadth of CST, even within the settled core, as evidenced by the
new *Compendium of the Social Doctrine of the Church*. Published by the Vatican
in 2004, it runs to 250 pages of text divided into 3 parts, 12 chapters and 583
sections.[4] The task also is complicated by the relatively long history of CST, by
differences of interpretation among theologians and Catholic political actors,
and by the internal disagreements over church discipline and the proper interpretation of the Catholic theological tradition between (for shorthand) "liberal" and "conservative" Catholics.[5] It will prove impossible to do justice to
these divisions, but it would be irresponsible to ignore them.

One can think of CST as a large ocean-going vessel with different factions
vying to navigate. Although all agree on the core principles (the vessel's

---

[3]I use the widely accepted abbreviation CST to refer to the broadly accepted principles of
Catholic social teaching. Other frequently used terms are "Catholic social thought" and
"Catholic social theory," each also conveniently abbreviated CST. Of course, these terms
suggest different levels of authoritativeness; *thought* and *theory* being less dogmatic than
teaching. In 2004 the Vatican's Pontifical Council on Peace and Justice issued the first compendium of CST but significantly employed the term *doctrine*.

[4]Pontifical Council for Peace and Justice, *Compendium of the Social Doctrine of the Church*
(Washington, D.C.: United States Conference of Catholic Bishops, 2005).

[5]Space and the reader's patience do not allow a full list of references; however, some of the
most important and useful works should be mentioned. Comprehensive accounts, each very
different in style, are the *Compendium;* and Judith A. Dwyer, ed., *The New Dictionary of Catholic Social Thought* (Collegeville, Minn.: Michael Glazier, 1994); and Kenneth R. Himes, ed.,
Modern Catholic Social Teaching: Commentaries and Interpretations (Washington, D.C.: Georgetown University Press, 2005). Helpful brief introductions are Rodger Charles, *An Introduction to Catholic Social Teaching* (San Francisco: Ignatius, 1999); Clarke E. Cochran and David
Carroll Cochran, *Catholics, Politics, and Public Policy: Beyond Left and Right* (Maryknoll, N.Y.:
Orbis, 2003); Michael J. Himes and Kenneth R. Himes, *Fullness of Faith: The Public Significance
of Theology* (Mahwah, N.J.: Paulist, 1993); Thomas Massaro, *Living Justice: Catholic Social
Teaching in Action* (Franklin, Wis.: Sheed & Ward, 2000); and Thomas Massaro and Thomas
A. Shannon, eds., *American Catholic Social Teaching* (Collegeville, Minn.: Liturgical Press,
2002). CST often defines itself in terms of the tradition of papal encyclicals (circular letters
addressed to the whole church or to the world at large) on social questions. Himes *(Modern
Catholic Social Teaching)* summarizes the principal encyclicals from 1891 to the present. Good
histories of CST may be found in Roger Aubert, *Catholic Social Teaching in Historical Perspec-
tive* (Milwaukee, Wis.: Marquette University Press, 2003); David A. Boileau, ed., *Principles of
Catholic Social Teaching* (Milwaukee, Wis.: Marquette University Press, 1998); Joe Holland,
Modern Catholic Social Teaching: The Popes Confront the Industrial Age, 1740-1958 (Mahwah,
N.J.: Paulist, 2003); Marvin L. Krier Mich, *Catholic Social Teaching and Movements* (Mystic,
Conn.: Twenty-Third Publications, 1998); and Michael J. Schuck, *That They Be One: The Social
Teaching of the Papal Encyclicals, 1740-1989* (Washington, D.C.: Georgetown University Press,
1991). For the specific American context, see Massaro and Shannon, *American Catholic;*
Patrick W. Carey, *American Catholic Religious Thought: The Shaping of a Theological and Social
Tradition* (Milwaukee, Wis.: Marquette University Press, 1987); and John T. McGreevy, *Ca-
tholicism and American Freedom: A History* (New York: W. W. Norton, 2003).

cargo), such as common good, social justice, subsidiarity, stewardship, human freedom and dignity, each wishes to sail by a different star. For some, generally on the left, world peace, protection of the rights of labor, government programs of assistance to the poor and needy, and economic justice are stars by which to navigate.[6] Others on the left reject tinkering with social life, replacing it with a vision of the church as an alternative community.[7] Others, more generally on the right, seek to steer according to free enterprise and the pursuit of political freedom and economic development at home and abroad.[8] Finally, others on the right seek to steer the vessel by the fixed stars of Catholic moral teaching's opposition to abortion, homosexuality and euthanasia.[9]

The varied navigational systems are expressions of the legitimate diversity of approaches to applying the stable core of CST to the variety of challenges presented by the political world. Arguments and differences of opinion on the church-state border reflect the reality that borders are essentially messy; they do not lend themselves to permanent, tidy solutions. This chapter argues that, in being faithful to its mission in the world, the Catholic Church displays different "faces" to the world. Its dealings with politics, culture and society will from time to time take on four different aspects: cooperation, challenge, competition and transcendence.[10]

Cooperation refers to the ways in which the church and its agents work in collaboration with government programs to meet social needs that each recognizes, such as hunger, family support and international relief. Examples are the network of Catholic Charities agencies and Catholic Relief Services programs largely financed by government grants and contracts, but manifesting the religious mission of the church.

Challenge signifies the myriad of ways in which Catholic institutions, groups and individuals lobby, demonstrate, agitate and sometimes disobey government in order to push it toward justice or correction of injustice. Pro-

---

[6]John A. Coleman, ed., *One Hundred Years of Catholic Social Thought: Celebration and Challenge* (Maryknoll, N.Y.: Orbis, 1991).

[7]Michael J. Baxter, " 'Blowing the Dynamite of the Church': Catholic Radicalism from a Catholic Radicalist Perspective," in *Paths That Lead to Life: The Church as Counterculture*, ed. Michael L. Budde and Robert Brimlow (Albany, N.Y.: State University of New York Press, 1999); Michael J. Baxter, "Reintroducing Virgil Michel: Towards a Counter-Tradition of Catholic Social Ethics in the United States," *Communio* 24 (1997).

[8]Michael Novak, *The Catholic Ethic and the Spirit of Capitalism* (New York: Free Press, 1993); Michael Novak, *Catholic Social Thought and Liberal Institutions: Freedom with Justice* (New Brunswick, N.J.: Transaction, 2001).

[9]The widely distributed *Voter's Guide for Serious Catholics* in the 2004 election <www.catholic.com/library/voters_guide.asp> (accessed November 16, 2005).

[10]Cochran, "Catholic Healthcare."

tests against the Iraq War or lobbying to maintain Medicaid funding for men-
tally disabled persons are examples of this mode.

Competition refers to Catholic institutions that directly compete with government programs: the network of Catholic schools, for example.

Transcendence signifies the mission that goes beyond any mission of the
state—eternal salvation. The church finds its essential orientation in the commission to "Go therefore and make disciples of all nations, baptizing them in
the name of the Father and of the Son and of the Holy Spirit, and teaching
them to obey everything that I have commanded you" (Mt 28:19-20). The state
has no business aiming to save souls; therefore, the church works to maintain
its distance from the state and to protect its ability to work outside of the con-
fining walls of both law and cultural expectation. Recognition of transcendence, of boundaries the state may not cross, acts also as a check on pride displayed in humanity's tendency to seek salvation through artifice and
technological prowess.

CST incorporates these four modes, recognizing a plurality of applications
to particular social and political questions, which gives Catholic social doctrine unique power and flexibility.

The Mission of the Church in Catholic Doctrine

Catholics, of course, are Christians. A rather basic point, but one often missed
or misunderstood by other Christians, especially fundamentalists in the
American South. Precisely because the design of this volume highlights differences among Christian traditions, it is necessary to reinforce that Catholics
share a mission with all Christians: to worship God (revealed by Jesus Christ
as Father, Son and Spirit) and to strive as disciples of Christ to live this truth
and spread its good news to all peoples. The Catholic Christian is called to "do
justice, and to love kindness, and to walk humbly with your God" (Mic 6:8).

No Christian can be entirely at home in the world, but all must live in the
world—sometimes cooperating with "powers," sometimes challenging them,
always looking beyond them to the kingdom. Catholics believe that the kingdom is now and not yet, fully present yet not fully actualized, and that the disciple of Christ strives to live as a citizen of the kingdom in both ecclesial and
civil life.

That said, there are distinguishing characteristics of Catholic Christianity,
and these stamp its interpretation of what it means to live in this world as a
pilgrim citizen of the kingdom. The distinctive Catholic understanding of the
Christian mission is incarnational, sacramental, social and committed to the
poor. Moreover, in its "methodology," Catholic theology relies on tradition,

reason and argument by analogy, characteristics supporting the claim that the Church's moral and social principles have universal applicability. These characteristics make Catholicism in principle a "public church."[11]

Incarnational. All Christians affirm that in Jesus, God became human. The second person of the Trinity assumed humanity in all aspects, save sin, thereby redeeming the human and material world.

This radical claim of the incarnation leads Catholics to believe that all persons "share humanity in common and so, to become like God, we should be as fully human as we can."[12] It is distinctly Catholic to value the natural world, including the naturally human. Grace, in the famous aphorism of St. Thomas, does not annul nature but perfects it. Thus the Church is not drastically opposed to the world but rather aims fundamentally to elevate the world to what God intended creation to be. Grace does not abolish human needs, desires and aspirations but elevates them to a new level.

This theological commitment entails that there is a natural justice and a natural common good. It is the duty of politics and government to respect and pursue them. Justice and common good then become central orienting principles of CST.

Sacramental. Catholicism is a sacramental communion. Religious life revolves around the weekly (for some, daily) celebration of the Eucharist, which the bishops of the Second Vatican Council (1962-1965) describe as the "source and summit" of the Church's life.[13] Baptism and confirmation are celebrated as moments of special grace in which the person enters fully into the life of Christ through the Church. The sacrament of reconciliation (confession) sacramentalizes the forgiveness at the heart of Jesus' mission, and anointing of the sick embodies the healing encounter of the patient with Christ. The central vocational calls of marriage and priesthood become sacramental signs of service to the world.

In Catholic theology these sacraments are uniquely graced encounters with Christ. Yet other signs, symbols and events also are sacramental in a very real way: rosaries, statues of saints, medals and holy water mediate encounters with Christ. In the same way, events of everyday life can become oc-

---

[11]Richard P. McBrien, *Catholicism*, new ed. (San Francisco: Harper, 1994), chap. 1. The idea of a public church is expressed most fully by José Casanova, *Public Religions in the Modern World* (Chicago: University of Chicago, 1994).

[12]Michael J. Himes, " 'Finding God in All Things': A Sacramental Worldview and its Effects," in *As Leaven in the World: Catholic Perspectives on Faith, Vocation, and the Intellectual Life*, ed. Thomas M. Landy (Franklin, Wis.: Sheed & Ward, 2001), p. 101.

[13]"The Constitution on the Sacred Liturgy" §10, in Austin Flannery, ed., *Vatican Council II: The Conciliar and Post Conciliar Documents* (Northport, N.Y.: Costello, 1975).

casions of intimacy with Christ, occasions mediated by material things (photographs, natural vistas, the touch of a hand, a gift given in love). It is the intensity and centrality of this sacramental principle that makes Catholic Christianity distinct from other forms of Christianity. Thus everything is potentially sacred; everyone is potentially holy, for everything and everyone may mediate God's love.

Sacramentality is indispensable in a social theology that evokes existence in tension, for human experiences of tension call upon emotions, commitments and actions that transcend words and rules of behavior. Sacraments communicate principally at the nonverbal level; quite literally, they embody meaning. Words, sentences and paragraphs as well as the rules, laws and principles into which words are formed fail to capture human and social complexity. A glance, a touch, a ritual or a symbolic exchange, however, can embody a range of meaning and human complexity beyond the capacity of words.

Sacramentality makes CST comfortable with the inevitable tensions, compromises and inexpressibilities of political life. Moreover, CST will be embodied as often in actions and institutions as in statements and manifestos.

Social anthropology. A third fundamental commitment of Catholic doctrine with substantial implications for CST is a social understanding of the human condition. Catholicism shares with all Christianity the idea that salvation depends on the response of the individual person to God's graceful invitation. However, the social relationships in which individual persons live always condition that response. God made humans for community. ("It is not good that the man should be alone.") Our lives and commitments, our abilities and our infirmities, reflect the communities that give shape and substance to our lives.

Although not denying personal responsibility, CST stresses the mutual responsibilities that human beings owe one another. Despite their significant differences, the various "schools" of CST share a fundamentally social vision of the world.[14] This social orientation is the point of convergence that makes it possible for Catholics to embrace political positions that transcend the liberal-conservative dichotomy that plagues most Christian and secular politics. The sacredness of human life in the womb deserves legal protection, CST teaches, because we have a mutual responsibility to protect the vulnerable. All citizens should have health insurance because the social virtue of solidarity demands it.

---

[14]John A. Coleman, "Neither Liberal nor Socialist: The Originality of Catholic Social Teaching," in Coleman, *One Hundred Years,* pp. 25-42.

Option for the poor. Although the "option for the poor" is a specific social and political principle, it is a larger theme in Catholic life. Catholicism reflects the Christian tension between the values of poverty and relief of poverty. In both respects, poverty and the poor are at the heart of Catholicism.

"Blessed are you who are poor" has a resonance for all Christians.[15] Catholicism frequently has taken literally the promise of blessings in poverty. Voluntary poverty for the kingdom has long been at the heart of Catholicism: from renunciation of all possessions by the desert fathers and mothers, through the monastic orders living austerely by the work of their hands, to the mendicant religious orders (Franciscans and Dominicans, for example) founded in the late Middle Ages, to the vows of poverty (and chastity and obedience) taken by all Catholic religious orders of women and men. Lay movements, such as Dorothy Day's Catholic Worker movement, have been inspired by the same motive: to live in poverty with and for the poor.

At the same time, many of these same religious orders (and their hospitals, orphanages and schools) devoted themselves to the relief of poverty in the form of alleviation of poverty (bread lines and soup kitchens) or of enabling skills that might break the cycle of poverty (education and health care, for example). The physician Paul Farmer describes the "option for the poor" as "making common cause with the losers" of the world.[16] Thus it is no surprise that by the late twentieth century the "option for the poor" had become a key element of CST. Although this commitment is most characteristic of the Catholic left, Catholic conservatives too stress that overcoming poverty is part of their fundamental commitment, left and right disagreeing principally on the *means* necessary to attack poverty.

Church as a public institution. The incarnational, sacramental, social and poverty-driven character of Catholicism, in aspiration if not always in performance, makes it essentially a public church; that is, a church inseparable from public life. This connection need not be, and is not today, understood in a theocratic sense, though there is no need to deny such a tendency in the past. What it does mean is that, in the words of the synod of bishops meeting at the Vatican in 1971, "Action on behalf of justice and participation in the transformation of the world fully appear to us as *a constitutive dimension* of the preaching of the Gospel, or, in other words, of the Church's mission for the redemption of the human race and its liberation

---

[15]This is Luke's formulation of the Beatitude (Lk 6:20). Matthew has "poor in spirit" (Mt 5:3).
[16]Quoted in Tracy Kidder, *Mountains Beyond Mountains* (New York: Random House, 2003), pp. 288-89.

from every oppressive situation."[17] The Church cannot be the Church without seeking justice through participation in the political and social life of the world.

This is so because if humanity is social, then justice (right relation with God) and redemption are social. This is so because if the Word became flesh, then the saving word preached must be enacted in the world. This is so because if the Church is a sacrament, then it judges the world and its power structures simply by being the Church.[18]

Although such theological language describing the Church is relatively recent, it reflects a historical reality that Catholics are particularly skilled at building institutions: religious orders, hospitals, schools, orphanages and charitable works as well as the more strictly ecclesial institutions of dioceses, parishes and the Roman Curia. Its institutions of charitable service and healing locate the Church substantially in the world, where social and political problems arise. The Church, then, is always engaged with the world, but also in tension with the world in this engagement.[19] For example, to be a Catholic hospital means to be both *Catholic* and a *hospital*. The former is defined by the moral and religious commitments of Catholicism; the latter by medical culture and public regulations. The two meanings are inseparably connected, but not always in harmony.

Moreover, because Catholic institutions are public in this way, they are sacramental. They embody meaning, sustain it in the persons who work and receive care in them, mediate it to succeeding generations and manifest it to the larger world. The world should encounter Christ when it interacts with a Catholic hospital or a Catholic Charities agency or a Catholic school. In short, the Church has no choice but to be related to the state, to the economy, and to society and culture. The choices involve *how* to relate to them. CST directs the Church's engagement to be tensional because it forbids one-

---

[17]"Justice in the World" §6, Roman Synod (1971), in *Proclaiming Justice and Peace: Papal Documents from Rerum Novarum Through Centesimus Annus, Revised and Expanded*, ed. Michael Walsh and Brian Davies (Mystic, Conn.: Twenty-Third Publications, 1991), emphasis added.

[18]This last point judges the Church itself for its failure to embody the gospel, especially as that gospel contradicts the political and economic structures of inequality and injustice. Catholic "radicals" make this point the focus of their critiques of the Church in relation to the world. See, for example, Baxter, "Reintroducing Virgil Michel"; Baxter, "Review Essay: The Non-Catholic Character of the 'Public Church,'" *Modern Theology* 11 (April 1995); Michael Budde, *The (Magic) Kingdom of God: Christianity and the Global Culture Industries* (Boulder, Colo.: Westview, 1997); Michael L. Budde and Robert W. Brimlow, *Christianity Incorporated: How Big Business Is Buying the Church* (Grand Rapids: Brazos, 2002); and Budde and Brimlow, eds., *The Church as Counterculture*.

[19]J. Bryan Hehir, "Identity and Institutions," *Health Progress* 76 (1995).

dimensional engagement. Rather, the Church's public interactions should be cooperative, challenging, competitive and transcendent.[20]

Purpose of the State

When it comes to the state and to politics more specifically, CST has evolved a number of principles, concepts and theories that orient its engagement.[21] Most central are that government is part of the natural order of creation, that the primary purpose of government is attainment of the common good and pursuit of justice, that the condition of the poor is a principal measure of common good and justice, and that solidarity with all persons and defense of human freedom and dignity are essential principles of governance. Moreover, the state has a responsibility to maintain order in the social and in the natural world; hence, stewardship of God's generous gifts is a prime responsibility of governance. Finally, CST embraces the principle of "subsidiarity," which entails that the commitments just stated are not the exclusive domain of a central government but are the joint responsibility of governments at all levels and of families, churches, economic enterprises and voluntary associations.

Government and the natural order. "The human person is the foundation and purpose of political life."[22] Because, following Aristotle and Thomas Aquinas, human persons are naturally social and political, government and politics are not something added onto humanity in order to remedy the effects of human sin and frailty, but are natural aspects of human life. Government indeed must respond to sin; however, government is *essentially* part of the natural, created order intended by God to advance natural purposes—flourishing of the human person, proper ordering of social life and pursuit of the common good of the whole community.

Collective human action, even under conditions of abundance, good will and high moral character, requires authority to choose a direction. Should we

---

[20]I develop these ideas more fully in Clarke E. Cochran, "Institutional Identity; Sacramental Potential: Catholic Healthcare at Century's End," *Christian Bioethics* 5 (1999); "Sacrament and Solidarity: Catholic Social Thought and Healthcare Policy Reform," *Journal of Church and State* 41 (1999); and "Taking Ecclesiology Seriously: Catholicism, Religious Institutions, and Healthcare Policy," in *The Re-Enchantment of Political Science: Christian Scholars Engage Their Discipline,* ed. Thomas W. Heilke and Ashley Woodiwiss (Lanham, Md.: Lexington Books, 2001). See also David Hollenbach, *The Global Face of Public Faith: Politics, Human Rights, and Christian Ethics* (Washington, D.C.: Georgetown University Press, 2003). The evolution of the American public church is described in Casanova, *Public Religions,* chap. 7.

[21]There is some variation in terminology and precedence of concepts as well as considerable differences in application of the principles to political, social, cultural and economic issues. See the works cited in note 5.

[22]*Compendium of the Social Doctrine of the Church,* p. 166. This discussion draws on chap. 8.

build the new elementary school here or there? Would it best promote the common good to place the new road there or here? These kinds of decisions do not arise out of human sinfulness but out of human nature itself. Political authority works toward an ordered and just community.

Individual sin and collective sin (war, racism and economic oppression) also require the organization of political communities to punish and deter harms, to right wrongs and to employ the law's educative force to teach right from wrong to persons only too inclined to follow their selfish interests.

Because in principle all persons can recognize the need for law and authority to direct action and to restrain the effects of evil, CST traditionally stressed the universality and rational accessibility of its principles. Typically, official ecclesial statements of and applications of CST to social problems have been addressed not only to Catholics but to all persons of good will. In other words, the ideas of CST are neither exclusively Catholic nor applicable primarily to Catholic persons or Catholic nations. Rather, they are principles of human reason that orient the governance structures and the public purposes of any political system.

Methodologically, universality has been most fully expressed in "natural law" theory as the ground of Catholic moral theology. In recent decades, without abandoning the idea of universality, papal and episcopal statements of CST (as well as more academic treatments) have stressed personalist and scriptural arguments. Pope John Paul II's study of Continental philosophy, especially Husserl and the phenomenologists, was a major influence in this regard. This influence can be seen in the structure of the Pontifical Council for Justice and Peace's authoritative 2004 *Compendium of the Social Doctrine of the Church*.[23]

Although the person-centered ground is compatible with natural law's appeal to reason, the more Scripture-based approach introduces some tensions within CST. The more CST emphasizes Scripture, the more sectarian it can seem to non-Christians. However, the scriptural aspect of CST may create a salutary tension, such that the challenge and transcendence modes of church-state interaction receive reinforcement.

---

[23]For the movement of CST to a personalist and scriptural orientation, see Charles E. Curran, "Catholic Social Teaching and Human Morality," in Coleman, ed., *One Hundred Years*, chap. 5; and Boileau, ed., *Principles of Catholic Social Teaching*, pp. 9-24. For a similar movement within the American episcopacy, see Michael Warner, *Changing Witness: Catholic Bishops and Public Policy, 1917-1994* (Washington, D.C.: Ethics and Public Policy Center, 1995). For a personalist political theory, see Thomas R. Rourke and Rosita A. Chazarreta Rourke, *A Theory of Personalism* (Lanham, Md.: Lexington Books, 2005).

The orientation of government to justice and the common good does not entail that all governments in all times will in fact be instruments of these principles. Indeed, government can be tyrannical, unjust and oppressive of human moral and religious values. In these instances the Church insists on the natural human right to resist unjust decrees and the religious duty to resist decrees that violate conscience. Although such resistance ordinarily should take peaceful and "passive" forms, such as political agitation, nonobedience and civil disobedience, under limited circumstances they may even entail the right to revolutionary violence.[24]

A more recent development (since the late 1950s) has been a focus on world community, including world government, and the promotion of peace. If humans are social and if the political community is naturally oriented toward good order, social justice and the common good, there is no good reason to limit its reach to current national borders. Indeed, since modern technology has rendered the means of communication and effective action global, CST now speaks of a global common good, of the obligations of wealthy nations toward poor ones and of an international order oriented toward justice and peace and directed by legitimate international organizations.[25] Moreover, the evolution of weapons of mass destruction and the horrors of nuclear violence revealed at Hiroshima and Nagasaki require new thinking about war and its underlying personal, social and economic causes. Popes from John XXIII in the 1950s through Paul VI in the 1970s and John Paul II in the 1980s and 1990s to Benedict XVI today have issued numerous statements condemning war in general and challenging many particular uses of military force to resolve international disputes.[26]

Common good. The preceding section alluded to the "common good" as the most general orienting purpose of the state.[27] Pursuit of the common good is the very reason for the authority granted to the state by God. Government has the responsibility to promote community among the variety of social groups

---

[24]*Compendium of the Social Doctrine of the Church*, pp. 172-73.

[25]Ibid., chap. 9.

[26]Ibid., chap. 11, and National Conference of Catholic Bishops, *The Challenge of Peace: God's Promise and Our Response* (Washington, D.C.: United States Catholic Conference, 1983).

[27]This section draws on *Compendium of the Social Doctrine of the Church*, pp. 72-75; David Hollenbach, "Common Good," in *New Dictionary*, ed. Dwyer, pp. 192-97; and Cochran and Cochran, *Catholics, Politics, and Public Policy*, pp. 8-9. See also Hollenbach, *The Global Face of Public Faith*; Hollenbach, *The Common Good and Christian Ethics* (New York: Cambridge University Press, 2002); and James W. Skillen, "The Common Good as Political Norm," in *In Search of the Common Good*, ed. Dennis P. McCann and Patrick D. Miller (New York: T & T Clark, 2005).

and individuals in society. The state's responsibility, however, does not deny but in fact requires the participation of the individuals and groups that constitute the political community (see sections on "Solidarity," "Freedom and Human Dignity" and "Subsidiarity").

In CST the common good is not an *aggregative* concept. That is, although the Church's language speaks of a "sum total of social conditions" that allows full human flourishing,[28] the common good is "common" because it belongs to everyone in the whole community. That is, the common good refers to the bonds of community that link persons together, bonds that depend on such specific goods as roads, schools, housing and health care. Because Catholic social anthropology insists that humans are social beings, the common good is a relational concept linking the unique personhood of each to the community that all share.

The concept of the common good thus steers CST between individualism and collectivism. The former is the temptation of liberalism—the insistence that the individual is the sole judge and possessor of goods. The latter is the temptation of socialism—the insistence that all goods come from cooperative relationships. CST, to the contrary, insists that being is *being* in relationship to God and to neighbor. Therefore, the common good is meaningless if it does not help each person flourish and if it does not, as part of that flourishing, facilitate each person's individual encounter with God. At the same time, an individual cannot attain fulfillment in isolation; inseparable from personal flourishing is the flourishing of the neighbor. Orientation to personal salvation and to subsidiarity deflect the temptation of collectivism, while orientation to being in relationship deflects the temptation of radical individualism.

Human finitude and the limits of natural resources mean that the common good is imperfectly realized in each political community. CST, however, sets it as the guiding principle for governments that they work to overcome and to limit the effects of sin and to integrate diverse experiences and ideas of good into a pattern that weaves together a human community from diverse individuals and groups.

The Catholic idea of the common good also draws on what CST calls the "universal destination of goods." "God destined the earth and all it contains for all men and all peoples so that all created things would be shared fairly by all mankind under the guidance of justice tempered by charity."[29] This principle entails that every human has the right to a share of the earth's goods nec-

---

[28]For example, *Compendium of the Social Doctrine of the Church*, p. 72.
[29]Ibid., p. 75 (quoting a document of the Second Vatican Council).

essary for one's own flourishing and the flourishing of the family and community of which one is a part. The use of private property ultimately must be compatible with this universal destination of goods and with the common good. This places CST in tension with capitalism and with those (even within the Church) who place unlimited trust in the market and in private initiative to promote material prosperity. Private property may be taxed, regulated for use and sometimes even appropriated in order to pursue the common good.

The universal destination of goods means also that the common good of an individual nation-state is ultimately limited by a universal or a global common good. If the earth is intended for *all* and if being is relational, there can be no justification for a nation's hoarding of goods or for unlimited preference for one's own. The needs of the poorest of the world, whose material and political rights are under gravest threat, have a substantial claim on the goods of the wealthiest nations.

Solidarity. The virtue of solidarity flows from the centrality of the common good to CST. Solidarity is the "Yes, I am my brother's keeper" affirmation of the bonds of common humanity. It is active caring for justice and the common good, flowing from identification with the needs and rights of others.

Solidarity is not a state of affairs or a goal, but a virtue that impels action. Although this concept has roots in earlier CST, it was John Paul II's encyclical *Solicitudo rei socialis [On Social Concern]*, issued in 1987, that brought the term to the forefront. Solidarity, he wrote, "is not a feeling of vague compassion or shallow distress at the misfortunes of so many people, both near and far. On the contrary, it is a *firm and persevering determination* to commit oneself to the *common good*; that is to say to the good of all and of each individual, because we are *all* really responsible for *all*."[30] "The unsurpassed apex of [solidarity] is the life of Jesus of Nazareth, the New Man, who is one with humanity even to the point of 'death on a cross' (Phil 2:8)."[31]

Although its immediate antecedent was the Solidarity Movement in Poland in the late 1980s, emphasis on solidarity lies in the paradox and tension between rising global human interdependence and stark inequalities in wealth, health and human freedom within and among nations. These inequities are not simply the result of individual human sinful choices but also of "structures

---

[30]Pope John Paul II, *Solicitudo rei socialis* (Washington, D.C.: United States Catholic Conference, 1987), §38. See also Charles E. Curran, Kenneth R. Himes and Thomas A. Shannon, "Solicitude Rei Socialis," in Himes, et al., *Modern Catholic Social Teaching*, esp. pp. 426-30. The explication of solidarity also draws upon *Compendium of the Social Doctrine of the Church*, pp. 84-87, and Matthew L. Lamb, "Solidarity," in *New Dictionary*, ed. Dwyer, pp. 908-12.
[31]*Compendium of the Social Doctrine of the Church*, p. 87.

of sin" built into the social arrangements of modernity.[32] These structures may be the exploitation of labor by capital in unregulated market economies, or they may be reliance on nuclear or other weapons, and indeed on war itself, in a world divided by ideology and religion, or they may be built-in structures of racial or ethnic stigma that divide humanity.

Solidarity, moreover, is an aspect of the Church's attempt to distinguish its social morality from such ideologies as individualism, collectivism and nationalism (and indeed of liberalism and conservatism). Solidarity reflects the social anthropology at the core of Catholic theology as well as the recognition that common humanity is mediated by cultural, ethnic, national and other forms of human particularity and diversity, which too are valuable and to be appreciated. Therefore, the virtue of solidarity is to apply both within national boundaries and across international borders, leading to a global solidarity that is the only guarantee of peace.

Social justice. A just society is one in which the common good is valued and pursued and, to the extent possible, realized in action. The broadest application of the concept of justice lies in the economic sphere, where it points to the need for a distribution of the world's goods that recognizes common humanity and human rights.[33]

Genuine community cannot exist where social and economic conditions exploit some members of the community or place members of the community at too great a distance from each other. Although individuals, businesses and the church itself have responsibility for establishing a just distribution of goods, government also must work to eliminate unjust social and economic conditions and to maintain fairness. Because lack of economic goods pushes many persons to the margins of society, beyond the pale of common membership, the condition of the poor and marginal is a particular test of social justice.

Social justice focuses particularly on the gap between rich and poor in the United States and the persistence of dire poverty in the Third World. Severe inequality and poverty make persons especially vulnerable to violations of human rights, economic exploitation, addiction, crime and violence. Moreover, a consumerist and materialist culture, derived from overcommitment to entrepreneurship and capitalist norms, undermines families and moral values, leading to a hyper-sexualized society, a culture of instant gratification, root-

---

[32]Ibid., p. 85.

[33]This discussion follows Cochran and Cochran, *Catholics, Politics, and Public Policy.* A review of CST and the economy may be found in Albino F. Barrera, *Modern Catholic Documents and Political Economy* (Washington, D.C.: Georgetown University Press, 2001).

lessness, dissatisfaction, and rebellion against the natural limits of the human condition. CST is concerned simultaneously with the ills of underdevelopment and "superdevelopment."

CST does recognize a right to private property and to the fruits of one's initiative, but it recognizes as well that all private property carries what the church calls "a social mortgage"; that is, private property must be directed ultimately by the principle of the universal destination of goods and by the common good. Moreover, individual initiative always depends on supportive social structures and the (often invisible) efforts and sacrifices of other members. Thus CST has no irrevocable commitment to any particular economic theory. Markets or government regulation or government ownership of productive capacity may conduce to social justice in different times and circumstances. The key is to prevent exploitation, to achieve relative social and material equality among citizens and to ensure basic human rights.

Not surprisingly, then, there is a substantial division among Catholic social theorists about economic justice. The "liberal" side of the spectrum argues that action on behalf of justice, particularly liberation of the economically and politically oppressed, is a "constitutive element" of the gospel and, therefore, of the Church's mission. The Catholic Church cannot be church without participating in the struggle for political and economic equality. The "preferential option for the poor" is especially strong in this strain of Catholic thought. On the left, there is also a small but significant group of thinkers who believe that the official church, even when liberal in economic orientation, is too committed to a capitalist, consumerist society that undermines the very foundations of the Church itself.[34]

On the other hand, there is a growing conservative voice, particularly among American Catholic theorists, in defense of free-market principles and practices as best embodying Catholic moral principles. What matters, on this account, is which economic system actually leads to greater equality, economic development and freedom. In the judgment of Catholic conservatives and neo-conservatives, the answer is free-market capitalism. In their view, that economic system embodies not only sound economic principles but a moral system congruous with Catholicism—freedom, human dignity, responsibility, thrift and generosity.

Freedom and human dignity. Human rights are grounded on the inviolable dignity of the human person made in the image of God, ennobled by the in-

---

[34]Budde, *The (Magic) Kingdom of God;* Budde and Brimlow, *Christianity Incorporated;* and Budde and Brimlow, eds., *The Church as Counterculture.*

carnation of the Son and redeemed by his passion, death and resurrection. Because of this dignity, persons have both rights and responsibilities. The rights include not to have one's dignity marred by violence or exploitation, the right to the means of sustenance for self and family, and the civil and political rights to participate fully in the life of one's society. The responsibilities include participation to advance the common good, respect for the dignity and rights of others, and protection of the weak and vulnerable.[35]

Again, CST attempts to mediate the tension between individualist and collectivist interpretations of rights and responsibilities. The human nature that bears dignity is social; therefore, rights and responsibilities are both individual and communal.

Because the human person is essentially oriented to transcendence, CST promotes religious freedom and toleration. Freedom of religious exploration and freedom of response to God are essential for the unfolding of transcendence. Conscience is inviolable; religious belief and practice must not be coerced. Protection of religious conscience demands separating the structures of faith and the structures of government. Separation, however, does not require prohibition of contact, nor does it forbid cooperation between church and state.

These teachings include the right and responsibility of Catholic Christians to participate in governance and in pursuit of justice and the common good. Although this responsibility does not mean that democracy is the *only* legitimate form of government, it does give democracy pride of place when such governments respect dignity, protect fundamental rights and advance the common good.

Freedom and democracy are *means*, not ends. The dignity of the human person is the soil out of which grow the common good, solidarity and justice. Particular freedoms (voting, press and assembly, economic enterprise) and democratic institutions are not ends in themselves. They are misused and abused if employed either to pursue selfish individual, class or national goals, or to defeat the common good or impair social justice.

It is no secret that certain aspects of CST's commitment to freedom and dignity are historically recent, being most dramatically expressed in the Second Vatican Council's 1965 *Dignitatis humanae [Declaration on Religious Liberty]*. Since that time, however, in many parts of the world, Church leaders relying on this commitment have become champions of human rights and strong crit-

---

[35]See *Compendium of the Social Doctrine of the Church*, chap. 3; Dwyer, *New Dictionary*; and Herminio Rico, *John Paul II and the Legacy of Dignitatis Humanae* (Washington, D.C.: Georgetown University Press, 2002).

ics of governments that violate the rights of their people. Yet tensions and paradoxes still abound. Many inside and outside the Church believe that its limitations on women with respect to ordination and its hierarchical structure violate rights and limit the very participation that the Church champions in secular life. An additional tension is that official Church documents argue strongly that it is the role of the *laity*, not the clergy, to advance CST in politics. Nonetheless, in practice the strongest voices remain those of the episcopacy, when it issues statements on human rights, health care, the death penalty, abortion or other social issues.

One final tension must be addressed. The most basic human right and freedom is the right to life itself, the foundation of all other rights. Unjustly to deprive a person of his or her life is a most grave violation of human dignity, of responsibility to the vulnerable and of the common good. This much is clear and shared by all schools of CST. This consensus, however, breaks down at the next level of analysis, and it disappears in political practice.

There is a minority but very influential opinion among theologians, bishops and lay activists that CST contains a clear hierarchy of life-related teachings that are absolute, exceptionless and nonnegotiable. Chief among them is the prohibition of abortion as a violation of the moral prohibition against killing of the innocent and an assault on human life and dignity in its most defenseless form. Included also, and on the same basis, are the wrongness of euthanasia, human embryonic stem-cell research and human cloning. So fundamental are these principles that government has the moral responsibility to prohibit all of these practices.

The majority of bishops and theologians, however, while not disagreeing with the graveness of these matters, does not agree that they belong in a separate and higher category of morality. Other assaults on human life, dignity and rights also have deep social significance, such as torture, the death penalty, war and threats of war, poverty, and lack of access to health care.

At the practical level the dilemma is that politicians and office holders seldom support all principles of Catholic moral teaching consistently. Moreover, there is disagreement about whether clear *moral* principles must always be fully embodied in *laws and public policies*. Whatever the level of theoretical agreement on life issues, there is considerable disagreement among Catholics in the pews and in positions of authority on the implications of CST for responsible Catholic electoral participation.[36]

Order and stewardship. The preceding discussion has alluded to ways in

---

[36]This, of course, puts the matter quite mildly.

which CST recognizes limits on the pursuit of justice, common good and human rights. These limits are of two kinds: limits of human goodness and limits of natural resources. The limits on human action imposed by the disorder of sin require government to create and maintain social order. The limits imposed by finite resources require government policies that steward the earth's resources.

Although many schools of Christian political thinking place order and the authority of government to punish evil first on the list of responsibilities, the Catholic impulse is to integrate this responsibility with the responsibility to pursue justice and common good. Government has purposes that flow from human nature in both its natural and its sin-damaged condition. Indeed, although conceptually it is possible to separate order-keeping from life-flourishing purposes, in practice they are intertwined. For example, criminal laws aim to prevent and to punish the effects of sin, but they also teach right from wrong. Punishment of criminals flows from sin but aims at reform by building on the good in all persons.

The Catholic tradition distinguishes ownership of goods from use of goods. Granting the right of private ownership of property requires that it be used for the common good. This principle ultimately means that humans do not possess the earth but are stewards of it under God's authority. Therefore, the political processes of debate and compromise must adjudicate competing demands for natural resources and insure the preservation of God's gifts into the future.

Church and State

The principles of CST just described produce no bright line of demarcation between church and state. These principles demand certain orientations and actions from government, but they demand corresponding orientations and actions from citizens and from the church itself. Both government and the church (and businesses and civil associations) have a deep concern for and responsibility toward the common good and social justice. Therefore, from the perspective of CST, it seems best to describe church, state and other institutions as interacting across a wide field of relationships, a complex intersecting borderland where territories, boundaries and responsibilities are shared, negotiated or fought over. The metaphor of tension that opened this chapter is apt for characterizing this terrain.

Seeking to separate church and state, whether from secular or sectarian motives, is really an attempt to eliminate necessary and healthy tension between church and state. In CST the *institutions* of church and state must be decisively divided. The church should not have the authority to write laws that govern the secular lives of citizens; the state must not have the authority to adjudicate proper forms of worship. This division of labor, however, does not separate the church from the state but rather frees it to pursue its mission and its principles, which will bring it into constant interaction with the state.

The tension recognized and advocated by CST with respect to state and politics is not foreign to the Christian life in general. Indeed, tension as a metaphor resonates with the core doctrines of Christian faith. What are the essential mysteries and paradoxes of Christian belief but forms of tension that have no final resolution, at least in human terms? The doctrine of the Trinity, for example, is the paradox of three persons in one God. As soon as we try to stress the oneness of God, we find ourself pulled back to the three. Similarly, the doctrine of the incarnation sees in Jesus one person with two natures, human and divine.

Given the tension between transcendence and collaboration, Christians are resident aliens, dissident loyalists, qualified patriots of whatever nation claims their citizenship. Some nations, or the policies of some nations, demand more than cooperation and transcendence; they may require Christians actively to challenge unjust policies or to found institutions to compete with the state in order to pursue the common good. If the only two possibilities were cooperation and transcendence, there would be some tension between church and state (or church and the world in general), but full tension emerges when all four dynamics interact simultaneously. Persons or denominations uncomfortable with this high degree of tension and ambiguity will try consciously or unconsciously to collapse competition and challenge into transcendence or collaboration. Or they will rule one or more of the dynamics out of order for Christians. CST requires all four to be held simultaneously.

These relationships do change from time to time. The degree of collaboration or challenge will vary from one historical period to the next, from one policy arena to another (from criminal justice to health care to war and peace) and from one nation to another. It is the same with transcendence and competition. There is no fixed amount of one or the other. The key is to respond appropriately to the demands of time and place. For example, in nineteenth-century America, Catholic institutions of social service existed largely apart from government. Catholic schools and orphanages, given the context of that time and place, offered a competitive alternative to often anti-Catholic government schools and sectarian orphanages. By the twentieth century, attitudes toward Catholics had changed; government social services had expanded dramatically and had become highly professionalized. In this new situation, Catholic social service agencies, especially charities and health care, became frequent collaborators with government, contracting for large sums in joint ventures to minister to the poor and to pursue the common good. At the same time, even with such collaborative relationships, Catholic institutions remained strong advocates, challenging government programs to achieve greater justice.[37] The present shape of social service provision in the United States requires Catholic institutions to work with a wide variety of public and private as well as secular and religious institutions that share some common goals and principles but diverge on others.

Given this complexity and the constancy of change, the Catholic approach is to stress political and social virtues rather than structural designs. The former are flexible; the latter tend toward rigidity. The political virtue par excellence in the Catholic tradition is prudence. Prudence is the practical wisdom to match application of lasting principle to transient circumstance. A proper relationship with a government agency in one policy arena may well be different from the proper relationship in a different arena or at a different time. In addition to prudence, the virtues of tolerance of ambiguity, respect for differences of perspective and opinion (between Catholics themselves and between Catholics and others), patience, and tolerance of complexity are essential. Finally, principles of institutional separation and wide scope for free exercise of religion allow maximum flexibility for strategies of collaboration, competition, challenge and transcendence.

Subsidiarity. The concept of subsidiarity, explicit in CST from 1931 with Pope Pius XI's encyclical *Quadragesimo anno [The Fortieth Year]*,[38] helps to flesh out the prudential character of Catholic political and social thinking.

Subsidiarity counsels that the primary purpose of the state is to assist ("grant help" = *subsidium*) the primary organs of social life (families, labor unions, businesses and other voluntary associations) to carry out their responsibilities. Secondarily, more comprehensive state institutions (such as the federal government) should provide assistance to states and local governments

---

[37]See Dorothy M. Brown and Elizabeth McKeown, *The Poor Belong to Us: Catholic Charities and American Welfare* (Cambridge, Mass.: Harvard University Press, 1997); and Christopher J. Kauffman, *Ministry and Meaning: A Religious History of Catholic Health Care in the United States* (New York: Crossroad, 1995) for the evolution of these trends in Catholic social services and Catholic health care.

[38]Christine Firer Hinze, "*Quadragesimo anno,*" in Himes et al., *Modern Catholic Social Teaching,* pp. 151-74; *Compendium of the Social Doctrine of the Church* §§185-88; Michael E. Allsopp, "Subsidiarity, Principle of," in *New Dictionary,* ed. Dwyer, pp. 927-29; Jonathan Chaplin, "Subsidiarity and Sphere Sovereignty: Catholic and Reformed Conceptions of the Role of the State," in *Things Old and New: Catholic Social Teaching Revisited,* ed. Francis P. McHugh and Samuel M. Natale (Lanham, Md.: University Press of America, 1993), pp. 175-202.

when these cannot fulfill their responsibilities to the common good from their own resources.

Subsidiarity generates both positive and negative injunctions. Positively, government has a moral mandate to act when voluntary associations, formed according to the natural right to associate and organize, encounter obstacles to their legitimate and necessary functions. Business and labor, families and schools have legitimate spheres of action and independence within those spheres. However, CST does not leave them to their own devices to sink or swim. Instead, there should be a collaborative relationship between government and associations, in which they respect government's purposes and government in turn assists them when necessary.

Negatively, government must not usurp legitimate functions of family, schools and other associations, nor is the national government to usurp the proper responsibilities of local governments. Instead, government's role is to *assist*. (Of course, government has roles that are uniquely its own and not assistive—criminal justice and national defense, for example.) It is wrong for "higher" associations, such as the national government, to take over what "lower" associations can do on their own. But it is also wrong for "higher" associations to withhold assistance when required.

Thus stated, subsidiarity constitutes a powerful recognition of human dignity, the rights of association and the indispensable contribution of the institutions of civil society to social justice and the common good. At the same time, subsidiarity is an abstract enough principle to invite misinterpretation. Economic conservatives invoke subsidiarity to advocate a "hands off" approach to the market and to advance a preference for state and local initiatives over national. Economic liberals invoke the principle to advocate government intervention and regulation as well as strong national policy, judging that associations such as labor unions, neighborhoods and local governments are too often under the sway of powerful interests and therefore require assistance to fulfill their goals.

Subsidiarity is best conceived as guidance for prudence rather than as a stand-alone principle. How much (if any) assistance and in what forms cannot be judged apart from specific policy arenas and specific circumstances. Putting this in terms of the four dynamics of church-state interaction, subsidiarity principally applies to judgments about the degree and form of collaboration required in particular policy arenas. For example, families frequently need assistance in fulfilling their mission of providing education, health care and material needs for their members. The forms of collaboration (and sometimes competition) between private social service organizations, local and state governments, and national government cannot be specified in the abstract but must be worked out in the daily push and pull of policy making, political debate and prudential judgment.

Church and the larger culture. Relationships between church and state operate within a larger cultural context whose influence should never be underestimated. Since the time of Constantine, the primary danger of culture to faith has been assimilation, the too-easy identification of the mission of the church with the dominant forces of the culture.[39] The Catholic Church has been guilty of this sin for much of its history.

Assimilation means loss of tension. The push and pull between faith and culture gives way to comfortable coexistence and mutual support. The church loses its edge; the state comes to depend on religion for legitimacy. Collaboration poses the greatest danger of assimilation, as the goals of church and state here are most congruous. Cooperation between government programs and faith-based service providers can blunt the edge of criticism and subtly mold the church in the direction of regime support.

Challenge and competition, although less subject to assimilation, are insufficient to avoid it because both too often take place on the terrain staked out by the larger culture. The church may challenge state institutions and practices, but in doing so it frequently relies on the language, images and terms set by the culture. The Right to Life movement, for example, strongly challenges the legalization of abortion, but does so by adopting the language of individual rights from cultural liberalism and applying that language to the child in the womb. This is an effective and necessary political strategy, but it leaves intact the dominant cultural paradigm even as it attacks one manifestation of it.

Competition as well often occurs on state terrain. Church-sponsored schools come to look very much like the public schools with which they compete. This result is not surprising; competition is the proper dynamic when an agreed-upon goal (education or health care) can be pursued by religious or by secular institutions. Necessarily, the practices to achieve the goal will share much in common. Church-related institutions then must expend considerable effort to maintain a distinctive identity in order to resist the pull of culture toward assimilation.

Necessarily, therefore, the transcendence dynamic bears considerable re-

---

[39]This is, of course, a very large generalization that cannot be defended here. And the church has shaped culture for the better in ways too numerous to count. See John W. O'Malley, *Four Cultures of the West* (Cambridge, Mass.: Harvard University Press, 2004). For the strongest version of the argument against assimilation, see Budde and Brimlow, *Christianity Incorporated*.

sponsibility for resisting assimilation. It is incumbent on Christians to remember Jesus and his refusal to bow to the dominant culture of his era (symbolized in the Gospel accounts of his three temptations in the desert), to sustain practices of transcendence (worship, retreats, renewal movements and monastic orders, for example) and to recognize the subtle temptations of culture. Therefore, all Christian religious communities need constant reminders of the difference between the faith and the world. For Catholic Christianity, these reminders are most prominent in the sacramental life of the church. The memory of Jesus, sacramentally expressed in weekly worship, in the life transitions of baptism, confirmation, marriage and anointing of the sick, as well as in the sacramental setting apart of ordained ministers in Holy Orders, has the potential to break social amnesia and to free the church from its cultural assimilation.[40]

Sacramental life constantly reinforces the mystery that is the heart of Christian faith—the mystery of the transcendence and immanence of God, of the reversal of life and death, of the unity of justice and mercy. Sacramental life in particular, and transcendence in general, are no guarantee that the proper degree of tension between church and state and between faith and culture will not be sundered. The danger of transcendence is separation into irrelevance. The mystery and transcendence of faith become so overwhelming that the world is dismissed as the realm of Satan, to be despised and rejected, or at best, ignored.

The *four* dynamics—held and practiced simultaneously—maintain the tension of existence. The principles of CST and their grounding in the distinctively incarnational and sacramental theology and practice of the Catholic Church fit the church for its encounter with state and culture. They furnish the tools for a "critical engagement" with government.[41]

Tension in Practice

Preceding sections referred to a number of policy issues. The present section employs Catholic health care and Catholic social services to illustrate CST's implications. Health care and social service provision represent very large sums of public money, extensive government regulation and intense policy debates. Catholic institutions are major participants in government programs of health care and social service. The idea of a "faith-based initiative" is nothing new for these institutions. They have been intimately involved with public programs for decades.

---

[40]Russell A. Butkus, "Dangerous Memory: The Transformative Catholic Intellectual," in Landy, ed., *Leaven in the World*, pp. 49-64.

[41]Skillen, *Common Good*.

Catholic health care and social services manifest the collaboration and challenge dynamics most clearly. The competitive dynamic is implicit, but not in the forefront. The internal challenge these institutions face is how to live transcendently and to embody a distinctive mission in the face of cultural, economic and public pressures to behave like other institutions with similar operations.

Catholic institutions are a strong presence in health care. In the hospital sector alone, over six hundred Catholic facilities constitute 12 percent of all community hospitals and 15 percent of all hospital beds, revenues, employees and admissions.[42] More than five million patients (without regard to religious affiliation) are admitted to Catholic hospitals in a given year. In addition, there are 1,400 Catholic day services and extended day services for people with health needs and another 1,400 continuing care facilities (such as assisted living and nursing homes). Thousands of parishes, missions and pastoral centers have health outreach ministries.

Similarly, hundreds of local agencies affiliated with Catholic Charities USA, as well as independent church-affiliated child care and adoption agencies, housing programs, job training, addiction treatment and programs for the elderly have for decades received public grants and contracts for their services. Catholic Charities across the nation provided help for about 6.5 million people regardless of religious, social or economic background in 2003. One hundred thirty-seven main Catholic Charities agencies and their 1,341 branches and affiliates provided a myriad of community-based services approximately 10.5 million times in 2003.[43]

Collaboration. Health care is a needed service for the community; government programs promote justice in access; Catholic facilities have a gospel mission to heal the sick and care for the poor. Cooperative arrangements, with tension arising over the details, are entirely natural and fitting.

Public programs, either in the form of health care financing (principally Medicare and Medicaid) or in the form of local, state and federal regulations regarding safety, quality of care and financial accountability dominate the U.S. medical system. Collaboration is the principal form of interaction between

---

[42]These and other data are for 2003 or 2004 and come from the Catholic Health Association of the United States. For historical perspective and contemporary description of the dynamics between church and state in Catholic health care, see Cochran, "Another Identity Crisis: Catholic Hospitals Face Hard Choices," *Commonweal*, February 25, 2000; Cochran, "Catholic Healthcare in the Public Square"; Cochran, "Institutional Identity; Sacramental Potential"; Cochran, "Taking Ecclesiology Seriously"; Hehir, "Identity and Institutions"; and Kauffman, *Ministry and Meaning*.

[43]See <www.catholiccharitiesusa.org/news/stats.cfm> (accessed February 13, 2006).

church and state for health care. Catholic facilities receive billions of dollars each year in the form of payment for services and, to a lesser extent, in the form of grants and contracts to provide health services for specific populations. In exchange for the tax exemptions that come with their legal not-for-profit status, Catholic health care facilities spend hundreds of millions of dollars on charity care for the poor, on community health outreach and prevention programs, and other forms of "community benefit." They comply (with much grumbling about complex and unnecessary regulations) with the thousands of pages of program requirements and reporting that accompany the funding and that govern health and safety codes.

The same is true of Catholic social service agencies. With a high percentage of funding from government grants and contracts for counseling of youth and families, job training, addiction services, and the like, collaborative relationships are typical. Just as with Catholic health care, such agencies hire on the basis of professional credentials and agreement with mission rather than religious affiliation. They serve persons in need regardless of creed. They do not require religious conversion or attendance at worship services as a condition of receiving assistance. Therefore, they have long met qualifications for public funding. The Bush administration's Faith-Based and Community Initiative (FBCI) did not represent a new opportunity for Catholic programs, nor did it represent a change in the way that these agencies do business with government.

In this light it is no surprise that the U.S. bishops and Catholic Charities USA were supportive of FBCI in principle and supported various specific legislative and administrative proposals. At the same time they were not favorable toward FBCI if it meant a *decrease* in federal funding to public assistance and social services or if it meant the *same* level of funding divided up among a larger number of religious or other nonprofit providers.[44]

Competition. To some extent there is competition between Catholic health facilities and government health facilities, especially where there are both local public hospitals and Catholic hospitals in the same community. However, there is generally plenty of medical need to go around and such competition seldom implies a Catholic dissatisfaction with the quality of care or other practices of public facilities. Competition, rather, is a historical byproduct of inde-

---

[44]Amy E. Black, Douglas L. Koopman and David K. Ryden, *Of Little Faith: The Politics of George W. Bush's Faith-Based Initiatives* (Washington, D.C.: Georgetown University Press, 2004); Jo Renee Formicola and Mary C. Segers, "The Bush Faith-Based Initiative: The Catholic Response," *Journal of Church and State* 44 (2002); Jo Renee Formicola, Mary C. Segers and Paul Weber, *Faith-Based Initiatives and the Bush Administration: The Good, the Bad, and the Ugly* (Lanham, Md.: Rowman & Littlefield, 2003).

pendent decisions about where to locate health care institutions.

Direct competition between public social service agencies and Catholic agencies is less common, principally because government does not directly operate many such agencies. The more common competition is between Catholic agencies and other religious and not-for-profit providers. Each seeks public funds to furnish particular services in the name of justice, charity and the common good.

Challenge. Although government programs with which Catholic facilities collaborate are oriented to the common good, to justice and to care for the poor, there are serious failures and shortcomings in those programs. Catholic health care spends considerable energy on public policy advocacy for program changes or for new programs to meet health care needs. For example, Medicaid programs are barely adequate the meet the health needs of poor and low-income persons, and they are frequently targets of budget cutting in Washington and state capitals. Catholic bishops and Catholic health systems advocate with legislators and program administrators for better administration and fuller funding. Catholic facilities have for the last three decades lobbied hard for universal health insurance, challenging official and public acceptance of 15 percent of the population uninsured.

These examples are cases of what might be called "offensive" challenge. That is, they are examples of how Catholics confront government when it does not live up to its obligations as CST understands them. The church does this, despite depending on funding that comes from the hands of those it challenges.

However, Catholic health care also spends considerable energy on "defensive" challenges to public programs. That is, policy sometimes interferes with or directly impinges on the ability of Catholic facilities to live their mission. These challenges come in the form of advocacy for more adequate reimbursement under Medicare, for example. Or they may take the form of resistance to legislative proposals to require Catholic health care facilities to provide services (abortion and contraception, most prominently) that violate their religious identity.

The situation is precisely the same with respect to Catholic Charities USA. It (and other Catholic agencies to a lesser extent) plays the same offensive-defensive lobbying/advocacy game. Despite its dependence on public funding, Catholic Charities is not shy about challenging the funders for increased funding and greater flexibility in the use of funds. Simultaneously, it must protect its agencies from mission-hampering or religious conscience-violating legislation.

Transcendence. Transcendence, it will be recalled, demands separation from state and culture, not primarily in the form of resistance (challenge) or rejection, but rather in the form of sublime indifference or even as suffering and death.[45] The church has a mission that it must pursue regardless of the actions (good, bad or indifferent) of the state. The difficulty in the health and social service sectors is that (as suggested earlier) cooperation with the state and with culture too often drives religious institutions toward assimilation. Collaboration demands taking on the initiatives and the directives of the public programs from which the institution derives the resources for its mission. Even to compete and to challenge public programs normally takes place on turf established by those programs. Therefore, it becomes too easy for Catholic institutions to lose vision in the midst of day-to-day collaboration and conflict.

These comments are not in any way meant to denigrate public programs or the professional norms of medical workers or social service providers. These may be (and certainly are in most cases) both admirable and convergent with Catholic norms and principles. However, they are not and should not be identical. The church has a mission in healing and in charity that transcends such naturally good principles. The danger is to forget the transcendent or to identify the naturally good with the transcendent.

Conclusion

The tension between transcendent and immanent mission varies over time. Although the Catholic tradition values both transcendence and immanence, they do not always rest comfortably together. But a healthy CST cannot lose tension, either by relaxing the difference or by stressing them so greatly that the tension snaps.

An ancient description of Christian life in the world wonderfully captures the tension and paradox:

> Christians are indistinguishable from other men either by nationality, language, or customs. They do not inhabit separate cities of their own, or speak a strange dialect, or follow some outlandish way of life. . . . With regard to dress, food and manner of life in general, they follow the customs of whatever city they have to be living in. . . .
>
> And yet there is something extraordinary about their lives. They live in their own countries as though they were only passing through. They play their full role as citizens, but labor under all the disabilities of aliens. Any country can be their homeland, but for them their homeland, wherever it may be, is a foreign

---

[45]A point suggested by Glenn Tinder.

country. Like others, they marry and have children, but they do not expose them.
... They pass their days on earth, but are citizens of heaven. Obedient to the laws, they live on a level that transcends the law.[46]

Appreciation of the tension between the multiple dynamics of Christian faith characterizes the Catholic approach to life on the border between church and state. The missions of charitable works and justice advocacy cannot be reconciled fully in earthly life, just as mercy and justice meld only in God. Yet each member of these pairs remains integral to Christian love,[47] lived according to the ecclesial and political disciplines required by a way of life patterned after Jesus' revelation that God is love and that the one who abides in love abides in God (1 Jn 4:16).

---

[46]From "Letter to Diognetus," in *The Liturgy of the Hours According to the Roman Rite,* vol. 2 (New York: Catholic Book Publishing, 1976), pp. 840-41.

[47]In notable continuity with this teaching of CST, the first encyclical letter of Pope Benedict XVI (*Deus caritas est,* published in early 2006) features this theme prominently.

Classical Separation Response

Derek H. Davis

Clarke Cochran's superb essay on the Catholic view of social justice reminds us that Catholics today possess a far more sophisticated and nuanced view of church-state relations than Catholics of past centuries. Church-state separationists often look to the medieval Catholic union of church and state (the so-called Constantinian Union) as the starting point for any discussion of the merits of separating church and state. The medieval experience produced a well-known parade of horribles—pogroms against heretics, inquisitions and religious wars—that make it relatively easy to celebrate religious freedom as a great modern advancement.

Especially since Vatican II, American Catholics have adopted a thoroughly modern view of church-state relations consistent with the American experience. Nevertheless, traces of the old view linger. Theses traces accommodate a close linkage between church and state institutions that sacralize the state in a way that, at least for me, offend the Founders' project. Thus when ideas like the Charitable Choice scheme arise, Catholics have little difficulty endorsing such proposals. In the case of Catholics, this is hardly necessary since, as Cochran makes clear, Catholics have a long history of working with state institutions to alleviate human suffering. They did this long before the Charitable Choice initiative appeared in the 1990s by receiving government funds for various social service projects. However, recipients were legally separate in structure from churches and other houses of worship, and they were not allowed to proselytize their clients or discriminate on the basis of religion in hiring. These rules were designed to protect the religious liberty of clients and to further the nation's commitment to nondiscrimination when using government dollars to finance a program. Successful organizations like Catholic Charities and Lutheran Social Services operated effectively with these rules for years. Under Charitable Choice, religious organizations can receive government funding directly rather than having to establish insulated social service organizations, and even Catholics, unfortunately, have endorsed this plan because in theory it will enhance delivery of social services.

The notion that America's apparent need to enlist the aid of government to assist churches and other faith-based institutions to administer social service programs has begun to soften the nation on one of its founding principles— the separation of church and state. For many, this softening is a welcome change. Legal scholar Carl Esbeck states that "to increasing numbers of Americans, strict separation presents a cruel choice between suffering funding discrimination or forced secularization."[1] These supposed coercive and discriminatory elements of church-state separation are common arguments among those favoring greater governmental accommodation of religious institutions of all kinds.[2] But church-state separation has served to benefit rather than harm American religious vitality. Furthermore, attempts to alleviate the alleged "harm" of separation inevitably involve the forfeiture of religion's sacred space under the First Amendment and the ultimate denigration of religious institutions to the status of social service organizations. Indeed, the kindly intent of bureaucrats to subsidize our religious institutions only can lead to irresolvable complexity and the despiritualization of those religious organizations that we depend on as a cultural counterweight to the often morally deficient bureaucracies of secular society.

To comprehend the potential damage to American religious vitality done by government benevolence, we first must recognize that the durability of a nation's spirit is conditioned heavily by the maintenance of separation between its two dominant institutional forms—the political and the religious. Baron de Montesquieu, recognizing the horrors of the church-state monism of eighteenth-century France, observed that the way to kill the vitality of religion is through government "favor." Similarly, Alexis de Tocqueville, having surveyed the American cultural landscape a century later, expressed his insight that "so long as a religion derives its strength from sentiments, instincts, and passions . . . it can brave the assaults of time"; however, "when a religion chooses to rely on the interests of this world, it becomes almost as fragile as all

---

[1]Carl Esbeck, "Equal Treatment: Its Constitutional Status," in *Equal Treatment of Religion in a Pluralistic Society*, ed. Stephen V. Monsma and J. Christopher Soper (Grand Rapids: Eerdmans, 1998), p. 13.

[2]Advocates of other governmental assistance programs such as Charitable Choice, which provides government funds and other resources to the social service organizations of religious groups, also employ this argument about the perceived discriminatory consequences of separation. For a more complete treatment of this topic, see Derek Davis and Barry Hankins, eds., *Welfare Reform and Faith-Based Organizations* (Waco, Tex.: J. M. Dawson Institute of Church-State Studies, 1999).

earthly powers."[3] For de Tocqueville, it was not coincidental that it is in America "where the Christian religion has kept the greatest real power over men's souls."[4]

The potential damage of the Charitable Choice initiative to the preservation of the unique American ethos observed by Tocqueville and others only can be discerned through recognition that the American constitutional system is uniquely susceptible to institutional subtleties, especially those that attempt to benefit religion through favor. There is considerable irony in the fact that the American church-state structure is able to withstand sledgehammer assaults like the great cultural schisms precipitated during the Civil War and Vietnam War, and the official attacks on liberal and pacifist denominations during the McCarthy era.[5] Yet in marked contrast to this resiliency there is vulnerability to the American system and to all church-state systems in modern pluralistic societies. That vulnerability is perhaps best illustrated in the church-state partnerships of modern Europe, where religion is given "equal treatment," yet statistics on religious belief and practice reflect a pale religiosity as compared to the United States with its tradition of church-state separation.

Do we not risk a similar decline in religiosity by adapting the same neutrality principle that has characterized much of Europe for decades, even centuries? Might it be true that the dynamism and vitality of religion in America is attributable to the separation principle? Is it not true that Americans voluntarily support their religious institutions because government declines to do it for them? Religion remains robust in America precisely because it is independent of government support and regulation. Americans possess a will to support their religious institutions because government does not do it for them. A new era of government benefits to religion could kill the voluntary spirit that sustains the vibrancy and dynamism of American religion.

If we are willing to take a lesson from our European friends, we will know that government aid and support is harmful rather than helpful to religion. Many Europeans today unfortunately look upon religion as just another government program. Attendance in most European churches is abysmal. The people have lost, to a very large degree, the will to support their own religious

---

[3]Alexis de Tocqueville, *Democracy in America*, ed. J. P. Mayer, trans. George Lawrence (1835; reprint, Garden City, N.Y.: Doubleday, 1969), p. 296.

[4]Ibid., p. 291.

[5]Robert S. Ellwood contends that McCarthyism not only attempted to subvert churches supposedly sympathetic to communism but tried to establish "an anti-Communist state church." See Robert S. Ellwood, *The Fifties Spiritual Marketplace: American Religion in a Decade of Conflict* (New Brunswick, N.J.: Rutgers University Press, 1997).

institutions because government does it for them. It would be a great tragedy indeed if America, where religion is alive and robust, adopted essentially the same patterns of government funding of religion that exist in many parts of Europe, where religion is experiencing a gradual death.

I make no pretense of understanding fully the dynamics that enables the church-state separation of American culture to contribute to a religious vitality far superior to the church-state accommodation of European countries, but the evidence is compelling. Because the essence of religion deals with the sacred rather than the temporal aspects of humanity, it differs in kind rather than degree from other aspects of life that government supports. Recognition of this fact provided the architectural wisdom that contributed to the subtle but ingenious wording of the First Amendment. If the United States adopts a system of "equal treatment" in church-state relations, it will be most difficult to return to genuine church-state separation even if it is recognized that equal treatment has been harmful to the country's religious vivacity.

It is also generally overlooked that those faith groups receiving public dollars will justifiably be subjected to government audits and monitoring. This will lead to excessive entanglements between religion and government and an unhealthy dependence of religion on government. Making religion the servant of government would likely inaugurate the decline of religion's current role as the nation's prophetic voice and conscience against ill-advised governmental policies. Religion with its hand out can never fulfill its prophetic role in society. Charitable Choice in some ways proves the point that many in America still fail to understand that religion is better off without government money.

Have Americans become so fearful of ideological diversity and the country's perceived moral decline that we are willing to place at risk our religious vitality, perhaps the most distinctive feature of American society? Our inability to come to agreement on the importance of our founding principle of church-state separation to the nation's identity and ethos is conditioned by William Lee Miller's observation that "religious liberty was more central to the nation's original moral self-definition than is comprehended."[6] The farther we drift in time from our nation's origin, the greater our disposition to tweak the system, to attempt to reshape our national ethos using the coercive power of government.

Advocates of Charitable Choice seem convinced that meeting the needs of the nation's poor and needy can only be achieved by enlisting the aid of

---

[6]William Lee Miller, *The First Liberty: Religion and the American Republic* (New York: Paragon House, 1985), p. 230.

faith-based institutions. But why does this also require an infusion of government money, with all of the attendant problems, both practical and constitutional? Congress could offer economic incentives (e.g., tax credits and multiple write-offs) to corporate America for donations to faith-based institutions. The possibilities here are endless, but the notion of corporations adopting and providing the financial means for charities, churches, synagogues and other faith-based organizations to administer social programs—in effect creating a new strain of partnerships to solve problems that government cannot solve—is an attractive prospect.

But apart from these possibilities, and even in the new world created by the Charitable Choice initiative, houses of worship and other religious organizations can still exercise the same option that has always been open to them: assist the poor and needy on their own terms, with their own financial resources, in an expressly religious environment, and with complete freedom to proselytize and teach their own religious beliefs. America's tradition of religious liberty could never be more faithfully or effectively exercised.[7]

---

[7]I am grateful to Chuck McDaniel, Baylor University, for his assistance in the preparation of this essay.

Principled Pluralist Response

Corwin Smidt

Rather than repeating certain preliminary points that I wish to make about each of the Christian perspectives examined in this volume, I would urge the reader to read first my opening paragraph of response to the classical separationist perspective (see p. 117). What is said in that paragraph applies also to the Roman Catholic perspective.

The principled pluralist perspective stands in agreement with much of the Catholic perspective. Of course, Catholic social teaching is quite broad in nature, covering a number of different topics and themes, and has a long history, with different perspectives emerging as to the proper interpretation of that theological tradition. As a result, Catholics of many different political perspectives can claim that they stand in agreement or conformity with the social teachings of the church. Consequently, it perhaps is not surprising that there are many points on which principled pluralists can claim to stand in agreement with Catholic social teaching.

Both perspectives stand together in their recognition of the role that civil society plays in public life. Catholic teaching does so through its principle of subsidiarity, while principled pluralists do so through the notion of sphere sovereignty. Consequently, Catholic social teaching at least allows for (and many Catholics support) legislative measures such as faith-based initiatives, a legislative endeavor that principled pluralists also support.

Principled pluralists stand in agreement with Catholic social teaching that the kingdom of God "is now and not yet, fully present yet not fully actualized, and that the disciple of Christ strives to live as a citizen of the kingdom in both ecclesial and civil life" (p. 42). The two also stand together in agreement that the church's mission is incarnational in nature, with justice and common good serving as the primary orienting goals or principles in terms of public engagement, and that God has created human beings as social creatures (though perhaps there are differences between the two perspectives, depending on how

"God made humans for community" might be understood).

Where the two perspectives tend to diverge (though not necessarily in terms of opposition) is on the Catholic emphasis of sacramental nature of the Christian mission and on its emphasis on the "option for the poor." This divergence occurs, with regard to the former, in that the principled pluralists follow the Reformed tradition with its somewhat different interpretation of the sacraments and its corresponding recognition of only two sacraments (baptism and Communion). Likewise, the "option for the poor" is different from, but related to, an emphasis on justice. There is agreement between the two perspectives on justice as a goal or principle. But, while the principled pluralist perspective is not opposed to "voluntary poverty for the kingdom," it has not been a feature of principled pluralism (though there is nothing inherent within principled pluralism to argue that it is contrary to Christian political engagement).

Perhaps the one place where principled pluralists and Catholic social teaching are most likely to diverge is with regard to the notion of "natural law," which stresses "the universality and rational accessibility" of Catholic social teaching, and the foundation of natural law in reason (though the author notes that, in recent decades, papal statements on Catholic social teaching have stressed scriptural arguments, without necessarily abandoning the idea of universality). The Reformed tradition too has long stressed the role of reason, reflected in part in its historical emphasis on the need to worship God with both heart and mind. However, for many within the Reformed tradition, reasoning occurs primarily within a particular system of thought. So, as was noted with regard to the social justice perspective, principled pluralists have frequently emphasized the presence of worldviews (i.e., systems of thought that are built on fundamentally different assumptions). This notion of worldview is tied to the "pluralist" component of the principled pluralist label, and it stands logically in opposition to the notion of natural law.

Whether the noted increased tendency of papal statements on Catholic social teaching to use arguments based on Scripture reflects a movement away from a natural law to a worldview perspective remains to be seen.

Anabaptist Response

Ronald J. Sider

In Clarke Cochran's masterful overview of Catholic social teaching, I find many things to approve. Here and there, I also have objections.

If the standard is biblical revelation, then it seems to me that most of Catholic social teaching is simply good, biblically grounded, orthodox Christian teaching. It may have been spelled out by Roman Catholic thinkers and documents, but to a very great extent it is what all Christians should affirm.

In fact, I would go further and argue that at some crucial points, Catholic social teaching approximates a biblical balance better than some evangelical thought and practice. Nowhere is this clearer than in the various ways that Catholic social teaching combines the individual and communal poles of human existence. Cochran shows how Catholic thought integrates on the one hand an emphasis on the unique personal identity of every individual called to a personal response to God, and on the other, an emphasis on our communal nature created for community and therefore unable to reach fulfillment as isolated individuals.

One sees this in many areas: in the way that the Catholic understanding of human rights embraces both personal and social rights, in the way the concept of the common good balances (and transcends) both Western individualism and Eastern collectivism, in the way the concept of the "universal destination of goods" (p. 50) both affirms and qualifies private ownership and market economies, and in the way government is understood—that government results not from the Fall but from our very created nature as communal beings, but also that because of the Fall, government must restrain evil.

Evangelicals—especially American evangelicals—have a lot to learn here. We have too easily and uncritically embraced Western individualism. Without abandoning the powerful truth of the dignity, importance and freedom of every single person, we need to grasp more fully the (biblical!) truth that we are also communal beings and therefore that the institutions of community, including government, have significant positive roles to play.

This is not to say that evangelicals should embrace every aspect of Catholic social teaching. I think Catholics are simply wrong on birth control. Historically, their view that human reason can discern the natural law in a way adequate to govern public life fails, I believe, to appreciate the extent to which sin has corrupted the mind. There is a (divine, natural) law written on our consciences, but sin has so obscured it that we need to rely primarily on biblical revelation for our understanding of the vision and norms for faithful Christian public engagement. (Fortunately, more recent papal encyclicals and Catholic bishops' statements rely much more on special, biblical revelation.)

One final comment. In his discussion of the recent Faith-Based Initiative, Cochran says that Catholics were generally supportive but also were largely satisfied with the arrangements for cooperation between Catholic social service agencies and government that had existed for decades. Catholic agencies like Catholic Charities, Cochran says, do not hire on the basis of religious affiliation and do not require conversion or attendance at worship as a condition for receiving assistance. This obscures a more basic question: Is there anything uniquely Christian about the way that Catholic social agencies do their work? The program may be sponsored by Catholics, have a Catholic name and have a few top Catholic executives, but are the activities and programs designed to produce some social outcome (e.g., freedom from drugs, successful workers through job training) any different from secular agencies? Are purely non-spiritual components adequate for changing people? If persons are spiritual beings as well as material beings, wouldn't prayer, personal faith in Christ and the inner power of the Holy Spirit also be highly relevant to a uniquely Christian social service agency? That does not mean we should demand that a client pray or worship before receiving social services from a Christian agency. But it does mean that staff must know that persons need both good material care (e.g., food, medical care) but also spiritual transformation. And that means that the vast bulk of the staff need to be praying Christians. One wonders if agencies like Catholic Charities have become far more secular than they acknowledge or that historic Catholic thinking would approve.

Social Justice Response

J. Philip Wogaman

I welcome this careful, at points elegant, presentation of Catholic social thought. It comes as a reminder of the ecumenical sea change represented by the papacy of Pope John XXIII and the Second Vatican Council. Before John XXIII and the Council (in the first half of the 1960s), the relationship between Catholics and Protestants in this country was strained. Catholics felt beleaguered in the dominant Protestant political culture—where Al Smith lost the presidency largely because of his Catholicism and John Kennedy was put on the defensive for the same reason, only narrowly gaining the White House. Protestants were fearful that their religious freedom would be undermined if Catholics gained political power, as seemed indeed to be the case in Spain and parts of Latin America. Even the philosophical and theological basis for social teaching was largely disparate—the Catholics wedded to a fairly narrow interpretation of Thomistic natural law (as exemplified, for example, in Pope Pius XI's encyclical *Casti connubii)* and Protestants' greater reliance on Scripture and uses of the social sciences (exemplified, to some extent, by the first three assemblies of the World Council of Churches). Catholics and Protestants, when not overtly hostile, were pretty much talking past one another.

But the refreshing breeze—one might almost say the benevolent hurricane—represented by Pope John and the Council brought a whole new recognition of commonality. My own professional life having begun just before the big change, I can attest its importance among Christian ethicists and moral theologians on both sides of the great divide. Since the mid-1960s, both Protestant and Catholic ethicists have been able to interact with comparatively few differences following along denominational lines. Some differences of style remain, but few of substance. Indeed, Cochran's use of the eloquent passage from the "Letter to Diognetus" helps emphasize the commonalities of shared tradition. That passage, also a personal favorite of mine, sets forth the paradoxical relationship between Christians and "the world" in terms most Christians can identify with.

And so it is that I find the main outlines of Cochran's essay to be compatible with much social teaching in the mainline Protestant denominations. Certainly the overriding advocacy for the poor and the witnessing for peace are shared concerns.

Cochran does well to acknowledge the untidiness of much Catholic teaching. This cannot be surprising in view of the long history and the immense geographical and cultural spread of that church. Certainly no Protestant can point the finger of judgment here, for if anything, Protestant teaching has been all the more untidy. Indeed, if I may say so, I am envious of the Catholic Church's greater deliberative care in arriving at major social teaching: the Vatican Council itself stretching over five years, papal encyclicals issued by popes but characteristically formulated carefully with the help of eminent Catholic scholars, the American Catholic bishops' 1986 pastoral letter on the U.S. economy (which I wish Cochran had referred to) developed over a period of years. Some Protestant church documents have been developed over time, but all too often the various church resolutions have been written in haste and adopted quickly by church bodies. I don't want to overstate this difference, but it is often real.

There remains, however, a still more important point of difference that Cochran has largely neglected. That is the role of the *magisterium* in authoritative Catholic teaching. That is the process whereby the church's teaching is expressed authoritatively. Often that has been understood to be through pronouncements by bishops, and especially the pope.[1] In most of the mainline Protestant denominations, teaching becomes authoritative through adoption by elected church assemblies. For example, the only body that can speak authoritatively for my United Methodist Church is the denomination's quadrennial General Conference—and one General Conference can change or even reverse what a preceding conference has enacted. In the Roman Catholic Church the definitive authority remains the pope. When Rome speaks, the matter is more or less settled. It is not unusual for a Catholic scholar or thinker to be at odds with the official teaching. But if dissent becomes too visible, it risks

---

[1] A number of Roman Catholic theologians have questioned whether hierarchical statements of bishops, or even of the pope, can be considered ipso facto authoritative. Charles E. Curran, for instance, has emphasized the legitimacy—even the necessity—of dissent from such statements when found to be inadequate expressions of the faith. See especially Curran's *Loyal Dissent: Memoir of a Catholic Theologian* (Washington, D.C.: Georgetown University Press, 2006).

heavy-handed disciplining, as Hans Küng and Charles Curran discovered.

Papal authority is rarely at issue in the matters of common good that are emphasized in Cochran's chapter. Not many significant Catholic moral theologians would disagree with the emphasis on the option for the poor or the witness for peace (usually expressed through a version of just-war theory) or religious liberty. But there remain deep, sometimes acrimonious, differences over the role of women, the morality of contraception and a few other issues. Pushed to their roots, some of the points of contention are related to the residual influence of a narrower conception of natural law. So hierarchical church authority continues to affect Catholic social teaching, though not nearly as tightly as during the pre-Vatican Council days—or so it seems to me.

Cochran has referred to the importance of that Council's "Declaration on Religious Liberty," which was indeed a landmark in Catholic teaching. Previously, official teaching had relied largely on what was known as the distinction between *thesis* and *hypothesis*. *Thesis* represented the norm, to be observed whenever social circumstances permitted. This norm provided that Catholic faith, perceived as objective truth, should be supported by the state and error should be suppressed. But where the church was not in a dominant cultural situation, it—still representing objective truth—should insist on policies of religious liberty. The new Vatican Council declaration abruptly turned away from this two-sided stance by flatly proclaiming that "the right to religious freedom has its foundation in the very dignity of the human person as this dignity is known through the revealed word of God and by reason itself. . . . [I]t is to become a civil right."[2]

That statement was truly a major move. In some respects, however, one could describe another of the Council's declarations as an even more significant support for religious liberty. That was the "Declaration on Non-Christian Religions," which spoke of positive values to be found in such religions and that these should not be repudiated by Catholics. Thus, so to speak, religious liberty is important not only as a matter of respecting the rights of others (who might still be considered to be objectively wrong in their religious views), but now as a recognition that they may have hold of some of the truth. Such a recognition is an excellent foreshadowing of that kind of interreligious dialogue the world so desperately needs.

By referring to the Catholic Church as a "public church," Cochran has clearly positioned that denomination more on the "church type" than the "sect

---

[2]"Declaration on Religious Freedom" 2, *The Documents of Vatican II* (New York: Guild Press, 1966).

type" side of the Troeltschian dichotomy (to which I refer in my response to the Anabaptist perspective [p. 212]). In this, Cochran is also more representative of the mainline Protestant churches, which also have a very positive conception of public participation. Still, one sees much affinity between Catholic and Anabaptist moral concerns. A striking emphasis in Cochran's Catholic view, however, is its "focus on world community, including world government, and the promotion of peace" (p. 49).[3] I am personally and wholeheartedly in agreement with that. I suspect that the Anabaptists would be less enthusiastic, being less persuaded that world community as such is possible or that world government could embody anything resembling Christian commitments. The mainline Protestant denominations are closer to that degree of world commitment, but on the whole—and to my regret—they may be more locked into nationalistic assumptions than the kind of Catholic teaching that Cochran represents.

At another point, Cochran has referred to Catholic recognition of "structures of sin" (pp. 51-52). That recognition, given substantial elaboration by the liberation theologians, is interestingly paralleled to the Social Gospel movement of American—mostly mainline—Protestant Christianity a century ago. One striking, brief formulation of the insight is contained in Walter Rauschenbusch's book *Christianizing the Social Order*, in which he defines an un-Christian social order as one in which good people are forced to do bad things—and a Christian social order in which bad people are forced to do good things.[4] Aside from all the caveats one must attached to such language, the central insight is that the way society is structured also structures the way good—or bad—people conduct their normal, everyday lives.

All of which is to say, the Cochran chapter illustrates well the basis for creative new forms of dialogue involving Catholics and Protestants (and others) about how all can contribute creatively to the public order.

---

[3]This focus gained significant impetus in Pope John XXIII's important 1963 encyclical, *Pacem in terris*. In that document, the pope employed the traditional concept of *subsidiarity* in a striking new way. Previously, *subsidiarity* had generally been taken as a protection of lower levels of social organization (such as families, local communities, churches and other institutions) from dominance by higher levels, such as the state. But in the encyclical, the pope asserted that "today the universal common good presents us with problems which are worldwide in their dimensions; problems, therefore, which cannot be solved except by a public authority with power, organization and means co-extensive with these problems, *and with a world-wide sphere of activity*. Consequently the moral order itself demands the establishment of some such general form of public authority" (sec. 137, emphasis added).

[4]Walter Rauschenbusch, *Christianizing the Social Order* (New York: Macmillan, 1912), p. 125.

2 | The Classical Separation Perspective

Derek H. Davis

In 1902 religious historian Sanford Cobb called religious liberty "America's great gift to civilization and the world."[1] Indeed, religious liberty stands as one of our nation's bedrock principles, yet seemingly it is always under siege—by those who fail to appreciate the complex thinking of the American Founding Fathers that caused them to write into the U.S. Constitution the principle that guarantees religious liberty: the separation of church and state.

The separation of church and state is blamed today for many things: the "unprecedented moral decline," the shootings at Columbine High School and other schools around the country, "rampant secularism," the spread of "cults and false religions," greed and materialism, even "God's judgment" against the United States resulting in the 9/11 terrorist attacks.

To remedy the so-called evils of the separation of church and state, many today attempt to rewrite history, telling us that the principle has been widely misunderstood. They suggest that the separation idea was only a political philosophy popular among a few radical Founding Fathers or that it was devised for expedience only—the inevitable result of religious pluralism in the new nation. Most often we hear that the principle originally prohibited only the establishment of one religion over others, thus permitting the advancement of religion by government if performed without discrimination against any particular religion. These critics suggest, for example, that there is no constitutional prohibition to prayer in public schools, provided we hear everyone's prayer; that we can help solve the moral decline with a program of nondiscriminatory government funding of churches and other religious groups to administer social programs and religious schools; and that we can post the Ten Commandments and other sacred texts that most Americans agree with in public schools, courtrooms, and other government buildings.

Of course, one rarely hears these suggestions from members of religious minorities. They know that a constitutional framework that allows government to

---

[1]Sanford H. Cobb, *The Rise of Religious Liberty in America: A History* (New York: Macmillan, 1902), p. 2.

actively support religion, even on a nondiscriminatory basis, will result in a virtual Christian establishment. This is because on the basis of virtually every poll, at least 80 to 85 percent of Americans still identify themselves as Christians. Thus minorities believe that allowing government to actively support religion will only result in the public sector being bathed in Christian prayer, language, programs, activities, symbols and messages. They fear being crushed under the weight of Christian majoritarianism—in a country where they are supposed to be "equal" in the eyes of government. And they are right. This is precisely what would happen, to the delight of many Christians who want a privileged place for Christianity in the nation but who fail to understand the profound theological foundation of the separation of church and state.

The principle of separation of church and state is ultimately founded on a theological basis. When the Founders, all religious men as far as we know, wrote in the Declaration of Independence that "all men are created equal," they had in mind that people are essentially equal in that they are created in the image of God and are "endowed by their Creator with certain unalienable rights," including the freedom to believe and practice one's religion. They believed that the *imago Dei* stamped upon every human being is the basis of the dignity and worth of every person. They understood that one's choices in the realm of religion must be made freely; otherwise a person's dignity and worth before God are not respected.[2] In other words, they believed in voluntarism, the right of every person to believe and practice his or her faith without coercion or interference from government, which can only be protected by a strong commitment to the separation of church and state.

In spite of its merits, the separation of church and state is a controversial subject in America today. This book presents five major views of the meaning

---

[2]For an excellent treatment of the theological dimensions of the American order, see Barbara A. McGraw, *Rediscovering America's Sacred Ground: Public Religion and Pursuit of the Good in a Pluralistic America* (New York: State University of New York Press, 2003), who argues that the roots of "America's Sacred Ground" are located in the ideas of John Locke, whose views were in turn accepted and expanded on by the American Founding Fathers. For Locke, natural law provides the essential rights (life, liberty and property) of humans and the necessary capacity (reason) to apprehend God and live according to conscience. His project was to remove from government the responsibility for crafting human souls and assign to it the new responsibility of protecting human rights, including the right to pursue religious truth according to conscience. Moreover, by decoupling church and state, religious institutions were to have no coercive political authority over anyone's pursuit of religious truth. McGraw argues convincingly that the underlying basis of the Founders' project is what she calls "America's Sacred Ground." This sacred ground, she claims, is the much-needed compass that provides the foundation for analyzing popular and political discourse about public religion and its fundamental role in shaping American values.

of the separation of church and state. The views presented hopefully will enable policymakers and other Americans to make sense of the debate and where they stand themselves. All of these views claim some measure of separation between church and state, but there are real differences in the positions presented. This chapter argues for what might be called "classical separation of church and state." It is classical because it captures, in my view, the original or "classical" spirit of the Founders' ideas and in fact became the fundamental framework of separation embraced by the U.S. Supreme Court until the 1980s.

The classical view should be distinguished from the "strict separationist" position, which countenances virtually no interplay between religion and government. This view is wisely excluded from consideration by the editor of this volume, who recognizes that strict separationists are almost nonexistent, that there were none among the Founding Fathers and that the category is a straw man erected today by critics of church-state separation to buttress their own antiseparation views. Classical separation takes the separation principle seriously, but is quite friendly to many aspects of religion in public life, as will be demonstrated. Although the U.S. Supreme Court once embraced this view, it began departing from it at least since the early 1980s, which I contend is an error of the first magnitude and portends days of significant trouble ahead for religious freedom in America. To explain classical separation, it is appropriate to look first at the constitutional provisions from which the principle emerged.

The Basic Debate: The Meaning of the Religion Clauses

The controversy over the meaning of the separation of church and state begins with the religion clauses of the First Amendment to the U. S. Constitution: "Congress shall make no law respecting an establishment of religion, or prohibiting the free exercise thereof." The two clauses (the "establishment clause" and the "free exercise clause") issue two separate mandates. The establishment clause was clearly intended to eliminate the possibility of an established church (e.g., as the Church of England was established in England) in the new nation; beyond that, full agreement among scholars as to the framers' intent ceases. The free exercise clause, whose original purpose is also much debated, generally was intended to preserve the right of the citizen to believe, following John Locke, "according to the dictates of his own conscience,"[3] free from civil coercion.

Much of the contemporary debate over the framers' intent in the wording of the religion clauses focuses on the establishment clause. This is because

---

[3]John Locke, "A Letter Concerning Toleration" (1685).

some of the key issues in American society today focus on the degree of permissible government sponsorship, promotion, advancement or support of religious activities, and it is accepted by all that the term *establishment* as contained in the establishment clause bears most directly on these issues.

There are two basic interpretations of what the constitutional framers intended the establishment clause to mean. Hereafter, for discussion purposes, I will refer to the classical separation position as simply the "separationist" position. The other four views presented in this book also prescribe some measure of separation, and while none of them will decry separation completely, they all call for a lesser degree of separation. These other positions will hereafter be referred to, separately or collectively, as "accommodationism," or the "accommodationist" position, due to the fact that they all call for a greater accommodation of religion in public life than the classical separation position, especially in allowing governmental financial assistance to religious institutions, even if it be only for the administration of programs that advance so-called secular interests—charitable endeavors, social justice programs, humanitarian measures and the like. Perhaps I am overgeneralizing a bit too much with respect to the other positions, so the reader should rely less on my comments than on the specific presentations of those positions located in this volume.

The separationist interpretation was first advanced by Justice Hugo Black for a five-to-four majority in the 1947 landmark case of *Everson v. Board of Education,* where he wrote, "In the words of Jefferson, the clause against establishment of religion by laws was intended to erect 'a wall of separation between church and State.' "[4] Elaborating further, the Court declared that the original purpose of the establishment clause was to create a significant separation of the spheres of civil authority and religious activity by forbidding all forms of government assistance for religion. That is, the clause went far beyond merely prohibiting the governmental establishment of a single church or of preferring one religious sect over another. The separation was not to be absolute, as will be explained later, nor should it be. As constitutional historian Leonard Levy has stated, "The heart of this broad interpretation is that the First Amendment prohibits even government aid impartially and equitably administered to all religious groups."[5]

---

[4]*Everson v. Board of Education,* 330 U.S. 1, 15-16 (1947).

[5]Leonard W. Levy, "The Original Meaning of the Establishment Clause of the First Amendment," in *Religion and the State: Essays in Honor of Leo Pfeffer,* ed. James E. Wood Jr. (Waco, Tex.: Baylor University Press, 1985), p. 44.

This separationist interpretation grows out of the views of many of the leaders, notably Thomas Jefferson and James Madison, in the eighteenth-century movement for religious liberty. For example, in Jefferson's "Bill for Establishing Religious Freedom" (1779) and Madison's "Memorial and Remonstrance" (1785), the idea is clearly expressed that religion should be totally independent of government interference.

In contrast to the separationist interpretation, the various accommodationist views generally hold that the framers intended the establishment clause to prevent governmental establishment of a single sect or denomination of religion over others. According to this interpretation, historian J. M. O'Neill has said that the framers purposed to prohibit "a formal, legal union of a single church or religion with government, giving the one church or religion an exclusive position of power and favor over all other churches or denominations."[6] Sometimes called "nonpreferentialists," proponents of this view permit governmental aid to religious institutions as long as it prefers no particular group or sect. Accommodationists hold that the wall of separation between church and state was not intended to create a sharp division between government and religion or to enjoin government from fostering religion in general.

The separationist-accommodationist debate also embraces the free exercise clause. The separationist position is that governmental bodies, having no inherent competence in matters of religion, should restrict the free exercise rights of individuals and religious bodies only to the extent that their religious exercise will endanger the health and welfare of themselves or others, or if it violates public policy in some serious way. As a legal standard, this became the accepted view of the Supreme Court as early as 1878 in *Reynolds v. United States*.[7] More recently, however, due to the views of an increasingly accommodationist Supreme Court, state and local governments have been given considerable freedom to regulate religious activity, so long as it occurs pursuant to "neutral" laws of "general applicability" not written to discriminate specifically against religious activity.[8] In this sense it is not religion being accommodated, as under the accommodationist interpretation of the establishment clause, but the majoritarian political process. This trend is troubling to separationists because it offers minority (and often unpopular) religions little

---

[6]J. M. O'Neill, *Religion and Education under the Constitution* (New York: Harper & Row, 1949), p. 56.

[7]*Reynolds v. United States*, 98 U.S. 145 (1878).

[8]*Employment Division of Oregon v. Smith*, 494 U.S. 872 (1990). The Religious Freedom Restoration Act, designed to deal with the harsh effects of the *Smith* case, became law on November 16, 1993.

protection or "separation" from legislative enactments that infringe on their religious practices.

Classical separation understands religious liberty as the absence of government constraint on individuals in religious matters. This emphasis on individual freedom, the protection of each individual's religious conscience, is the fulcrum on which issues of church and state turn.[9]

The accommodationist position deemphasizes individual action while giving greater attention to the communal aspects of religion.[10] Accommodationists emphasize that the religion clauses were never intended to deal harshly with religion and interpret them to make religious liberty a positive right, the individual and communal exercise of which is to be encouraged, if not initiated, by government. This position is significantly different from that of separationism and leads to markedly different contemporary policies and practices.

In sum, accommodationists consider that the operative ideal of the early republic was a posture of support of religion by government on a nonpreferential basis. In turn, that posture seems to point toward a twenty-first-century ideal of governmental accommodation to religion in ways that promote virtue among the citizens and generally secure the greater common civil good. Classical separation holds that direct, especially financial, support of religious institutions inevitably compromises their religious mission, causes dependence on governmental support, politicizes religion and ultimately causes religion to lose its prophetic role and its ability to provide the moral foundations that the nation needs.[11]

Both positions have their strengths and weaknesses. The surviving data of the founding period, especially the debates of the Founding Fathers in formal session, as well as the records of the states' ratification proceedings, are regrettably inadequate in their treatment of the subject and certainly leave room for more than one interpretation. Nevertheless, it is submitted that on close examination of the deliberation process engaged in by the drafters of the religion clauses, it can be demonstrated that the separationist position is indeed far more compatible with the drafters' views and should therefore be adhered to today.

The First Congress and the Emergence of the Religion Clauses

James Madison had been among those who argued that a bill of rights was un-

---

[9]John F. Wilson, "Religion, Government, and Power," in *Religion and American Politics: From the Colonial Period to the 1980s,* ed. Mark A. Noll (New York: Oxford University Press, 1990), pp. 79-80.
[10]Ibid., p. 80.
[11]Ibid., pp. 80-81.

necessary. He insisted that the national government had no power to infringe on individual rights. He soon came to appreciate the honest fears of the delegates to the state conventions, however, who insisted on a clear prohibition of federal infringement on the rights of conscience as well as other individual liberties. It was largely on the basis of his assurances that he would seek to secure before the first Congress the kinds of amendments that the states wanted that most of the states were willing to ratify the Constitution.[12]

The proposals. After the Constitution was ratified, Madison, feeling "bound in honor" to secure amendments,[13] was true to his word and offered a number of proposed amendments to the first Congress. On June 8, 1789, at the opening of the first Congress, Representative Madison proposed, among others, the following amendment: "The civil rights of none shall be abridged on account of religious belief, nor shall any national religion be established, nor shall the full and equal rights of conscience in any manner or in any respect be infringed."[14]

As stated earlier, most of the controversies about church-state separation in the United States revolve around the establishment clause. While every proposed wording of the religion clauses differentiated establishment issues from free exercise and other issues, due to space limitations only the establishment issues will be addressed here. Accommodationists claim that the word *national* in Madison's proposal is proof that Madison intended nothing more than a prohibition against the preference of one religion over another. Yet a number of facts suggest that Madison might have opposed more than just the establishment of a national church.

Madison had led a fight in 1785 in the Virginia legislature against a bill calling for a general tax assessment for the support of not one but of all Christian religions. In his renowned "Memorial and Remonstrance," Madison repeatedly referred to the assessment bill as an "establishment of religion."[15] After his retirement from the presidency, Madison in 1817 expressed his disapproval

---

[12]James E. Wood Jr., E. Bruce Thompson and Robert T. Miller, *Church and State in Scripture, History, and Constitutional Law* (Waco, Tex.: Baylor University Press, 1958), pp. 101-2.

[13]*Annals of the Congress of the United States, The Debates and Proceedings in the Congress of the United States*, 42 vols., compiled from authentic materials by Joseph Gales Sr. (Washington, D.C.: Gales and Seaton, 1834), 1:441; reprinted in *The Founder's Constitution*, ed. Philip B. Kurland and Ralph Lerner, 5 vols. (Chicago: University of Chicago Press, 1987), vol. 5: Bill of Rights, no. 11, at 21-32.

[14]*Annals of the Congress*, 1:451, as appearing in Kurland and Lerner, *The Founder's Constitution*, vol. 5: Bill of Rights, no. 11, at 25.

[15]Robert A. Rutland, ed., *The Papers of James Madison*, 9 vols. (Charlottesville: University of Virginia Press, 1976), 8:298-306.

of tax-supported chaplains for Congress and the armed services as well as presidential proclamations of days of thanksgiving. Significantly, he described these as "establishments" and "the establishment of national religion."[16] All of this makes it difficult to know conclusively what Madison meant when he submitted his proposed amendment prohibiting the "establishment" of a "national religion." He may have been signifying not that the federal government had no business preferring one church or religion over others but that national action on behalf of any or all churches or religions was outside the purview of permissible government action.

Madison's proposed amendment was referred to a specially formed House select committee, of which Madison was a member. The committee subsequently considered four alternative proposals. Space does not permit elaboration on these proposals, but generally they had separationist leanings.[17] For example, one proposal, submitted by Samuel Livermore of New Hampshire, said, "Congress shall make no laws touching religion, or infringing the rights of conscience." This proposal has a decidedly separationist flavor and seems to be a reaction to possible nonpreferentialist notions among certain other committee members. Congress's inability to pass any laws "touching" religion would arguably foreclose any kind of law that would benefit or sponsor religious projects or institutions. But the language was apparently unsatisfactory, thus the House committee entertained other proposals.

On August 21, 1789, the committee finally agreed on this language: "Congress shall make no law establishing religion, or prohibiting the free exercise thereof, nor shall the rights of conscience be infringed." There is contemplated here far more than the prohibition of a national church or the preference of some religions over others; thus the separationist perspective seems to be in view. The only account of the debate, in the *Annals of Congress*, provides only a paraphrase of the proceedings and does not help resolve the questions about the members' meaning. Without debate, this proposal was adopted by the necessary two-thirds of the House. The amendment was submitted to the Senate.

The Senate began deliberations on the House amendment on September 3 and continued through September 9. In considering the House's draft, a Senate motion was first made to strike out "religion, or prohibiting the free exercise thereof" and to insert "one religious sect or society in preference to

---

[16]Elizabeth Fleet, ed., "Madison's Detached Memoranda," *William and Mary Quarterly* 3 (1946): 554-59.

[17]See Derek H. Davis, *Original Intent: Chief Justice Rehnquist and the Course of American Church-State Relations* (Buffalo, N.Y.: Prometheus, 1991), pp. 55-62.

others."[18] Thus the first new Senate version read: "Congress shall make no law establishing one religious sect or society in preference to others, nor shall the rights of conscience be infringed."[19] The establishment clause in this proposal appears to revert to a nonpreferentialist perspective, since only a prohibition against favoring some religions over others is contemplated. The same is generally true of four subsequent proposals.

Considerable disagreement exists among church-state scholars as to the meaning that should be given these Senate drafts. For example, Levy,[20] as well as legal scholar Douglas Laycock, argues that all of these drafts favored the "no preference" viewpoint, but all were rejected because the Senate clearly wanted a wording favoring the broad interpretation of the establishment clause. Laycock comments, "At the very least, these three drafts show that if the First Congress intended to forbid only preferential establishments, its failure to do so explicitly was not for want of acceptable wording. The Senate had before it three very clear and felicitous ways of making the point."[21] Another legal scholar, Gerard Bradley, however, holding to the narrow interpretation, seems to suggest that the rejected versions all were aimed at prohibiting a national church, indicating, despite the fact that all three versions were rejected, the dominant idea among the Senators—no national church.[22]

The Senate's final form of the amendment, adopted on September 9, read, "Congress shall make no law establishing articles of faith or a mode of worship, or prohibiting the free exercise of religion."[23] Like most of the previous Senate drafts, however, this proposal has the unmistakable meaning of prohibiting acts that prefer one church or sect over others—clearly a narrow intent. The Senate version of the amendment was then sent to the House, which rejected it. This action indicates, in all likelihood, that the House was not satisfied with merely a ban on the preference of one church or sect over another— clearly, a broad intent.

The religion clauses emerge. A House-Senate joint conference committee was created to resolve the disagreement over the religion amendment. A compromise amendment was eventually agreed to on September 25, and

---

[18]Linda Grant DePauw, ed., *Documentary History of the First Federal Congress of the United States of America,* 3 vols. (Baltimore: Johns Hopkins University Press, 1971), 1:151.
[19]Ibid.
[20]Levy, "Original Meaning of the Establishment Clause," p. 60.
[21]Douglas Laycock, " 'Nonpreferential' Aid to Religion: A False Claim About Original Intent," *William and Mary Law Review* 27 (1985-1986): 880.
[22]Gerard V. Bradley, *Church-State Relationships in America* (Westport, Conn.: Greenwood, 1987), pp. 93-94.
[23]DePauw, *Documentary History,* 1:166.

passed by both houses: "Congress shall make no law respecting an establishment of religion, or prohibiting the free exercise thereof."[24] The joint
committee left no records of its deliberations, but the congressional action
was completed. The religion clauses, comprising a mere sixteen words, had
been approved.

What are we to make of this final language? At best we can say that it reflects considerable disagreements over what the religion clauses were intended to achieve. The final wording reflects a compromise, but clearly reverts
to the more separationist language that dominated the House proposals. One
thing is clear: the no-preference understanding of the establishment clause
was rejected. We may not be able to state precisely what the establishment
clause means, but the committees had language, no less than five times, that
favored a nonpreferentialist perspective, but five times it was rejected. Whatever the merits of the no-preference perspective, it is enlightening to know that
it was so closely considered, yet so frequently rejected.

The religion clauses, with other amendments, were submitted to the thirteen state legislations for ratification. Much to the disappointment of students
of American constitutional law, there are no surviving records of the states' debates. By June of 1790, the necessary nine states had approved of ten amendments—the Constitution's Bill of Rights.[25]

The search for meaning. It is unfortunate that in all of the developmental
process, the framers left no record of any attempts to define terms so as to enable succeeding generations to determine with precision the intended meaning of the religion clauses. This problem is exacerbated by the paucity of
records of the debates in Congress and the state ratifying conventions. Regarding the debates of the first Congress, Leonard Levy adds: "Not even Madison
himself, dutifully carrying out his pledge to secure amendments, seems to
have troubled to do more than was necessary to get something adopted in order to satisfy popular clamor and deflate anti-federalist charges."[26]

Despite the absence of perspicuous meanings in the religion clauses, it is
submitted here that what we know of the process indicates at least a leaning
toward a broad, separationist interpretation of the establishment clause rather
than a narrow, nonpreferentialist perspective. It is instructive, to say the least,
that the drafters of the religion clauses had so many opportunities to endorse
nonpreferentialist language but five times rejected it.

---

[24]*Annals of the Congress,* 1:913; DePauw, *Documentary History,* 1:181.
[25]Levy, "Original Meaning of the Establishment Clause," pp. 61-65.
[26]Ibid., p. 58.

Classical Separation of Church and State as an Evolving Movement

The separation of church and state must be viewed as the principal means of ensuring an evolving movement for religious liberty merely "in process" at the time of the founding and whose advanced maturity lay in the future. The movement is still maturing, in fact, as America's revolutionary experiment in religious liberty is ongoing. The early stages of this movement can be seen by briefly examining three of its component parts: the disestablishment movement, the movement to end religious oaths for holding political office and the movement to decriminalize religious behavior. The error of looking too keenly at only the proceedings of the drafters of the Constitution and the Bill of Rights, ascertaining therefrom the drafters' "original intent," is not only an elusive task, given that they were not all in agreement about the meaning of the religion clauses, but it can easily skew one's understanding of the revolutionary events occurring at the state and federal level that would ripen into a more complete commitment to religious freedom.

The disestablishment movement. Broadly speaking, the disestablishment movement was gaining a momentum that would accelerate dramatically in the tumultuous Revolutionary War years. When America declared independence in 1776, only four states had no established churches—Delaware, Rhode Island, Pennsylvania and New Jersey. By the time of the convening of the Constitutional Convention in 1787, Virginia, New York and North Carolina had also abandoned monetary governmental support of religion. In all seven states, government support of any church or churches was considered contrary to the basic principles of religious liberty. The remaining six of the original thirteen states were eventually convinced on this point, but it took forty-six more years before Massachusetts, the last holdout, was to join the disestablishment movement.[27]

Far too many critics of church-state separation examine only the proceedings of the Constitutional Convention and the first Congress to ascertain the framers' intent. Taking a "snapshot" of these proceedings reveals far too little about the larger movement for religious liberty that was happening around the country. The disappearance of church establishments in the United States in the early nineteenth century was the culmination of a movement for disestablishment that had been active from the very time of the settlement of

---

[27]The disestablishments among the remaining six states occurred in the following order: South Carolina (1790), Georgia (1798), Maryland (1810), Connecticut (1818), New Hampshire (1819) and Massachusetts (1833).

Rhode Island in the 1630s. While the meaning of the First Amendment's prohibition against Congress's passing laws "establishing" religion was open to
some debate, clearly the growing conviction in the late eighteenth and early
nineteenth centuries was that it meant at least that churches were to receive no
financial support from the federal government. It was the appeal and the success of this model that led all of the states to enact similar provisions against
the financial support of churches.

While the meaning of religious liberty has always had many dimensions,
the revolution for religious liberty that occurred in America from the 1630s to
the 1830s had as its chief component the proscription of financial support of
churches by civil authority. This was a revolution "in process" in 1787, the full-
est expression of which was in Virginia. But the point is that it was a revolution
that had barely begun when the Constitution and Bill of Rights were written.
The delegates to the Congress understood at that time that a diversity of
tightly guarded establishments still existed in the colonies and that the legal
status of those establishments lay outside of their authority.

The movement to ban religious tests for civil office. Following Old World
practices, all of the thirteen original colonies required an attestation of religious belief or affiliation as a prerequisite for holding public office. These oaths
were viewed as instruments of social control, given the traditional view that
citizens were only trustworthy as civil servants if they were willing to affirm
their allegiance to basic religious tenets. All of the colonial oaths went beyond
requiring only a belief in God, often mandating a belief in the Trinity, the Scriptures or, in some cases, a commitment to Protestantism.

In the eight-year period following independence, eleven of the thirteen
original states adopted new constitutions. Many of the states ended their religious establishments, but most continued to require religious oaths for civil
officeholders. Only Connecticut and Rhode Island failed to adopt new constitutions, but the constitutions of both states required officeholders to be Protestants.[28]

Among the states adopting new constitutions, most simply reaffirmed the

---

[28]John F. Wilson, "Religion Under the State Constitutions, 1776-1800," *Journal of Church and
State* 32 (1990): 764. As Wilson explains, Rhode Island's requirement that officeholders be
Protestants was not enacted until 1719. This is somewhat of a surprise, he notes, "because
at the time of Roger Williams, in 1665, a law provided that no religious tests for office or voting were allowed, which made it the most tolerant state in the colonies, and possibly in the
Western World" (p. 764). But freedom atrophied in Rhode Island after Williams's death in
1683, and the colony often tended thereafter, at least until the revolutionary era, to persecute
non-Protestants even more so than its other New England counterparts—Massachusetts,
Connecticut and New Hampshire.

religious tests that had been in force during the colonial era. The states that limited state officeholders to Protestants were Georgia (1777), Massachusetts (1780), New Hampshire (1784), New Jersey (1776), North Carolina (1776), South Carolina (1778) and Vermont (1777). One only had to be a Christian in Delaware (1776), Maryland (1776) and Pennsylvania (1776), although Delaware required a belief in the Trinity, and Pennsylvania and Vermont required a belief in the Scriptures (both Old and New Testaments).[29]

Of the new state constitutions adopted prior to the Philadelphia Convention of 1787, only the Virginia and New York constitutions declined to require religious oaths for civil servants.[30] Nevertheless, the "no religious test" clause of the federal Constitution became a model that many of the states adopted. Before the turn of the century, the states of Georgia (1789), South Carolina (1790), Delaware (1792), Vermont (1783) and Tennessee either prohibited or removed their constitutions' religious tests. Moreover, as a newly admitted state, Kentucky, in its 1792 constitution, opted not to require a religious test for its civil officeholders.[31] Other states retained their religious tests, however, often well into the nineteenth and even the twentieth centuries.[32]

Again, we see that another significant aspect (religious tests) of what we might refer to as a two-hundred-year movement for religious liberty in America (the 1630s to 1830s) was in process, still undeveloped, still incomplete in the founding era, where we typically look for original intent. If we were to take only a snapshot of the proceedings of the Constitutional Convention and the first Congress, we would be affected very little by this movement that was in its very early stages. It is only by looking ahead to the nineteenth century that we find in the case of religious test bans, as with state disestablishments, the more mature notion of religious liberty, guaranteed increasingly by the separation of civil and religious institutions.

The movement to decriminalize religious behavior. Colonial legislatures were wont to pass all manner of legislation to strictly curtail unwanted and unconventional religious practices. In seventeenth-century Virginia, for example, a parent who did not baptize his child was fined two thousand pounds of tobacco, and the death penalty loomed over those who might deny the Trinity

---

[29]Ibid.

[30]Daniel L. Dreisbach, "The Constitution's Forgotten Religion Clause: Reflections on the Article VI Religious Test Ban," *Journal of Church and State* 38 (1996): 267.

[31]Ibid., pp. 272-73.

[32]See Anson Phelps Stokes, *Church and State in the United States*, 3 vols. (New York: Harper & Brothers, 1950), 1:358-446; and Carl Zollman, "Religious Liberty in the American Law," *Michigan Law Review* 17 (1991): 355.

or disparage the clergy. In Connecticut a person could be imprisoned if he or she did not specifically repudiate the pope and transubstantiation. In the seventeenth century, Maryland actually had a law that divested Catholic parents of real estate ownership in favor of a child willing to repudiate Catholicism.

As America matured in its embrace of religious freedom, these kinds of laws gradually disappeared, although many of them persisted long into the nineteenth century. But many of these laws, which most Americans would find repulsive and absurd today, were still on the books in the founding era. Thus, taking only a snapshot of the founding era would not reveal the gradual decline of these kinds of laws that penalized religious behavior.

In sum, by noting the gradual progress of the movements to disestablish churches, to end religious test oaths and to decriminalize religious behavior, we are better able to appreciate the growth of the separation of church and state as a staple in the American public philosophy in a way that could never be appreciated by analyzing the founding era in isolation.

Classical Separation of Church and State Is Not an Anti-God Statement

Contrary to the impression of many critics today, the separation of church and state, at least in the classical sense, was never intended to negate or minimize religion. In fact, separating religion from government was intended to energize religion to supply the moral virtue in the citizenry that the nation would need for success. Thus the seemingly secular character of the Constitution, specifically the decision of the Founding Fathers to break with tradition by not directly placing the nation under divine authority, can be very confusing on the issue of the place of God in the constitutional framework.

Actually, the apparently secular nature of the new Constitution rested to some degree, for many of the leading thinkers, on the way that God was thought to govern the universe. With the spread of Enlightenment rationalism, the pervading theological metaphor for God's method of controlling the universe was a constitutional paradigm. This provided the political leaders with a vocabulary they could use to express the new concepts of a federal constitutional government. Thus Americans could accept Thomas Paine's characterization of the republican system of government as "always parallel with the order and immutable laws of nature, and meets the reason of man in every part."[33] Madison also defended the idea of a constitutional government by ap-

---

[33]Thomas Paine, *The Rights of Man*, quoted in David Nicholls, *God and Government in an Age of Reason* (London: Routledge, 1995), p. 106.

pealing to its progenitor as God, "the supreme lawgiver of the universe."[34] And John Adams would note to Jefferson that the "general principles of Christianity are as eternal and immutable as the existence and attributes of God; and that those principles of liberty are as unalterable as human nature and our terrestrial, mundane system."[35]

The kind of constitutionalism conceived by the founders was infused with a divine imprimatur—a necessary advantage to obtain and sustain the support of the Constitution in the hearts and minds of the people. Thus the Constitution was never presented as a completely secular document; the idea of the providential hand of God was consistently retained. This image was effectively used by James Madison in *The Federalist* when arguing for acceptance of the Constitution: "It is impossible, for the man of pious reflection, not to perceive in it a finger of that Almighty Hand, which has been so frequently and signally extended to our relief in the critical stages in the revolution."[36]

The concept of a federal constitution was in turn planted and nurtured within the minds of the people through sermons and the clergy's drawing analogies between an earthly and a divine constitution. God was presented as governing the universe according to the laws of a constitution that he himself established, in keeping with his own rational nature.[37] The Constitution was granted a sacred status by such clergy as Abraham Williams, a Congregationalist minister who extolled the virtues of a constitutional government by likening it to the manner in which God governs the universe: "Government is a divine Constitution founded in the nature and relation of things. God is the head . . . and supreme governor."[38] Williams thanked the "great governor of the world" for "placing us under a government so wise and good in its constitution and administration."[39] Similarly, Congregationalist minister Stanley Griswold concluded that the constitution was "the palladium of all that we hold dear. Let it be venerated as the sanctuary of our liberties and all of our best interests. Let it be kept as the ark of God."[40]

---

[34]John Madison, "Memorial and Remonstrance Against Religious Assessments (1785)," quoted in Nicholls, *God and Government*, p. 108.

[35]Letter from Adams to Jefferson, June 28, 1813, quoted in Nicholls, *God and Government*, p. 108.

[36]Madison, *The Federalist 37*, quoted in Nicholls, *God and Government*, p. 108.

[37]Nicholls, *God and Government*, pp. 105, 114.

[38]Abraham Williams, "An Election Sermon (1762)," quoted in Nicholls, *God and Government*, p. 118.

[39]Williams, "Election Sermon," quoted in Nicholls, *God and Government*, p. 119.

[40]Stanley Griswold, "Overcoming Evil With Good (1801)," quoted in Nicholls, *God and Government*, p. 121.

The Baptist Contribution

The Baptist contribution to the American tradition of religious liberty, especially of the principle of the separation of church and state as the essential foundation of religious liberty, is often overlooked. The American tradition of religious liberty, ensconced in the Constitution of 1787, and more fully elaborated in the Bill of Rights, owes much to Baptist belief and practice, especially Baptist leaders like Roger Williams, Isaac Backus and John Leland.[41] An examination of the contributions of these men leads to the inescapable conclusion that the separation of church and state, as conceived and elaborated during the American founding era, was indeed a concept more theological than secular.

The paramount importance placed on religious liberty in America today is undoubtedly due in part to the bold and enduring religious pilgrimage of Roger Williams. Williams came from England as a Puritan pastor to Massachusetts in 1631, but he was banished in 1635 because of his criticism of the colony's theocratic political order and overt suppression of religious dissenters. Using the Bible, and for a period as a Baptist, he contested New England's theological justifications for church and state cooperation within the colony. For Williams, Massachusetts had violated the biblical doctrine of soul freedom through its intolerance of religious diversity and convergence of church and state. Williams adamantly objected to mandatory church attendance for all citizens within the colony. In addition, he objected to religious tests for holding public office and to the colony's "Freeman's Oath," which required an oath to God before one could obtain citizenship. He argued that, for non-Christians, such an oath was tantamount to the state's coercion of prayer, and for Christians, it could not be taken since only the kingdom of heaven, not the temporal state, is to be established by oaths to God.[42]

Roger Williams was convinced that the separation of church and state is necessary to ensure that the state performs its essentially secular tasks and the church is free to perform its spiritual tasks. He was America's first separationist and was clearly far ahead of most political thinkers of his day.

The Baptist Isaac Backus (1724-1806) would lead the charge in pursuit of religious liberty during the tumultuous period of the American Revolution. Backus recognized the importance of church-state separation and freedom of the soul, and emerged to a position of preeminence, carrying the torch of religious liberty first lit by his predecessors a century before. Dartmouth historian

---

[41]E. Y. Mullins, *The Axioms of Religion* (Philadelphia: American Baptist Publication Society, 1908), p. 57.
[42]Ibid., pp. 128-29.

John Mecklin acknowledged Backus's importance: "Patient, tolerant, wise and brave in the face of institutionalized intolerance and petty persecution, he illustrated, in simple and unpretentious fashion, principles which were later to become embodied in organic law and made the guarantee of our democratic liberties."[43]

Backus argued that the enforcement of religion led to much bloodshed and suffering, exacerbating the spread of infidelity under the Christian banner and serving as the greatest form of tyranny known to humankind.[44] Conversely, Backus posited that the church was to refrain from interference in governmental affairs. There could be a harmony between the church and the state, but the nature of their work was vastly different and prohibited them from ever being successfully united.

A generation later, John Leland (1754-1841) carried on the struggle of Backus and his predecessors. Religious liberty dominated Leland's writings and constituted much of his life's work. Leland was a widely read and well-informed evangelist and agitator throughout most of his life. Though a native of Massachusetts, Leland labored tirelessly for fifteen years in Virginia from 1776 to 1791. As a vibrant and bold preacher, Leland promoted the Baptist message during these crucial years of Virginia's struggle for religious liberty.

His passionate defense of liberty coincided with the efforts of Thomas Jefferson and James Madison, who were at the forefront with Leland in Virginia's fight for religious liberty. Leland championed the Baptist notion of rights of conscience as inalienable to every man. As such, he labored vigorously to sever any remaining ties between Virginia and the Episcopal Church, concluding:

> Government has no more to do with the religious opinions of men, than it has with the principles of mathematics. Let every man speak freely without fear, maintain the principles that he believes, worship according to his own faith, either one God, three Gods, no God, or twenty Gods; and let government protect him in doing so.[45]

Leland was supported in his struggle by Thomas Jefferson and James Madison, and he was instrumental in helping to gather signatures for Madison's legendary *Memorial and Remonstrance*, "even as he lobbied for enough votes to

---

[43]John M. Mecklin, *The Story of American Dissent* (New York: Harcourt, Brace, 1934), p. 221. See also J. M. Dawson, *Baptists and the American Republic* (Nashville: Broadman, 1956), p. 46.

[44]T. B. Maston, *Isaac Backus: Pioneer of Religious Liberty* (London: James Clark & Co., 1962), p. 71.

[45]John Leland, quoted in H. Leon McBeth, *The Baptist Heritage* (Nashville: Broadman, 1987), p. 275. See also L. F. Greene, ed., *The Writings of John Leland* (New York: Arno, 1969), pp. 179-92.

help pass Jefferson's Bill for Establishing Religious Freedom."[46]

Madison and Leland had a meeting in 1788, which was instrumental in striking a "deal" between them, thereby gaining Baptist support for the Constitution. Madison agreed to introduce amendments to the Constitution "spelling out the freedoms which the Baptists desired."[47] While Madison's suggested wording was considerably modified once presented to Congress, its fundamental ideas survived, including the principles of no establishment and free exercise, which are the heart of the American tradition of religious liberty. While most Americans would hail James Madison as the man most responsible for American religious liberty, Baptist historian J. M. Dawson put forth the notion that if James Madison was asked who was responsible, he would quickly reply, "John Leland and the Baptists."[48] It is definitely the case that Madison received much insight and inspiration from the Baptists, and perhaps, asserted Dawson, "[w]ithout the Baptists Madison might never have been."[49]

While the contribution of the Baptists to the American principle of separation of church and state is undeniable, their basic position is fundamental to most Christians. This is because religious liberty, which depends on the separation of church and state for its fulfillment, is rooted ultimately in a theology of the nature of God and his dealings with humankind. Religious liberty is a corollary to the biblical truth that God has chosen to make himself known in love and that he does not use coercive means to bring men and women to himself. We are at liberty to believe whatever we wish to believe about God; any coerced faith, indeed any faith that results from anything less than the completely free choice of the human actor, is an empty faith and a false allegiance.

Moreover, Genesis 1:26 teaches that humans are made in God's image. Following Reformers such as Martin Luther and John Calvin, many early Americans believed that humanity's likeness to God includes a moral likeness. God must by his very nature be free; an omnipotent, all-powerful God could be nothing less. If humans are made in this moral likeness, then we too are free and must be given the ability to make our own choices about things pertaining to God. This, in turn, suggests that state power should be limited, so that the state cannot interfere with a human's free choices about God. The New England Puritan theologian John Cotton recognized as much: "All power on

---

[46]Edwin Scott Gaustad, "The Baptist Tradition of Religious Liberty in America" (Waco, Tex.: J. M. Dawson Institute of Church-State Studies, Baylor University, 1995), p. 12.

[47]McBeth, *Baptist Heritage*, p. 282.

[48]Dawson, *Baptists and the American Republic*, p. 117.

[49]Ibid.

earth must be limited, church power or other."[50] Divesting the state of the power to guide humankind's religious choices, that is, separating church and state, therefore respects God's free nature and the freedom of choice he has granted to all men and women. Religious historian James E. Wood Jr. puts it this way: "God's sovereignty is man's most transcendent loyalty, which necessarily supercedes one's loyalty to human and civil authority. The limited state stands as a safeguard against an uncritical exaltation of the state, one inevitable consequence of which is the abridgement of religious liberty."[51]

Religion's Role in the New System

All of this points to a federal system of government that had only begun to think in separationist terms during the constitutional era. There were strong objections to the apparent secularity of the document, but those who understood it knew that it was in no way hostile to religion. Historian Walter Berns says the Constitution was ordained to secure liberty and its blessings, not to acknowledge God or move people to faith in God.[52] Had the framers desired to create a Christian commonwealth, calculated to cause Americans to endeavor to keep God's laws, they could easily have done so. But they chose not to because in their minds, the government derived not from God but from the people. Religion was to be subordinate to liberty; liberty was to free all persons to exercise their faith, absent government prescription. Because the nation was not founded on religious truth, it would act to protect the right of all citizens to believe and act on divergent views of religious truth. Religious liberty was a natural human right, with which the federal government had no right or authority to interfere.

In the minds of many government leaders, of course, this arrangement still did not contemplate a radical separation of religion from government. In their view the happiness of the people and the good order and preservation of civil government still depended on religion and piety. If the nation was not theocratic in the primary sense, it remained so in a subordinate sense. This was the position of John Turner at the Massachusetts ratifying convention, who stated that "without the prevalence of Christian piety and morals, the best republican

---

[50]John Cotton, *An Exposition upon the Thirteenth Chapter of Revelation* (London: L. Chapman, 1655), p. 72.

[51]James E. Wood Jr., "Theological and Historical Foundations of Religious Liberty," *Journal of Church and State* 15 (1973): 251.

[52]Walter Berns, "Religion and the Founding Principle," in *The Moral Foundations of the American Republic,* ed. Robert H. Horwitz, 3rd ed. (Charlottesville: University Press of Virginia, 1986), p. 214.

constitution can never save us from slavery and ruin."[53] John Adams declared: "Statesmen may plan and speculate for liberty, but it is religion and morality alone which can establish the principles upon which freedom can securely stand."[54] In his later years Adams added that the Constitution "was made only for a moral and religious people. It is wholly inadequate to the government of any other."[55] Moreover, George Washington, in his inaugural address in 1789, gave thanks "to the Great Author of every public and private good" and suggested that Americans must "acknowledge and adore the invisible Hand which conducts the affairs of men."[56] There is no specifically Christian message here, but certainly it is proof that Washington acknowledged a connection between religion and the sustaining of the new nation. A similar perspective appears in Washington's Farewell Address:

> Of all the dispositions and habits which lead to political prosperity, religion and morality are indispensable supports. . . . Let it simply be asked where is the security for property, for reputation, for life, if the sense of religious obligation desert the oaths, which are the instruments of investigation in courts of justice? And lest us with caution indulge the supposition that morality can be maintained without religion. Whatever may be conceded to the influence of refined education on minds of peculiar structure, reason and experience both forbid us to expect that national morality can prevail in exclusion of religious principle.[57]

Accommodationists are understandably pleased by statements like those just quoted, since they are evidence that the framers did not intend to withdraw religion from public life. Yet while all of these statements exalt religion as a necessary support for human government, none of them express the view that it is *government itself* that must promulgate religion. Such statements might, in fact, be looked upon as arguments for separationism as much as for accommodationism. Separationists usually look to religion to supply the civic virtue so essential to successful democratic government, but hold that human government should play a limited role, if any, in promulgating religion as the underlying source of civic virtue. There is strong evidence that many of the

---

[53]John Turner, quoted in Bernard Schwartz, *The Bill of Rights: A Documentary History,* 2 vols. (New York: Chelsea House, 1971), 2:709.

[54]John Adams, quoted in Lynn R. Buzzard and Samuel Ericsson, *The Battle for Religious Liberty* (Elgin, Ill.: David C. Cook, 1982), p. 180.

[55]John Adams, quoted in Charles Frances Adams, ed., *The Works of John Adams, Second President of the United States,* 10 vols. (Boston: Little & Brown, 1850-1856), 9:229.

[56]George Washington, quoted in *The Writings of George Washington,* ed. John C. Fitzpatrick, 39 vols. (Washington, D.C.: U.S. Government Printing Office, 1931), 30:291-96.

[57]Ibid., 35:229.

founders decidedly became proponents of this view.[58] Thus today most separationists contend that it is the nonpublic sphere that must be respected as the domain of religion and that will supply, in turn, the morality and virtue so essential to the successful functioning of democratic government.

Accommodationists, in arguing that the founders believed that the federal government should have a role in nurturing religion, also point to later presidential proclamations by John Adams and many later presidents who have offered presidential prayers and thanksgiving proclamations, usually in general language acceptable to most faiths. But even if it is conceded that such proclamations and prayers do indeed assign to the federal government a role in nurturing religion, there is contrary evidence. There were a number of men of the first Congress who objected to the practices. James Madison, for one, had strong reservations about such practices. He held that "thanksgiving and fasts . . . seem to imply and certainly nourish the erroneous idea of a national religion" and called them "establishments."[59] He remained flexible on the subject, however, proclaiming several days for thanksgiving, reportedly because he found extenuating circumstances in the fact that he was president during the time a war was fought on American soil.[60] Thomas Jefferson, too, opposed official prayer, believing that it was best left in the hands of the people, "where the Constitution has deposited it."[61] Andrew Jackson shared Jefferson's views and steadfastly refused to issue any thanksgiving proclamations.

It is probably best to conclude from these diverse perspectives that the framers were, on the whole, unclear and in some disagreement about the role that religion should play in national life. There is no dispute that as a body they were firmly of the view that the federal government should not interfere with the free exercise of religion so long as it did not disrupt peace and order. A major part of promoting social justice in the new nation centered on freeing all citizens to worship according to the dictates of conscience. They were also of the view that the government should disaffirm any special competence in religious matters. They were of differing opinions, however, about whether the federal government might exercise some subordinate, supportive role that would encourage religion or acknowledge the government's accountability to

---

[58]See Derek H. Davis, *Religion and the Continental Congress, 1774-1789* (New York: Oxford University Press, 2000), chap. 10.

[59]John Madison, quoted in "Madison's Detached Memoranda," ed. Elizabeth Fleet, *William and Mary Quarterly* 3 (1946): 560, 554-59.

[60]Ibid., p. 560.

[61]Thomas Jefferson, quoted in *Wallace v. Jaffree*, 105 S.Ct. 2479 (1985) at 2514 (Rehnquist, J., dissenting).

God as a human institution. Early presidential thanksgiving proclamations, congressional chaplaincies and legislation reciting the merits of religion (such as the Northwest Ordinance) are evidence that many of the framers believed that the establishment clause should be read to countenance at least a very indirect role for religion in national life.

Classical Separation Is Not Strict Separation

With these propositions in mind, it should be said that classical separation of church and state is somewhat relaxed on many aspects of religion and its penetration into public life. The American system must be understood as embracing three distinct yet interrelated sets of rules: separation of church and state, integration of religion and politics, and accommodation of civil religion. All of the various rules, customs and practices that shape the unique relationship between religion and state in America can be assigned primarily, though not always exclusively, to one of these three categories. With an appreciation of these three categories, their interrelationship and the way in which they combine to promote democratic principles, it is readily seen that classical separation is quite friendly to many aspects of religion in public life.

Separation of church and state. Separation of church and state has become the customary way of describing the relationship between religion and state in the American system.[62] Yet the phrase is too broad to accurately describe the whole system because in many respects there clearly is no separation. How can a system that proclaims "In God We Trust" as its national motto, invokes the names of God in its pledge of allegiance, observes a national day of prayer, and sanctions government-paid legislative chaplains be committed to the separation of church and state? Obviously, the American tradition of separation

---

[62]The separation principle is explained in a large range of ways. Among the best of accommodationist interpretations are Chester James Antieu, Arthur L. Downey and Edward C. Roberts, *Freedom from Federal Establishment: Formation and Early History of the First Amendment Religion Clauses* (Milwaukee: Bruce, 1964); Walter Berns, *The First Amendment and the Future of American Democracy* (New York: Basic Books, 1976); Michael J. Malbin, *Religion and Politics: The Intentions of the Authors of the First Amendment* (Washington, D.C.: American Enterprise Institute for Public Policy Research, 1978); and Robert L. Cord, *Separation of Church and State: Historical Fact and Current Fiction* (New York: Lambeth, 1982). Among the best of separationist stances are Leo Pfeffer, *Church, State and Freedom,* 2nd ed. (Boston: Beacon, 1967); Leonard Levy, *The Establishment Clause: Religion and the First Amendment* (New York: Macmillan, 1986); Anson Phelps Stokes, *Church and State in the United States: Historical Development and Contemporary Problems of Religious Freedom under the Constitution* (New York: Harper & Brothers, 1950); and Isaac Kramnick and R. Laurence Moore, *The Godless Constitution: The Case Against Religious Correctness* (New York: Norton, 1996).

of church and state does not mean that a separation of religion from government is required in all cases.

A better way to think of separation is as a term that describes an *institutional* separation of church and state. In other words, the Constitution requires that the institutions of church and state in American society not be interconnected, dependent on or functionally related to each other. The purpose of this requirement is to achieve mutual independence and autonomy for these institutions based on the belief that they will function best if neither has authority over the other. Affected are the institutional bodies of religion (i.e., churches, mosques, temples, synagogues and other bodies of organized religion) and the institutional bodies of governmental authority (state and federal governments but also small local bodies such as school districts, police departments, city councils, utility districts, municipal courts, county commissions and the like). Consequently, churches and other houses of worship receive no direct governmental funding, nor are they required to pay taxes. Government officials appoint no clergy; conversely, religious bodies appoint no government officials. Governments, even courts, are not allowed to settle church disputes that involve doctrinal issues. And religious bodies, unlike the Catholic Church in the Middle Ages, have no authority to dictate law or public policy.

The institutional separation of church and state is observed most frequently and most controversially in judicial decisions that limit religious activity in the public schools. Court decisions limiting schools' ability to entertain vocal prayers and Scripture readings, to post the Ten Commandments and other religious texts or to advance a particular religious worldview are intended to protect the sacred domain of religion from state interference. These are nonnegotiable issues for most classical separationists. It is important to remember that in the public school context, it is the precepts and practices of *institutionalized* religion that are prohibited from being embraced or proscribed. Courses that teach comparative religion, the historical or literary aspects of religion, or the anthropological dimensions of religion are permitted, even encouraged.[63]

Likewise, court decisions that place restrictions on the ability of government to fund private religious education are the product of the institutional separation of church and state, and thus fundamentally important to classical separationists. Generally, the courts have held that these programs, administered by bodies of institutionalized religion, tend to advance religion in a sectarian manner and therefore violate the establishment clause. But funding of "secular" components of private religious schools is permitted. Consequently,

---

[63]*Abington v. Schempp*, 225.

the courts have permitted governments to purchase, by way of example, text-books, computers, equipment for diagnostic testing, and other miscellaneous expenditures on behalf of private religious schools because these aid programs are not endorsements of religion.[64] Programs that provide benefits that might be used for promoting or advancing religion, however, such as teacher sti-pends or open-ended subsidies that might be used to purchase religious texts, erect religious statues or finance field trips in which religious instruction might take place, have been held unconstitutional.[65] These limitations are nevertheless being eroded, based on recent, more preferentialist-oriented decisions by the Supreme Court.[66]

The institutional separation of church and state affects other areas of religion-government interaction as well. In recent years government has passed a set of measures that attempt to provide government funding of churches and other religious institutions that are willing to administer social service pro-grams—soup kitchens, drug and alcohol rehabilitation programs, clothing pantries, homeless shelters, youth anticrime programs and the like. Theoreti-cally, these programs advance secular ends, thus passing constitutional scru-tiny. But they are a bold challenge to prevailing constitutional doctrine, which holds that churches, temples, mosques and other houses of worship are "per-vasively sectarian," which means that their mission and purpose is so per-vaded by religion that it is virtually impossible for them to ferret out "secular" aspects of their activity. This legislation, dubbed Charitable Choice because program beneficiaries may choose either a government-funded religious or secular provider, is a challenge to traditional separationist judicial interpreta-tions of the establishment clause.[67]

At the heart of promoting social justice is the principle of nondiscrimina-tion. Government programs that fund so-called secular programs of religious institutions, such as education and social service delivery, while well in-tended, ultimately lead to greater discrimination. If funded, the Constitution requires that all religious groups receive their share of benefits. As there are now approximately two thousand identifiable religions and sects in America,

---

[64]See *Board of Education v. Allen*, 392 U.S. 236 (1968); *Mitchell v. Helms*, 530 U.S. 793 (2000); *Levitt v. Pearl*, 413 U.S. 472 (1973), respectively.

[65]See *Lemon v. Kurtzman*, 403 U.S. 602 (1971); *Pearl v. Nyquist*, 413 U.S. 756 (1973); *Wolman v. Walters*, 433 U.S. 229 (1977).

[66]See, for example, *Mitchell v. Helms*, 530 U.S. 793 (2000), and *Zelman v. Simmons-Harris*, 536 U.S. 639 (2002).

[67]On Charitable Choice legislation generally, see Derek Davis and Barry Hankins, *Welfare Reform and Faith-Based Organizations* (Waco, Tex.: J. M. Dawson Institute of Church-State Stud-ies, 1999).

it would be impossible to fairly and equitably distribute government monies among them all. Instead, governments at all levels would be forced to make hard choices about which faith groups would receive public money, which would necessarily result in weighing the utility of certain religious programs. Inevitably, those with the most financial resources and political clout would get the largest share of the pie; smaller, less popular faith groups would be forced to the periphery in the new climate of destructive competition among America's communities of faith. Moreover, to operate nondiscriminatorily, government would be forced to fund unorthodox religious groups holding little public trust or confidence.

Moreover, making religion the servant of government would likely inaugurate the decline of religion's current role as the nation's "prophetic voice" and conscience against ill-advised governmental policies. Religion with its hand out can never fulfill its prophetic role in society. What is so wrong with a system of requiring religion to rely on its supporters and, ultimately, on God for sustenance? Benjamin Franklin's counsel is surely appropriate here: "When a Religion is good I conceive that it will support itself; and when it cannot support itself, and God does not care to support it, so that its Professors are obliged to call for the help of the Civil Power, 'tis a sign, I apprehend, of its being a bad one!"[68]

The institutional separation of church and state is a novel experiment in human history. Most societies throughout history have operated on the assumption that government should be a moral agent, that it must play a leading role in crafting the human being. It became customary in ancient times for governments to sponsor, even require, religious worship and instruction as the means of inculcating morality into citizens' lives. The American founders were convinced that successful nation-building would be impossible in the absence of a moral citizenry, but they believed that moral training, insofar as it was religiously based, must derive primarily from the faith community, not government.[69] The establishment clause was the founders' attempt to end government's coercive role in directing the religious course of citizens' lives; the free exercise clause reflected their goal of putting religion in the hands of the citizens to enable them to shape their own religious commitments. It was a bold experiment, but one that is now central to the American public philosophy. As

---

[68]Benjamin Franklin, *The Works of Benjamin Franklin,* ed. Jared Sparks (Chicago: MacCoun, 1882), 8:505.
[69]See Davis, "Virtue and the Continental Congress," in *Religion and the Continental Congress, 1774-1789.*

Supreme Court justice Wiley Rutledge once declared, "We have staked the very existence of our country on the faith that complete separation between the state and religion is best for the state and best for religion."[70] Justice Rutledge understood that *complete* separation between church and state is impossible, but his words are a powerful reminder of how central the principle of separation is to the American way of life.

Integration of religion and politics. Separation of church and state is indeed important to the American way of life, but it does not describe all aspects of the interplay between religion and state. This is readily seen in the way that the American system encourages the participation of religious voices in the political process. Were the system one of *total* separation, it would not countenance the active involvement of religious persons, faith communities and religious organizations that vigorously enter public discourse, seeking to persuade government officials of the merits of framing law and public policy to reflect their distinctly religious outlooks.

The right of churches and other religious bodies to engage in political advocacy and to make political pronouncements has never been seriously questioned by classical separationists. Today virtually all of the major religious groups in America and many religious coalitions have public affairs offices in Washington, D.C., to lead their lobbying efforts on a range of issues, including economic and social justice, war and peace, abortion, civil rights, poverty and world hunger.[71] These groups, for the most part, do not consider these offices to exist for the promotion of their self-interests but as an effective means by which they give witness in public affairs based on their own understanding of their mission in the world. To ignore the active and vigorous voice of religious bodies in the political process would be to deny the central role that religion has played throughout American history in shaping law and public policy. Classical separation affirms the political involvement of America's diverse religions.

The United States Supreme Court has not seriously challenged the right of

---

[70]*Everson v. Board of Education*, 330 U.S. 1, 59 (1947).

[71]For excellent treatments of religious lobbying, see Ronald J. Hrebenar and Ruth K. Scott, *Interest Group Politics in America* (Englewood Cliffs, N.J.: Prentice-Hall, 1982); Jeffrey M. Berry, *The Interest Group Society* (Glenview, Ill.: Scott, Foresman, 1989); Allen D. Hertzke, *Representing God in Washington: The Role of Religious Lobbies in the American Polity* (Knoxville: University of Tennessee Press, 1988); Jeffrey M. Berry, *The New Liberalism: The Rising Power of Citizens Groups* (Washington, D.C.: Brookings Institution Press, 1999); Daniel J. B. Hofrenning, *In Washington, but Not of It: The Prophetic Politics of Religious Lobbyists* (Philadelphia: Temple University Press, 1995); and Luke Eugene Ebersole, *Church Lobbying in the Nation's Capital* (New York: Macmillan, 1951).

religious bodies to be active participants in the American political process. The strongest affirmation of this right was given by the Court in *McDaniel v. Paty* (1978), a case striking down the last of the state statutes prohibiting ministers from seeking state office. The Supreme Court affirmed the importance and protected status of religious ideas in public debate: "Religious ideas, no less than any other, may be the subject of debate which is uninhibited, robust, and wide-open.... That public debate of religious ideas, like any other, may arouse emotion, may incite, may foment religious divisiveness and strife, does not rob it of its constitutional protection."[72]

Supreme Court pronouncements such as these, however, should not lead one to assume that organized religion in America enjoys an absolute right to participate in the making of public policy, free from governmental interference of any type. These groups are subject to losing their tax exemptions, for example, for *substantial* political expenditures[73] or for endorsing political candidates ("lobbying").[74] Nevertheless, they enjoy essentially the same rights as secular groups to participate in the political process. The principles of democracy prevail here, such that the rights of every person or group in American society, religious or secular, that wishes to contribute to democratic governance is free to do so, even encouraged to do so, even though such participation constitutes a technical violation of the principle of church-state separation.

While religious arguments are commonplace in American political discourse, legislation that advances a religious purpose generally is not, because of the Supreme Court's requirement, pursuant to the *Lemon* test, that governmental action reflect a secular purpose, that it not have the primary effect of advancing or inhibiting religion and that it not create an excessive entanglement between religion and government.[75]

---

[72]*McDaniel v. Paty*, 435 U.S. 618, 640 (1978).

[73]Though there is no clear rule for defining *substantial*, one case suggests there is a "safe harbor" if an organization's lobbying expenses do not exceed 5 percent (*Seasongood v. Commissioner*, 227 F.2d 907 [6th Cir. 1955]). In another case a court held that a church spending approximately 22 percent of its revenues on members' medical bills under a church medical plan was engaged in a "substantial nonexempt activity" (*Bethel Conservative Mennonite Church v. Commissioner* 80 T.C. 352 [1983], rev'd., 746 F.2d 388 [7th Cir. 1984]). Another court has held that a percentage test is inappropriate (*Haswell v. United States*, 500 F.2d 1133 [Ct. Cl. 1974], cert. denied, 419 U.S. 1107 [1975]). Still, according to one source, no more than 20 percent of expenditures would be deemed "insubstantial" (see Lynn R. Buzzard and Sherra Robinson, *I.R.S. Political Activity Restrictions on Churches and Charitable Ministries* [Diamond Bar, Calif.: Christian Ministries Management Association, 1990], pp. 53-59).

[74]*Lobbying* is defined in the Internal Revenue Code Section 4911 (d)(1). Various regulations, rulings and court decisions on the meaning of *lobbying* are explained well in Buzzard and Robinson, *I.R.S. Political Activity Restrictions*, pp. 42-52.

[75]*Lemon v. Kurtzman*, 403 U.S. 602 (1971).

American adherence to the integration of religion and politics also means that potential candidates and officeholders are free to speak about their religious views. The free exercise clause gives them the freedom to speak freely about matters of faith, even, for the most part, when acting in their official capacities. It is unlikely that a candidate for president could be elected in America without some candid talk about his or her religious views. America is diverse in its religious makeup, but it is unmistakably one of the most religious nations on the globe, and the American people generally demand to know their representatives' religious beliefs. The Constitution forbids the administration of formal religious tests for holding public office (and most states have followed suit), but this is different from the unofficial expectation that an officeholder have at least some religious commitments. This expectation is the product of a religious culture, of a body of citizens who "are a religious people whose institutions presuppose a Supreme Being."[76]

Accommodation of civil religion. If in the American system the establishment clause is relaxed in sanctioning an integration of religion and politics, it is equally relaxed in accommodating various expressions of civil religion, according to the classical view of separation. According to Robert Bellah, the most celebrated scholar on American civil religion, civil religion is about those public rituals that express the nexus of the political order to the divine reality.[77] By most accounts, civil religion is a form of religion that gives sacred meaning to national life. It is a kind of theological glue that binds a nation together by allying the political with the transcendent. Civil religion is a way for Americans to recognize the sovereignty of God over their nation without getting bogged down in theological differences.

Many Americans affirm the separation of church and state, but this does not remove their belief that the nation—as a civil entity—is still somehow obligated to God. For them, nationhood makes little sense unless it is part of a universe ruled by God; consequently, they believe that the body politic should have a religious dimension. Stated in another way, religion is not merely private; it is inescapably public too. Bellah acknowledges this, arguing that separation of church and state does not deny the political realm a religious dimension.[78] The classical notion of church-state separation likewise allows for a religious component within the civil realm.

---

[76]*Zorach v. Clauson*, 343 U.S. 306, 313 (1952).
[77]See Robert N. Bellah, *The Broken Covenant: American Civil Religion in Time of Trial*, 2nd ed. (Chicago: University of Chicago Press, 1975), esp. p. 3.
[78]Ibid., pp. 169-70.

The most common symbols of American civil religion are the national motto, "In God We Trust," which also appears on U.S. currency; the invocation of God's name in the pledge of allegiance, recited daily by students in many of the nation's public schools; observance of a national day of prayer; the utilization of government-paid chaplains in the military, U.S. Congress and state legislatures; and the frequent allusion to God and America's religious destiny in political, especially presidential, speeches (every president has acknowledged God in his inaugural address). These civil religious expressions are not promoted exclusively by the state or exclusively by the religious community. Rather, they are promoted by both, serving to imbed in the national civil order an unmistakable religious quality.

Civil religion is a sociological reality in every society. It manifests itself in different ways in different contexts, but French sociologist Émile Durkheim (1858-1917) was probably correct in suggesting that every society at its deepest foundations is religious, and the sovereign must act responsibly to respect and acknowledge this, lest the society itself deteriorate and pass into oblivion.[79] For most Americans, of course, a nation that takes steps to acknowledge the sovereignty of God, even if in generic, symbolic ways, is not merely accommodating the wishes of the citizenry in the sense of filling a sociological need, but acting to affirm the divine reality. In any case, the accommodation of civil religion can be said to prevent the nation from steering too far in the direction of a secularized culture.

The U.S. Supreme Court occasionally acknowledges the evidence of civil religion in American life. Legislative prayer, legislative and military chaplaincies, Christmas and Hanukkah displays, and graduation prayers in public schools, as expressions of civil religion, have all been challenged as violations of the "separation" requirements of the establishment clause.[80] The Court tends to sanction those civil religious traditions that are generic, longstanding and not likely to offend persons of tender age. Thus in the case of legislative prayer, the Supreme Court has held that the practice is constitutional because it has a long and unbroken tradition in American political life.[81] In the public school context, however, given the impressionability of young persons, similar prayers are prohibited as violations of the in-

---

[79]Émile Durkheim, *The Elementary Forms of the Religious Life,* rev. ed. (New York: Free Press, 1965).
[80]See *Marsh v. Chambers,* 463 U.S. 783 (1983); *Abington v. Schempp,* 374 U.S. 203 (1963), 296-97 (Brennan concurring); *Lynch v. Donnelly,* 465 U.S. 668 (1984); *Allegheny v. Pittsburgh ACLU,* 492 U.S. 573 (1989); *Lee v. Weisman,* 505 U.S. 577 (1992); respectively.
[81]*Marsh v. Chambers,* 463 U.S. 783 (1983).

stitutional separation of church and state. The same contrary set of rules, applied in the respective contexts of legislative halls and public school classrooms, can be said to apply to the posting of the Ten Commandments and other sacred texts.[82] Legislative and military chaplaincies are likewise affirmed as longstanding traditions, although it is doubtful that courts would endorse the concept of public school chaplains because of the impressionability and potential for indoctrination of the students. Holiday displays have been held not to violate the establishment clause if their religious message is muted by surrounding secular symbols.[83] Prayer offered by a clergyperson at a public school graduation ceremony, however, has been held to violate the establishment clause as an inappropriate government sponsorship of religion.[84]

The federal courts have struggled in their efforts to assess the constitutional propriety of these kinds of public acknowledgment cases. The difficulty in evaluating such cases is that the religion advanced is typically nonsectarian, symbolic and without specific theological content—in short, civil religion. The courts, with lawyers sitting as judges, have not been particularly sophisticated in their ability to distinguish civil religion from traditional religion. Occasionally, the Supreme Court has applied a vague concept called "ceremonial deism" to justify some practices of civil religion.[85] The Court has never defined *ceremonial deism;* the term seems to be mere shorthand for the Court's judgment that a practice ought to be constitutional because it is not really religious, either because it has culturally lost the significance it once had or because it is used only to solemnize a public occasion.

All of these civil religious traditions are violations of a strict notion of the separation of church and state. Yet they form a rich tradition of practices that are culturally and judicially accommodated. The classical view of the separation of church and state sanctions these practices and never insists on a strict separation that would not countenance civil religion as part of an accepted and necessary part of the American cultural order. Undoubtedly some civil religious symbols offend many, but they are for the most part generic practices

---

[82]*Stone v. Graham,* 449 U.S. 39 (1980).

[83]*Lynch v. Donnelly,* 465 U.S. 668 (1984): Christmas crèche paid for with public monies constitutional when surrounded by Santa Claus, reindeer, elves and related secular Christmas decorations; *County of Allegheny v. ACLU,* 109 S.Ct. 1086 (1989): Jewish menorah displayed on public property constitutional when located next to a Christmas tree and a sign saluting liberty.

[84]*Lee v. Weisman,* 505 U.S. 577 (1992).

[85]For example, see *Lynch v. Donnelly,* 465 U.S. 668 (1984), 716 (Brennan, J., dissenting), and *County of Allegheny v. ACLU,* 492 U.S. 573 (1989).

that are not coercive in the way that, for example, audible school prayers in the public schools are. Civil religious practices tend to respect religious and ethnic differences and therefore complement rather than impede efforts to promote social justice. Indeed, these practices are accepted and celebrated by most Americans, and they contribute to a unique, nuanced, and sometimes contradictory set of concepts, principles, customs, beliefs and symbols that comprise the American tradition of religion and state.[86] Civil religion has its dangers, of course, such as the use of civil religion for political purposes, but such matters are beyond the scope of the present discussion.

Conclusion

The classical idea of the separation of church and state resulted from the religious pluralism that was an outgrowth of the Reformation and the accompanying recognition that religion is perhaps more a matter of private conscience than public concern. The atrocities of the Middle Ages and the Reformation, in which hundreds of thousands died in inquisitions, witch hunts and religious wars, were thought to be the result of government having too much authority in matters of religion. The evolution of individual rights, which began in earnest in the fourteenth century, led human government, in the West at least, to abandon its previous role of causing all people to conform to a common faith in favor of a new role of protecting individual rights, including the free exercise of religion.

America was the first nation to construct a constitutional framework that officially sanctioned the separation of church and state. It was a noble experiment in the founding era and remains so today. The experiment was undertaken by the framers in the hope that it would enable America to escape the persecutions and religious wars that had characterized the Christian West since Emperor Theodosius made Christianity the Roman Empire's official religion in A.D. 380. The First Amendment's religion clauses have proved to be, in the words of the celebrated Catholic theologian John Courtney Murray, "Articles of Peace."[87] Religion of all persuasions is accorded a greater respect in the United States than in any other civilized society.

---

[86]This position is consistent with the Supreme Court's doctrine of "benevolent neutrality," first expressed in *Walz v. Tax Commission*, 397 U.S. 664 (1970). Benevolent neutrality is appropriately sensitive to the institutional difference between religion and government that was intended by the framers while simultaneously allowing for some governmental expressions of religion in public life.

[87]John Courtney Murray, *We Hold These Truths: Catholic Reflections on the American Proposition* (New York: Sheed & Ward, 1960), p. 45.

Far too many Christians in America undervalue the separation of church and state. In Matthew 22:21, Christ said that Christians are to "give therefore to the emperor the things that are the emperor's, and to God the things that are God's," thus affirming that spiritual commitments are distinguishable from political commitments. God is due worship but Caesar is due taxes and submission to governmental authority (Rom 13:1). But the interests of God and the interests of Caesar are not necessarily synonymous. While Christians might often find that divine claims on their life do not conflict with their obligations to the state, the two may occasionally clash dramatically. Early Christians, for example, were sometimes persecuted or even executed for failing to bow the knee to Caesar, for refusing to participate in state-sanctioned pagan sacrifices or even for possessing copies of Christian scriptures. The Christian frequently was forced to make a choice: obey the commands of Caesar or follow the will of God as he or she understood it. Because the Roman Empire assumed jurisdiction over religion, it readily exacted punishment upon those who failed to comply with the tenets of the state religion. In the modern context, the separation of church and state, if nothing else, is a recognition that the state should not, insofar as it is possible, interfere with a citizen's religious beliefs and practices. Modern states have learned, moreover, that granting religious freedom to its citizens increases the citizens' willingness to develop bonds of loyalty and patriotism.

Consequently, in the United States today, because the separation of church and state is a reality, Christians typically are proud to be Americans and find it relatively easy to be good citizens. Meanwhile, they are free to vigorously pursue the spiritual mission of the church, which is to do good to all people (Gal 6:10) and to spread the gospel (Mt 28:19-20). They might call on the government to assist them in the first task, but not in the second. They can expect government to assist those who struggle against the common enemies of humanity—tyranny, poverty, disease and war—but to expect the government, or attempt to use the government, to spread the gospel is a perspective that is absolutely foreign to the Bible. In fulfilling the first task, Christians participate with other citizens who share membership in our nation to bring about social justice. In fulfilling the second, they look only to the Christian community, what the apostle Peter called a "holy nation" (1 Pet 2:9). This approach pays a healthy respect to the principle of separation between church and state. If Christians want absolute freedom to spread the gospel, they must refuse to make America a religious state with the authority to define its religious character in ways that might impede their ability to determine God's truth for themselves and to share it with others.

It can be said that from America's earliest days, many political and religious leaders have strongly advocated the separation of church and state—for the protection of religion, for the protection of human conscience in religious matters and for the efficient operation of civil government. The result has been a formal national commitment to the twin pillars of freedom—religious liberty and the (classical) separation of church and state.

Catholic Response

Clarke E. Cochran

While the most significant weakness of Sider's account of Anabaptist perspectives is neglect of a theory of the state, Derek Davis's account of classical separationism suffers from minimal attention to the church. The Catholic perspective, as I understand it, requires and supplies a robust description of the nature and purposes of both church and state. Although there is much to agree with in classical separationism (and much that the Catholic Church has learned from it), there are serious divergences at the theoretical and practical level.

Theologically, Davis's position begins from an individualist account of the human person. It emphasizes free will and conscience. Because these are foundational, substantial distance must be kept between church and state, lest the powers of government coerce conscience and lest church attempt to use the powers of government for the same purpose. The *implicit* picture of church then is a voluntary assembly of free and equal persons who covenant or contract together for strictly religious purposes in accordance with their individual understandings of the divine. So long as these understandings are compatible, the assembly stays together. The members of the church protect each other's liberty of belief and avoid the temptation of imposing belief on others.

From the Catholic point of view, this account (never explicitly argued in Davis's essay) is defective in a number of respects. The Catholic understanding of the human person is social. Human beings are meant for each other ("It is not good for the man to be alone," God muses in Genesis). Cut off from family, friends and other intimate associations such as religious bodies, the individual becomes lonely, isolated and (often) mad. This does not mean that Catholic political theory disparages individual free will and conscience. It honors and values them. It must be admitted that Catholic theory learned a greater respect for these from the Protestant and Enlightenment traditions, as well as from the history of disestablishment, that ground Davis's argument. Freedom, however, according to the Catholic account is learned and exercised in community. So there must be interplay between person and community, even a tension between them that seems not part of the classical separationist position.

The neglect of church and the social nature of humanity produces another theoretical problem for Davis. In his essay, the relationship between church and state is all about protecting the individual. Their relationship is characterized by "mutual independence and autonomy." In the Catholic account, however, genuine mutual though tension-filled *inter*dependence must be present. Tension between church and state protects individual freedom but also demands pursuit of social justice and the common good. These are primary purposes of the state, and the church must challenge the state when it neglects this duty. These are also social goods enjoyed in community. The neglect of social justice and the common good in Davis's account flows from his tradition's disregard of the social dimension of the human person. He does recognize the integration of religion and politics (along with the separation of church and state), but he describes that integration in *process* terms, as the right of religious persons to participate and advocate policy positions. He does not acknowledge the *substance* (justice, common good and option for the poor), which is essential from the Catholic perspective. Davis's account is only *implicitly* aware of the creative tension between church and state that is good for each and that lies at the heart of my account of the Catholic tradition.

Finally, Davis's accommodation of civil religion and his seeming willingness to accord "sacred status" to the Constitution is deeply troubling from the Catholic perspective. To associate religious status with the state or its founding documents is to weaken the necessary tension between faith and politics and to imperil the very liberties that the separationist tradition cherishes.

Despite these areas of fundamental disagreement, I want to acknowledge again the genuine debt of the Catholic tradition to the separationism that Davis defends. The Catholic turn toward freedom of religion, liberty of conscience and global human rights in the middle of the last century owes much to the Catholic Church's flourishing under the American regime of church-state separation.

At the practical level too there is much to agree with, but also some to disagree with, Davis's classical separationism. He criticizes the Supreme Court's recent free exercise clause jurisprudence and the weakening of protection for minority religions through the "neutrality" principle articulated in the *Employment Division v. Smith* case. I agree entirely, as do most American Catholic political theorists. Our agreement on the free exercise clause, however, is mirrored by disagreement on the establishment clause. In saying this, I must be careful to speak only for myself, because there are a wide variety of points of view on establishment clause issues among Catholic thinkers.

Most (including myself) agree with Davis that *institutional* separation of church and state is obligatory. However, the meaning in practice of institutional separation produces different perspectives. I agree that prayer and religious exercises in the public schools are a mistake from the theological perspective as well as a violation of the establishment clause. However, I believe that a large part of the mistake is public school prayer's promotion of civil religion, a reason different from Davis's. On other matters, it seems to me (and to most Catholic commentators) that a properly designed and properly limited school-voucher program could maintain the needed institutional separation between church and state while affording support for individual conscience, social justice and recognition of subsidiarity in education. The same is true of the Faith-Based and Community Initiative (FBCI) that Davis criticizes. Although there can be (and perhaps have been) implementations of that program that violate the proper relationship between church and state, my understanding of the Catholic tradition would be more supportive of that initiative than in Davis's classical separationism. The cooperation entailed in the FBCI is indeed proper (and does not violate church-state relations) when it is part of a dynamic that includes as well competition, challenge and transcendence.

Principled Pluralist Response

Corwin Smidt

Each of the five different positions articulated in this volume are based on the Christian faith understood within a historically orthodox framework of interpretation, and each seeks to be true to the Christian faith. These different positions emerged, in part, because Christian people in different contexts, experiencing different circumstances, came to understand and interpret their Christian faith in light of the particular circumstances they found themselves in. Moreover, each interpretation has evolved over time, responding to particular problems or criticisms, becoming more refined and internally consistent in nature. No one position is necessarily more, or less, Christian in its perspective; each position takes certain Christian principles, teachings or emphases and contends that that position best reflects the "heart of the gospel" or contends that it more fully reflects the totality of the Christian perspective. As a result, it should not be surprising to learn that no two perspectives articulated here necessarily stand in total opposition to each other. There are points of convergence and points of divergence with which the principled pluralist perspective (or any other perspective) stands in relationship to each of the other four positions articulated in this volume. Even where two positions diverge, there may not be any great disagreement, except when each position is pushed to its more logical extreme endpoints.

The classical separationist perspective is less a theological than a historical and philosophical argument. Clearly there is a theological basis, but it is more a secondary than a primary foundation of the perspective. All five perspectives discussed here would likely agree that, since human beings are made in the image of God, every human being has dignity and worth and all are equal in the sight of God. However, such a theological perspective does not necessarily lead logically to the classical separationist position. In terms of the argument presented in the chapter, the primary basis for the classical separationist perspective is twofold: (1) that its position is far more compatible with the

Constitutional drafters' views and should therefore be followed today within the American context, and (2) that religious faith, to be a true faith, must be freely chosen, and that the freedom of choosing a religious faith can only transpire within a context of religious liberty. Consequently, this response focuses on these two primary arguments.

It is unlikely that any of the five perspectives would deny that a religious faith, to be a personal faith that is truly embraced by the individual, has to be freely chosen by that person. One's religious faith or lack thereof, regardless of what one publicly professes, is always freely chosen. Laws and legal systems can never compel belief; at best, they can only compel behavior. Thus, the important issue is whether a particular religious faith can be freely practiced without legal punishment or personal detriment within any legal provisions outside a classical separation framework. And clearly the answer is yes, as a nonpreferentialist framework does not necessarily punish or penalize religious groups for practicing their religious faith. Moreover, adherents of all five perspectives might well place certain restrictions on freedom of religious practice (e.g., all such perspectives would almost certainly call for legal restraints on a religious faith that practiced human sacrifice). Thus the issue relates more to the parameters within which religious liberty may be exercised.

Davis argues that the classical separationist position is the classical interpretation because it best captures the original spirit of the founders' ideas. He rightfully acknowledges that there is an ambiguity in terms of the framers' intent. This ambiguity is evident, in part, because of the absence of historical records. But it is also due to the fact that the framers viewed the role of religion politically as being a double-edged sword. Religion could have both potentially positive (fostering virtue) and negative (fostering conflict) consequences with regard to politics. Despite this ambiguity, Davis contends that the classical separationist interpretation best reflects the founders' ideas, and he advances a plausible argument for why it should be viewed so (namely, that the drafters at various points in the process had opportunities to endorse more nonpreferentialist language but ended up rejecting such language).

However, there can be both political and philosophical reasons for the framers' choosing to support (or oppose) the particular wording of the religion clauses (as well as for us today to support or oppose the wording of a particular piece of legislation). We can never know with certainty what the true motives were supporting the particular wording the framers adopted. Even if they had chosen to reveal to us their motives, we would nevertheless be dependent on the truthfulness of their revelations (which potentially can always be questioned politically). Thus we do not (and never will be able to) know exactly just why the more nonpreferentialist language was not adopted—whether it reflected opposition on the basis of particular philosophical principles or whether it was not adopted for other, more strategic, political calculations. Thus it may be possible to argue the classical separationist position is classical in some logical sense, but any argument that this is the classical position historically is weaker (though not implausible), as there have always been a wide variety of interpretations advanced with regard to the meaning of the religion clauses of the First Amendment. It is these different dimensions of logic and history that enable Davis to contend that what he has outlined is the "classical" interpretation but yet acknowledge that "the separationist interpretation was first advanced by Justice Hugo Black . . . in the 1947 landmark case of *Everson v. Board of Education*" (p. 84).

However, the greatest problem associated with the classical separationist perspective is a more pragmatic consideration—namely, its capacity to be swallowed by the strict separationist position and the lack of constitutional standing for the set of rules related to the "integration of religion and politics" and the "accommodation of civil religion." In fact, it is the rise of the strict separationist perspective—namely, that religion is and should be a strictly private matter—that has given rise to the growing advance of more nonpreferentialist arguments.

Finally, Davis acknowledges that religion in American politics is somewhat accommodated through the presence of American civil religion and that all societies display some form of civil religion. However, this argument too is somewhat problematic. First, within the field of sociology of religion, the notion that all societies exhibit a civil religion is based on a functionalist (as opposed to a substantive) understanding of religion. The functional perspective contends that in every society religion functions to provide social cohesion in society; accordingly, whatever serves to provide cohesion in society functions as its religion. So if sports function as the basis of cohesion in society, then sports serves as the civil religion of that society. Thus, according to the functionalist perspective, no society, by definition, is without religion (even if not a single person in that society believes in some divine being, prays, meditates or attends any religious ceremony). Similarly, there is no such thing as secularization under the functional definition, as religion does not disappear but only relocates (as long as society exists according to the functionalist approach, there needs to be some beliefs or practices that serve to generate and provide cohesion in society). However, based on a substantive understanding of religion, civil religion may or may not exist within American society, and even if it currently exists within the American context, there is no guarantee that it always will continue to do so.

The second problem with having civil religion serve as a means by which religion is accommodated within American political life is that civil religion can easily become distorted by nationalistic tendencies and the danger for Christians of making the United States an idol that is worshiped and served uncritically. At its best, American civil religion does not exhibit these qualities, and a certain level of nationalism in terms of pride of place is normal and perhaps even healthy. But what must be avoided is any proclivity of Americans to use their civil religion as a basis for jingoistic nationalism.

In conclusion, in contrast to the classical separationist perspective, the principled pluralist position does not permit any slide into a strict separationist position. It allows for religious tolerance and diversity through the accommodation of secular as well as alternative religious perspectives. The principled pluralist perspective, like the classical separationist perspective, permits the integration of religion and politics, and it does so without relying on some potentially problematic civil religion as a means of integrating religion within public life.

Anabaptist Response

Ronald J. Sider

I am not a historian of American legal and constitutional history, so I will not try to evaluate Derek Davis's basic historical analysis.

Since Davis claims that the more accommodationist decisions of the Supreme Court since the 1980s (which fit well with things like Charitable Choice legislation and President George W. Bush's Faith-Based Initiative) represent an error of "first magnitude," I find it surprising and disappointing that he spends almost no time wrestling with and critiquing the accommodationist arguments. And the very short section he does devote to this critique is not very compelling. For example, his argument that a constitutional implementation of a faith-based initiative providing government funding for social services run by faith-based organizations would require government to fund all the two thousand current religions in the United States is very weak. Only a few apply. Government has secular criteria for judging which programs run by faith-based applicants produce effective public goods (e.g., good job training) and rightly only fund effective programs.

At least twice we see a clear hint of Davis's view that religion is essentially something personal and private. On page 101 he says, "Today most separationists contend that it is the nonpublic sphere that must be respected as the domain of religion." And in the first paragraph of his conclusion, he says that "religion is perhaps more a matter of private conscience than public concern." Unfortunately, that is to adopt an individualistic, privatized understanding of Christian faith that is fundamentally contrary to historic Christianity. Christianity is not just a private, personal relationship between me and Jesus. At the heart of Christian faith is (1) the claim that Christ is now Lord of all, ruler of the kings of the earth, and (2) the church as a visible community that is public and speaks as a community to other parts of the culture, including the state. That does not mean the church as an institution should want to or demand that it have the legal right to directly force the state to do things (except insofar as it participates in societal debates and peacefully persuades a majority to share its views). But Davis seems to underestimate the communal, visible, public character of the church. If he understood this better, he would be more open to the accommodationist understanding of the First Amendment.

It is probably the same misunderstanding that leads him to the astonishing conclusion that it is a "technical violation of the principle of church-state separation" when organized religious groups seek to participate in the political process (p. 106). That is only true if the First Amendment means that there must be an absolute separation. But that would violate the free exercise clause if one remembers that historic Christianity understands Christian faith to claim that Christ is now Lord of all of life, not just some personal, private sphere, and therefore Christians (both the individual Christian and the church as a visible public community) must speak to the total society about justice, peace, life, freedom and the common good based on its biblical worldview.

Finally, I find Davis's defense of civil religion inconsistent with his basic principles. In a society of theists, polytheists and atheists, how is it not an establishment of one specific religious view (monotheism) to have a pledge of allegiance or coins that declare "In God We Trust"? To speak of God rather than "gods" or nature (understood, as atheists do, in purely naturalistic terms) is not, as he claims, to use language that lacks "specific theological content." "In God We Trust" is a monotheistic, not a polytheistic or naturalistic, statement.

Social Justice Response

J. Philip Wogaman

I find this chapter a bit different from the others in this volume in that its primary focus is more ideological than theological. Davis does argue, briefly, that what he calls the "classical theory of separation" is "ultimately founded on a theological basis" (p. 82). That basis, as understood by early American supporters of freedom, lies in "humanity's likeness to God [that] includes a moral likeness. God must by his very nature be free; an omnipotent, all-powerful God could be nothing less. If humans are made in this moral likeness, then we too are free and must be given the ability to make our own choices about things pertaining to God" (p. 98). Such a brief theological reference is, however, overshadowed by a quite extensive and useful discussion of the historical development and application of the First Amendment to the U.S. Constitution. Ideological exploration is not, as such, to be discounted. I have argued elsewhere that much of our ethical thought is either consciously or unconsciously framed by ideological perspectives.[1] That being the case, much then depends on the adequacy of the ideology in light of our deeper faith perspective. Much also depends on our willingness to be flexible enough in light of that perspective, should unforeseen historical circumstances warrant change. Moreover, when we are theologically well-grounded in our ideological commitments, we can more readily distinguish the important from the trivial in application of those commitments.

That said, I am not uncomfortable with much of Davis's discussion. I am genuinely appreciative of his careful review of the historical development of the First Amendment. I also note with appreciation his unwillingness to carry "separation" to the point of hostility toward religion and his flexibility about some minor issues like the slogan "In God We Trust" on coins and chaplaincies

---

[1]See chap. 9 of J. Philip Wogaman, *Christian Moral Judgment* (Louisville: Westminster John Knox, 1989). In that chapter I suggest that we tend to place the burden of proof against actions or policies that appear to be in conflict with our ideological predispositions.

in legislative bodies.[2] Such issues are hardly worth major attention, although they should be seen—as Davis suggests—from the standpoint of those who are in the religious minority.

Davis aptly quotes John Courtney Murray's judgment that the First Amendment provisions were "articles of peace"—that is, that they were prudently adopted by the founders as a basis of keeping the peace in a pluralist society and avoiding the bloody interreligious warfare that plagued Europe in the first two centuries of the Protestant era. But Davis also goes further than Murray in holding that such articles are more universally applicable. The liberty clause is a necessary protection of even the tiniest minority and is a recognition of a spiritual nature in every person that is to be respected and protected by government. The establishment clause also serves as a bulwark for religious freedom, protecting religious minorities from overbearing cultural dominance by majorities. But it serves as well to protect the integrity of even, and maybe especially, the majority religious institutions from becoming manipulated by the state—while also protecting the state from theocratic control by religious groups that would thereby also diminish the rights of minorities. For many years the big Protestant anxiety was over possible Roman Catholic theocracy, quite overlooking the actual extent of Protestant theocracy in much of early America.[3]

Classical church-state theory notes a historical distinction between theocratic and Erastian tendencies. The former involves control of the state by religious institutions and authorities, the latter, control of religious institutions by political leaders for political ends. Both of these tendencies have been illustrated in the last few decades: Erastianism, especially by a number of communist countries before the end of the Cold War, and theocracy, especially by some

---

[2]Some years ago I accepted the invitation to pray in the U.S. House of Representatives. I trust that God was present there, as well as everywhere else. But, as is typically the case, only a handful of representatives were on hand. In deference to the separation principle, the House was only gaveled into session after the prayer was concluded. I must confess that, in retrospect, I am even less comfortable than Davis with this feature of civil religion. Might it not be better for Congress to begin, as does the U.N. General Assembly, with a moment of silence, thus acknowledging the seriousness of human spiritual existence but with respect to the presence of persons of differing faith traditions? The issue was presented in an almost bizarre way in late 2006, when minor controversy erupted over whether a newly elected Muslim congressman would be permitted to place his hand on the Qur'an in taking the oath of office.

[3]A surprising footnote on this is supplied by Franklin H. Littell's discovery that even Thomas Jefferson—cited so approvingly by Davis and other separationists—required University of Virginia students to attend Protestant chapel services when he became rector of that state-supported institution (see Franklin H. Littell, *From State Church to Pluralism: A Protestant Interpretation of Religion in American History* [Garden City, N.Y.: Doubleday, 1962]).

of the contemporary Muslim countries such as Iran. It can be argued that historically what begins as theocratic quickly becomes Erastian, and what begins as Erastian, stays Erastian.[4] So Davis is clearly right in arguing that the separation principle is, perhaps above all, a protection of the integrity of churches.

The discussion of religious liberty requires further elaboration. I have elsewhere sought to distinguish between three different forms of religious freedom.[5] *Absolute religious freedom* is freedom of conscience: not being required to say as truth what we do not believe to be true. *Qualified absolute freedom* is freedom to express our views and to worship in accordance with our faith, qualified only to the extent that such expression is incontrovertibly injurious to others. But this must be considered to be *almost* absolute. And *qualified freedom*, which is freedom to *act* on the basis of one's religious motivations unless a clearly demonstrated interest of state is put at risk. That view was expressed in the Religious Freedom Restoration Act during the Clinton administration, but the act was reversed by the Supreme Court, and the status of the principle is tangled in American law. Without elaborating these distinctions further, they may suggest something of the complexity of the subject of religious freedom, along with its importance.

One objection to the separationist position, to which Davis does not respond directly, is the charge that the position actually creates a new establishment of secularism (or secular humanism) as national religion. Of course it could, if carried to the point of driving all expressions of religion from the public sphere. The point should be that separation is appropriate because the state takes religion seriously, not because it doesn't. This might well mean that deliberate space should be provided in public spaces for religious observances and symbolism, provided that all are treated equally. That can pose dilemmas at the margins, for there exist bizarre and even fraudulent religious organizations and there also exist canons of good taste. But as the old legal saying goes, "hard cases make bad law." Society should not be unduly inhibited by the fact of the bizarre and tasteless—although it can well monitor the fraudulent. Though not a Roman Catholic, I was not offended when, on his first visit to Washington, D.C., Pope John Paul II conducted a Mass on the National Mall,

---

[4]I have discussed this and other issues in church-state relations more fully in chap. 13 of J. Philip Wogaman, *Christian Perspectives on Politics: Revised and Expanded* (Louisville: Westminster John Knox, 2000).

[5]J. Philip Wogaman, *Protestant Faith and Religious Liberty* (Nashville: Abingdon, 1967), pp. 182-90. That discussion was greatly influenced by the earlier work of A. F. Carrillo de Albornoz, *The Basis of Religious Liberty* (Geneva: World Council of Churches, 1964), pp. 20-26.

assuming that Protestants, Jews, Muslims, Sikhs, Hindus, Buddhists, Baha'i, Wiccan and other forms of religion could also use such a space in an orderly way to hold events or services of particular importance to them.

Similarly, as Davis has noted, it is quite in order for the public schools, in age-appropriate ways, to expose our young to the contributions of a broad diversity of faith traditions. I myself experienced this in a high school English class many years ago when the teacher invited every student to take a few minutes of class time to explain their "philosophy of life" (which really meant their faith tradition). Other students could ask questions, but criticism and ridicule were off-limits. That was an excellent exercise, flawlessly executed, with resultant mutual understanding and appreciation. School prayer is another matter, for it does place children and youth under pressure to conform to majority practices or at least to feel that their own traditions are viewed by public authority as less worthy. There is nothing to prevent any child or youth from praying silently (it being understood that prayer is not a substitute for preparation for an examination!). Moreover, I am inclined to agree with the proposal of a moment of silence at the beginning of a school day—again in the manner of the U.N. General Assembly—provided it can be done in a way that underscores mutual respect while acknowledging the transcendent context of human life and values.

The Principled Pluralist Perspective

Corwin Smidt

The principled pluralist perspective is closely tied to and derived largely from what might be called the Reformed tradition of the Christian faith.[1] The Reformed tradition arose largely out of the theological perspectives advanced by John Calvin, John Knox and Ulrich Zwingli during the Reformation of the sixteenth century. While these theologians did not advance the principled pluralist position per se, their theological formulations provided the foundation on which that perspective was later advanced. Not all Reformed Christians necessarily hold the principled pluralist view with regard to politics, and some who so advance the perspective may not be thoroughly Reformed in their theology. Nevertheless, the perspective largely arises out of a Reformed theological understanding, and its proponents have generally worked out of a Reformed perspective.

Broadly speaking, principled pluralism may be viewed as a framework of understanding that serves to explain and accept the diversity evident in public life, that recognizes different structures of authority that operate within different spheres of social life, and that provides a basis for opposing both totalitarianism and individualism in political life. Thus principled pluralism accepts the state as a social structure possessing legitimate authority within a particular domain of life, but it sees other social structures as possessing legitimate authority within other domains of human and social life. The state is one, but not the only, structure to which God has delegated authority.

Most, if not all, biblically based social and political perspectives see God's rule as mediated through offices or representatives on earth and hold that God has instituted multiple authorities and institutions. Principled pluralism, however, develops this common understanding further and forms it as a fundamental foundation for its political philosophy. Though God mediates his power on earth through various offices or representatives rather than exercising it directly, he remains ultimately sovereign. This delegated authority is

---

[1]I would like to thank Tracy Kuperus, Nick Lantinga, Stephen Monsma, Stanley Carlson-Thies and Darren Walhof for helpful comments on earlier drafts of this chapter.

never concentrated in any one person or earthly institution. In God's diverse and differentiated creation, no single structure—political, economic or cultural—should dominate the others. Families have particular purposes and powers, as do economic, religious and other institutions. This understanding provides a framework that legitimizes constitutionally limited governmental power, human rights and citizen participation—while avoiding both the excessive individualism and the diminution of community that is associated with modern liberalism.[2]

The Theological Basis of Principled Pluralism

Reformed theology provides the primary basis for the principled pluralist perspective.[3] What then distinguishes the Reformed view theologically, and how does that theological understanding shape and color the way in which Reformed Christians approach the political world? Reformed theology places great emphasis on the creation-fall-redemption narrative. The outline of this narrative is simple: All has been created good, including the full range of human cultures that emerge when humans act according to God's design. But all have been corrupted by evil, including not only culture but also the natural world. So all—the whole cosmos—must be redeemed by Jesus Christ the Lord. What follows is that all of life is sacred: the whole of it stands under the blessing, judgment and redeeming purposes of God.[4]

While other Christian traditions also recognize and emphasize this thematic scheme, what distinguishes the Reformed tradition is the centrality of this narrative in its theological understanding and the implications drawn from it. To more fully grasp the approach of Reformed Christians to political engagement, it is necessary to briefly explore the ramifications of this narrative for understanding governmental authority.

Creation: The cultural mandate. First, God created the world; all things that exist have their being as a result of his original creative act. When God finished

---

[2]Lawrence Adams, *Going Public: Christian Responsibility in a Divided America* (Grand Rapids: Brazos, 2002), p. 120.

[3]While principled pluralism is historically tied to the Reformed tradition, there is a growing recognition that it shares important similarities with the notion of subsidiarity within the Catholic social justice/natural law tradition. As a result, principled pluralism is increasingly a merger of Catholic social justice/natural law tradition and the Reformed tradition. For a discussion of subsidiarity, see Jonathan Chaplin, "Subsidiarity as a Political Norm," in *Political Theory and Christian Vision: Essays in Memory of Bernard Zylstra*, ed. Jonathan Chaplin and Paul Marshall (Lanham, Md.: University Press of America, 1994).

[4]Cornelius Plantinga Jr., *Engaging God's World: A Reformed Vision of Faith, Learning, and Living* (Grand Rapids: Eerdmans, 2002), pp. xv-xvi.

this act of creation, God pronounced all things good, including the entire natural realm and the human race. Adam and Eve are described as the sole human beings within the creation narrative; no governmental institutions or broader society exist within the creation story at the end of the sixth day. Thus Genesis 1—3 does not mention families (no children were yet born), art or recreation, nor institutions of worship, education or vocation. As a result the biblical text in Genesis does not record that these endeavors or institutions were thereby explicitly pronounced good. Yet, to the extent that these endeavors and institutions are implicit within the creation story, they too can be considered to have been pronounced good.

Creation entails more than just this primary formative act; it is an ongoing process in which human creatures themselves take part. Within Reformed thinking, the opening pages of Genesis reveal that the Creator assigns the first human pair a "cultural mandate." God said to Adam and Eve, "Be fruitful and multiply, and fill the earth and subdue it" (Gen 1:28). While the first command (to be fruitful and multiply) can be viewed, in part, as a mandate to reproduce the species,[5] the second command (to fill the earth and subdue it) cannot be so simply interpreted. Rather, the "filling" of the earth can be viewed to be a cultural activity. Thus, when our early ascendants fashioned rudimentary tools in order to accomplish certain tasks more easily, when they named the animals and created basic labeling systems, or when people began to create schedules in order to organize their lives, human beings were not only building on the potential of the original creation, they were doing so as a means of fulfilling the cultural mandate given by God in the Garden.[6] Thus creation is both finished (in the sense of the original creation) and ongoing. Creation continues to unfold "through the task that people have been given to bringing to fruition the possibilities of development implicit in the work of God's hands."[7]

It is clear that God has given humankind tasks to perform on earth. These tasks are not merely perfunctory duties but are creative acts as well. As such, they are a major part of the way in which we, as humans, reflect and embody the "image of God"; in other words, we act creatively in imitation of God's creative nature. In instructing humans to "fill the earth," God has delegated some of his authority to humans by giving them a measure of influence and respon-

---

[5]However, the command to be fruitful can also have several meanings—not simply procreation. To be fruitful can also entail culture creation.

[6]Richard Mouw, "Creational Politics: Some Calvinist Amendments," *Christian Scholar's Review* 23 (1993): 182.

[7]Albert Wolters, *Creation Regained: Biblical Basics for a Reformational Worldview* (Grand Rapids: Eerdmans, 1985), pp. 37-38.

sibility over the rest of the created world, even though he remains ultimately
sovereign over all things.

Some Christians see in this cultural mandate the foundation of public authority. As humans pursue the task of tending the garden of this planet, government would likely develop naturally. Assume, for example, that Adam and
Eve had not eaten of the forbidden fruit, that they had been fruitful and multiplied, that many generations had been born and had further multiplied, that
technological developments had transpired as part of the creation process and
that sin still had not entered the garden. Even in this sinless garden, there may
well be a need for some kind of state authority that would, for example, make
decisions as to where to install traffic lights and determine how those at such
intersections should proceed. It would not be wise to allow traffic lights to be
put up simply by anyone who wished to do so. Such actions may not be morally wrong (sinful) per se, but the ability of individuals to install random traffic
lights could well result in confusion, frustration and possibly chaos.

State authority would also likely come into play in terms of the need to establish rules related to the use of such traffic lights. For example, some uniform
system of colors would be needed, with each different color representing the
same particular command at each intersection. It would be chaotic if one set of
lights employed a system of red, yellow and green lights, while a second set
utilized a system of purple, orange and blue lights, and a third set had a system of pink, green and brown lights.

Finally, even in this sinless world there would be a need for some kind of
authority that held a legitimate right to have its rules followed. Different people cannot choose to follow different rules at each intersection where traffic
lights are installed; identical rules must prevail across the different intersections. Once the legitimate authority establishes the rules, all parties must agree
to follow these "arbitrary" rules.[8] Thus even in a sinless world, there may well
be a need for a state authority that determines for the larger community the
particular standards and procedures to be followed by those within the community (e.g., where traffic lights should be placed, the rules to be followed related to such lights, and the authority to bind all within the community to obey
the rules related to those lights).

For those who see the state to be simply the result of sin, the political sphere
primarily has a negative justification and task: to hold back sin. While many

---

[8]To some degree, such rules are arbitrary in nature. For example, there is no inherent reason
why the color green as opposed to the color blue on a traffic light should be mandated as the
particular color to indicate "go" at a traffic intersection.

Christians hold this view, Reformed theology provides for a more positive view of the state that is derived from its theological understanding of the cultural mandate and the unfolding of creation. The state not only holds back sin, it also enables members of society to accomplish more in their life together and fare better than they would on their own.

Fall: Common grace. Although humans may have had certain needs (e.g., food and sleep) and desires (e.g., the desire to eat, sleep and perhaps to have sexual relations) in the Garden, these were not distorted, resulting in gluttony, sloth or lust. When God made humans, he established a system of norms by which humans are to live and by which they are to govern the interrelationships of all created things. If humans had continued to obey God's directions, any emerging culture could have continued to grow and develop—without sin—as human beings followed the God-given norms for relationships in this world.

Such harmony, however, was not to be. Before any such societies or authorities could develop, humankind disobeyed God's perfect design and thus corrupted the natural relationships God had instituted. As humankind's will became corrupted in the act of sin, so every relationship involving human beings became corrupted—whether these relationships were with God, each other or the rest of the created world. However, this corruption was not total or complete. Sin affected everything in creation and all aspects of life, but everything was not absolutely or totally corrupted. The Calvinist concept of total depravity relates to the breadth rather than the depth of the corrupting effects of sin. Humankind continues to bear much of the image of God even though this image is distorted. Thus even those who reject God or who worship idols can still do good works; those who are not Christians can be benevolent, kind and generous.[9]

There is, therefore, a second component to Reformed theology that shapes the principled pluralist perspective. This is the theological distinction between what might be labeled "particular grace" and "common grace." While those who are called by God (and who respond to that call)[10] experience a particular

---

[9]To a certain extent this appearance of benevolence, kindness and generosity relates to human rather than divine perception. The Bible notes, for example, that our righteousness is like filthy rags before God. Moreover, others argue that while good works done by nontheists may be in conformity with what is good, such works still lack the right disposition allowing them to be done for the sake of being good.

[10]Reformed theology emphasizes election because it does not want to suggest that humans in any way "earn" their salvation. Any emphasis on the need for individuals to respond to God's call may suggest that, through one's act of responding, one "earns," in part, one's salvation. Hence, Calvinists tend to downplay human agency, while Arminians tend to emphasize human action.

kind of grace, the Bible notes that God continues to bestow his goodness to all men and women, believers and unbelievers alike. There is a "common grace" that all humanity shares which is to be distinguished from God's "special grace" or "particular grace."

Common grace is that grace afforded to all people, regardless of religious belief. As Jesus declares in Matthew 5:45: "[God] makes his sun rise on the evil and on the good, and sends rain on the righteous and on the unrighteous." The common grace of God is experienced in the ordering of nature, the restraint of evil and the ability of unbelievers to reason and perform acts of civil good. The doctrine of common grace holds that God bestows on humanity a grace that, while not "saving," enables unbelievers to develop many virtues and express many truths.

Therefore, as Christians, we do not believe that all insights and wisdom of, or accomplishments associated with, unbelievers are necessarily bad and are to be rejected as totally corrupt and fallen.[11] Not only can "achievements in politics and scholarship, arts and technology, . . . not motivated by faith . . . still be cherished gifts of God," but cooperation between Christians and unbelievers may be possible and even necessary at times.[12] It is this common grace that provides us with certain shared ground with unbelievers, which gives us a basis for Christian engagement with the larger society.[13]

However, as a result of the sinfulness of human beings, the nature of public authority has had to be modified and broadened in scope. Instead of existing simply to facilitate greater cooperation between spheres of society within the perfect divine order, the state must now also exist as a means to curtail sinful behavior, "bearing the sword" to restrain evil and coerce prescribed or good behavior if need be. In addition, public authority or government has also now become tainted by sin. Government is led and administered by sinful human beings. As a result, governmental leaders may try to abuse their God-established roles; even if they devoutly seek to perform their tasks in a pious fashion, they cannot fill their role perfectly because they are separated from the fullness of God's wisdom due to the Fall. And so, though it serves in part as a means to restrain wrongdoing, government itself can become a perpetrator of wrongdoing. And since it wields the sword, its wrongdoing can at times be extremely vicious.

---

[11]H. Henry Meeter discusses three different ways in which the Bible has noted that the works of evil men can be counted as good. See his *The Basic Ideas of Calvinism*, 6th ed., rev. Paul Marshall (Grand Rapids: Baker, 1990), p. 72.

[12]James Bratt, "The Dutch Schools," in *Reformed Theology in America*, ed. David Wells (Grand Rapids: Eerdmans, 1985), p. 146.

[13]Richard Mouw, *He Shines in All That's Fair* (Grand Rapids: Eerdmans, 2001).

Redemption: Cosmic in scope. However, God did not leave this fallen world in a hopeless situation. In order to fulfill his divine purpose for the world, God sent Jesus Christ to redeem *all* things (individuals; social life, communal and national relationships; and natural life, including the environment and animal life)—and to reconcile everything to himself and each other. Redemption is thus not only individual in nature—it is social, natural and cosmic in scope. Jesus came not only to save individuals, but to restore his whole creation and to reestablish the proper function of family, religious life, state and all other institutions. As Paul discusses in Romans 8:18-23, creation "has been groaning in labor pains" (recall that labor pains were part of the curse associated with the Fall), and it "waits with eager longing" to be "set free from its bondage to decay." Likewise, when the apostle John talks about a new heaven and a new earth in Revelation, he is not referring to some destruction of the present earth and a creation of a new planet. Rather, he is pointing to a new earth that has been refined and purified, as in a refiner's fire, where the dross is removed to purify the metal. Thus John can later note in Revelation 11:15, "The kingdom of the world has become the kingdom of our Lord / and of his Messiah."

Redemption in the creation-fall-redemption narrative, therefore, is not limited to personal salvation; it has a much broader scope. Just as the fall touches and affects all aspects of creation, redemption in Jesus Christ also seeks to "reclaim" all facets of creation. As Paul notes in Colossians 1:20, "through him [Christ Jesus] God was pleased to reconcile to himself all things, whether on earth or in heaven, by making peace through the blood of his cross." Redemption therefore entails "the recovery of creational goodness through the annulment of sin and the effort toward the progressive removal of its effects everywhere."[14]

This task of redemption is not an effort to restore creation to some original, relatively pristine yet primitive form. Rather it "means a restoration of culture and society in their present stage of development."[15] While the historical developments of increased literacy, industrialization and urbanization have been shaped by their own distortions or evils, these are not necessarily processes that should be entirely reversed or eradicated. Instead, the coming of the kingdom of God demands that they should be reformed, made answerable to their creational structure and subjected to the ordinances of the Creator.[16] As Wolters notes, "Perhaps the most fitting symbol of the development of creation from the primordial past to the eschatological future is the fact that the

---

[14]Wolters, *Creation Regained*, p. 69.
[15]Ibid., p. 71.
[16]Ibid., p. 64.

Bible begins with a garden and ends with a city—a city filled with 'the glory and the honor of the nations.'"[17]

Christians have an obligation to facilitate this task of redemption. Certainly God is at work saving his creation. Yet we who know God's salvation are saved not simply because God loves us, but in order to fulfill God's tasks for his people in the world—whether in farming, building, manufacturing, educating or engaging in political life.[18] As redeemed people work to reconcile structures of public authority to their right condition, such entities may themselves become agents of redemption (not in terms of salvation but of transformation) in the society and world at large, fulfilling their original purpose by bringing about a right ordering of human interrelationships.

Conclusion. Calvin's *Institutes of the Christian Religion* made important statements about the comprehensive character of the kingdom of God and the task of believers in hostile pagan and apostate environments. In terms of the relationship between church and state, Calvin articulated what might be called a "two-powers" view, though his theocentric impulse led him to a restrictive view of the power of all human authorities and legal institutions. The unifying theme in Calvin's worldview was the sovereign rule of God in Jesus Christ over every part of life. Thus for Calvin all human authority stands under the authority of God and his law. It was this conviction that led Calvin to reject the longstanding paradigm of shared jurisdiction between church and state that had dominated Western Christianity for the twelve hundred years following the rule of Constantine.

Calvin's two-powers view, which became the Reformed view, is distinct from another major sixteenth-century Protestant understanding of the relationship between church and state. Martin Luther's two-kingdom view separates the two domains of church and state, with each operating independently; Christians, in turn, owe their allegiance to both domains. In contrast, the Reformed view recognizes a close and mutually interdependent relationship between the two authorities, even though they remain autonomous spheres. God gives power and authority to both spheres, but each sphere has a responsibility to defend the other. Thus, despite Calvin's differentiation between church and state, Calvin still presumed that the state had some churchly responsibilities—as the state should not only provide for the safety of the church and of believers, but it should battle against heresy as well.

---

[17]Ibid., p. 41.

[18]Paul Marshall, *Thine Is the Kingdom: A Biblical Perspective on the Nature of Government and Politics Today* (Grand Rapids: Eerdmans, 1984), p. 35.

At the same time, however, the Reformed two-powers view teaches that should the state fail in its responsibilities, the church has the prophetic responsibility of calling the state to account for the conduct of its affairs. When participating in political activities, Christians have a right and duty, if necessary, to oppose civil authorities. Because all human authority is under the purview of God and his law, human beings have the natural right to resist civil authority if obedience to the legal authority conflicts with God's law.

Principled Pluralism

Although Calvin enunciated political principles that "broke new ground," he did not construct a fully developed theory of the state; this task was largely left for future generations of Calvinists to do.[19] Later followers would wrestle with Calvin's "theocratic" understanding of the state's task, asking how such a state could honor the religious liberty of all citizens and whether it implicitly treated government as being too much like the church.

Reformed theologian and Dutch politician Abraham Kuyper took on this issue most directly, expanding on Calvin's two-powers perspective by emphasizing what has been called "sphere sovereignty." Kuyper (1837-1920) was a dominant figure in the religious and political life of the Netherlands for nearly half a century.[20] Not only was he a theologian and devotionalist, but he served as prime minister of the Netherlands, founded a major university and served as editor of a major newspaper. Kuyper's ideas continue "to inspire an international school of thought."[21]

Particularly problematic for Kuyper was Calvin's support of governmental intervention in matters of religion and the legacy of article 36 of the Belgic Confession, a confessional standard of the Reformed churches, adopted in 1566. Article 36 entrusted the government with the task of preserving the sanctity of the church by dealing with false religion. Even as late as the end of the nineteenth century, many Calvinists still assumed that the state should enforce Christian beliefs and morality. But for Kuyper, these problematic aspects of Calvinism were best understood as remnants from the medieval period. As a result, he held that the only system supported by Calvinism was simply "a free church in a free state."[22]

---

[19]Meeter, *Basic Ideas of Calvinism*, p. 72. For a brief discussion of the ways in which Calvin's political thinking helped to shape later political philosophy, see ibid., pp. 72-73.
[20]Peter Heslam, *Creating a Christian Worldview: Abraham Kuyper's Lectures on Calvinism* (Grand Rapids: Eerdmans, 1998), p. 1.
[21]Ibid.
[22]Ibid., p. 161.

Kuyper argued that society was made up of various spheres (such as the family, business and education), and these spheres derived their authority neither from the church nor the state but directly from God, to whom they are ultimately accountable. The phrase he used to denote this theory was "sovereignty in the individual spheres," which today is frequently termed "sphere sovereignty."[23] The idea of sphere sovereignty holds that God has ordained, as part of the creational order, various spheres of authority; each has a reason for existence and its own particular right to exist.[24] These spheres represent the various domains in which different authority structures operate. The state, the family, schools and business have different God-given tasks to perform; each area has the authority and responsibility to fulfill these tasks. These spheres in society are not ultimately sovereign since they are subservient in their relationships to God. However, they do possess a certain level of sovereignty both within their domain and in their interrelationships with each other: "Each sphere has its own identity, its own unique task, its own God-given prerogatives."[25] Each of the authority structures within these different areas is "sovereign," in that "each sphere in society has its own independent authority; no one sphere should dominate or usurp the role of the others."[26]

Because Kuyper insisted on the autonomy of the various social spheres, the role he reserved for government was limited and restricted, yet also "elevated" in importance. On the one hand, the state is like other concerns, with distinct powers and responsibilities; it simply occupies a place alongside all the other entities. And the state is restricted in that it is not permitted to compel the authority structures of other social spheres to conform to the state's will. Nevertheless, under certain circumstances the state is supreme in its influence over other domains. First, the state is to maintain parity between the different spheres. Thus it has an obligation to enforce mutual respect for the boundary lines separating the different spheres of authority whenever a conflict arises between areas or when one sphere steps over its boundary of authority into the domain of another. Second, the state is to prevent authorities within a particular sphere from abusing their power by acting unjustly toward those who are relatively powerless within that sphere. Finally, the state has the right to impose

---

[23]Ibid., p. 154.
[24]Gordon Spykman, "Sphere-Sovereignty in Calvin and the Calvinist Tradition," in *Exploring the Heritage of John Calvin*, ed. David Holwerda (Grand Rapids: Baker, 1976), p. 167.
[25]Ibid.
[26]Gordon Spykman, "The Principled Pluralist Position," in *God and Politics*, ed. Gary Scott Smith (Phillipsburg, N.J.: Presbyterian & Reformed, 1989), pp. 79-80.

taxes in order to support the apparatus of government and to facilitate its task of maintaining the health and vitality of the commonwealth. Thus while the state is merely one among various social spheres, it does enjoy supremacy and sovereignty over these other spheres; in turn, the state is to be regulated by means of both constitutional law and representative government.[27]

The principled pluralist perspective draws and builds on this understanding of sphere sovereignty. First, principled pluralism recognizes the empirical presence of various structures of authority within human life (structural pluralism) and acknowledges that human beings live within and across (and are constrained by) different structures of authority. Individuals do not experience life simply within the social frameworks associated with church and state but within a variety of other social structures wherein positions of authority exist (e.g., parental authority; educational authority, such as teachers and school administrators; workplace authority).

But principled pluralism does not stop there; it goes further and normatively contends that this kind of pluralism is good. Not only do human beings live within a network of human relationships, ordered along and through different social structures, but "people fulfill their callings within a plurality of communal associations, such as family, school, and state."[28] Principled pluralism ties the empirical presence of these different spheres to the creation order and to the command to "fill the earth." Thus, for principled pluralists, structural pluralism is good in that God has ordained different spheres of activity as part of the original order, and together these different spheres constitute community life.[29]

While principled pluralists view structural pluralism as tied to creational norms, there is a historical dimension to the differentiation and development of each of these different types of activities and the structures of authority that govern them. Once differentiated, each of these types of activity displays its own characteristic qualities.[30] Thus, while government has authority and certain distinct responsibilities related to particular facets of life, other social structures have their own moral bases and competence. And, building on Kuyper's arguments about the role of the state, principled pluralists argue that "as society differentiates into an ever more complex array of social structures," it is the task of government to secure

---

[27]Heslam, *Creating a Christian Worldview*, pp. 158-59.
[28]Spykman, "Sphere-Sovereignty," p. 79.
[29]Ibid.
[30]James Skillen, *Recharging the American Experiment* (Grand Rapids: Baker, 1994), p. 83.

justice through the recognition and protection of these different structures of authority, and through that protection, help to secure the legal integration of the whole society.[31]

Along with the presence of structural pluralism, the principled pluralist perspective recognizes the existence of a second kind of pluralism as well—confessional pluralism. Clearly, contemporary social life is characterized by the presence of multiple religious confessions. Given this reality, what should the state (as well as the church collectively or Christians individually) do about it? Principled pluralists use the term "confessional pluralism" to denote the right that different religious groups have, not only to exist within society but to promote their own views and develop their own patterns of involvement in public life through formation of their own associations—whether in terms of schools, political parties, labor unions or churches.[32] In the United States, the First Amendment to the U.S. Constitution specifies that the government is not to prohibit the free exercise of religion. In part, the presumption that undergirds this restriction on governmental authority is that government is not competent to decide, for purposes of eternal salvation, what the religious obligations and orientations of its citizens should be. This incompetence, coupled with the state's responsibility to establish justice, "leads to a civic-moral conclusion that there should be fair and equitable confessional pluralism."[33]

The state's recognition and tolerance of different social groups holding divergent worldviews is not an assessment that the beliefs and values of all such individuals and groups are equally "right and true" or that there is no particular group that holds the truth. Rather, confessional pluralism simply reflects the recognition that it is not the function of the state to discern the ultimate truth for those under its rule.[34]

This recognition of confessional pluralism does not, for principled pluralists, constitute an acceptance of relativism. Instead, principled pluralists assert that it is God's responsibility, not the Christian community's, to separate the false from the true in the field of harvest. The parable of the wheat and tares (weeds) found in Matthew 13:24-30 and Jesus' explanation of the parable indi-

---

[31]Ibid., p. 84.
[32]Spykman, "Sphere-Sovereignty," p. 79.
[33]Skillen, *Recharging the American Experiment*, p. 84.
[34]One might also note that the acknowledgment and declaration of one's own identity enables a better understanding of those who are different. When I clearly know who I am, then I can more easily recognize who you are, and that you are different. Relativism reflects confusion, not tolerance.

cate that the Son of Man, not his disciples, will separate the wheat from the tares and that this separation will be done neither shortly after the weeds are first planted nor while they are growing together with the wheat, but only at the time of harvest (Mt 13:36-43). Hence, the task of weeding is not the Christian's responsibility here on earth, whether through political or other means. Religious pluralism rests on God's sovereignty within his created order and on his Word that this separation between true and false belief is not to be effected during the present era but at the time of Christ's return.

Political Principles

Even with this relatively brief discussion of the theological emphases and social theory of the Reformed tradition, we can discern some of the important political themes the Reformed tradition and principled pluralism stress. However, it should be noted first that, given the purposes for which it was written, the Bible is not a political treatise that outlines and explicates some detailed political philosophy. Rather, there are various passages within the Bible that relate to politics, some directly and others indirectly. Moreover, those passages that do relate to politics must be assessed to determine whether they are instructions that transcend time and place or are instructions for a particular historical audience (certain statements, for example, may relate specifically to certain kings or kingdoms in the Old Testament). At the same time, even those passages containing specific instructions for a particular time and place may nevertheless involve political principles that hold across time and space.

Certainly there are biblical instructions related to politics that remain true for contemporary political life. These political principles need to be discerned, as the particular context in which the principle is applied may color, but not necessarily negate, the principle itself. The principle may remain the same, but its application may vary based on context. While the Christian faith makes an absolute claim about the nature of Jesus of Nazareth (he is the Christ) and the redemption and salvation his life accomplished, the Christian religion is always a "religion in or even of a particular society, wherever and whenever we encounter it."[35] As is true of any religious faith, there is a contextual nature to the Christian faith. Therefore, in the end, what can be drawn from biblical texts regarding political life are principles that should govern political life across time and space rather than detailed prescriptions

---

[35]H. M. Kuitert, *Everything Is Politics but Politics Is Not Everything* (Grand Rapids: Eerdmans, 1986), p. 62.

about political institutional arrangements that transcend time and space.[36]

The vital role of communities. Principled pluralists, much like other pluralists, emphasize the social nature of human beings, the intrinsic existence of
communities and associations in society, and the vital contributions such entities make to society.[37] First of all, principled pluralists believe that human beings are fundamentally social beings. As Kuyper stated, "Human life . . . is so
constituted that the individual can exist only within the group and can come
to full expression only in community."[38]

Second, given the social nature of human beings, principled pluralists believe that communities and associations are an intrinsic feature of society. Thus
society is not composed of some isolated particles that are fused together by the
power of the state. Rather, society is "made up of social groups, related organ-
ically, rather than of individuals related impersonally."[39] Because human beings naturally form social groupings (communities, associations, social groups)
and experience their lives, establish their identities and form their values
within the social structures of these groups, such social groups and structures
are viewed to exist "prior to and in a real sense independent of the state."[40]

Third, principled pluralists affirm the vital role of communities and associations in creating a healthy polity, an emphasis that stands between the extremes of the individualism associated with laissez-faire liberalism and the
collectivism advanced by socialist and nationalist ideologies. This assertion of
the social nature of human beings compels principled pluralists to oppose individualism (at least in its extreme forms) while the emphasis on structural
and confessional pluralism compels principled pluralists to oppose collectivism and totalitarianism as well. In addition, because Reformed thinking con-
fers authority and integrity to social associations and institutions outside the

---

[36]Theonomists, however, argue that God's law is eternal and that the laws given to Israel in
the Old Testament continue to be the laws that God expects the state to proscribe and implement today. Thus, while theonomists recognize a distinction between church and state,
they tend to do so in "an ahistorical fashion" (James Skillen, *The Scattered Voice: Christians at
Odds in the Public Square* [Grand Rapids: Zondervan, 1990], p. 171). In the words of Gary
North, a noted theonomist, "Christians must confront the fact that God requires them to impose His law for the state upon all men, whether men like it or not. The universe is not a
democracy, but a Kingdom. If Christians do not impose God's laws upon non-Christians,
then non-Christians will impose man's laws upon Christians" (quoted in Skillen, *Scattered
Voice*, p. 171).

[37]Stephen Monsma, *Positive Neutrality: Letting Religious Freedom Ring* (Westport, Conn.:
Greenwood Press, 1993), p. 146.

[38]Abraham Kuyper, quoted in Spykman, "Sphere Sovereignty," pp. 182-83.

[39]Dirk Jellema, "Abraham Kuyper's Attack on Liberalism," *Review of Politics* 19 (1993): 482.

[40]Monsma, *Positive Neutrality*, p. 145.

state, it advances what many political philosophers deem to be an important safeguard of individual rights and liberties—namely, the presence of mediating structures.[41] These structures (associations, organizations and institutions) provide a sense of community, while shielding their members against any aggrandizing tendency of state authority.

The nature of the church. The church too is a kind of community. Because principled pluralists articulate a political philosophy, they are much more prone to discuss matters related to the nature of the state than of the church. But Reformed theology does discuss such matters. Within Reformed theology, human beings are spiritual as well as material beings. And because they are spiritual beings, humans tend to seek meaning and purpose in life and religious fellowship with others.

However, not all congregations of religious people necessarily constitute a true church, that is, a properly formed worshiping community. Within Reformed theology the marks of a true church entail three specific features: (1) the preaching of the Word, (2) the administration of the sacraments and (3) the maintenance of standards of Christian discipline.[42] Internally, the church is first of all a community that listens to God's Word. Second, it is a community that, through the sacraments, is being served by the God who calls it together. And finally, it is a community that is experiencing a process of growth through discipline and discipleship.

However, this formulation of the marks of a true church relates primarily to the internal life of the church as an institution. The institutional church is the formal, more ceremonial center of the life of the Christian community in which Christians are, in an important sense, a gathered people. But in many important ways the church is also much broader than this institutional base. This is recognized in a variety of ways: in discussions that differentiate between the visible and the invisible church, between the church as an institution and the church as a mystical communion, between the church as herald and the church

---

[41]Mediating structures are defined as "those institutions standing between the individual in his private life and the large institutions of public life" (Peter Berger and Richard John Neuhaus, *To Empower People: The Role of Mediating Structures in Public Policy* [Washington, D.C.: American Enterprise Institute, 1977], p. 158). Principled pluralism shares certain affinities with, but also diverges from, mediating institutional theory. From the perspective of mediating institutional theory, nongovernmental institutions serve primarily as devices to shield individuals from state power; such institutions simply function as a means to protect the individual from, and serve as a check to, the overaggrandizing tendencies of state power. For principled pluralists, such nongovernmental institutions are viewed more as ends in themselves, and any "shielding" that results is more a byproduct of their formation.

[42]The following three paragraphs draw heavily from the discussion found in Richard Mouw, *Politics and the Biblical Drama* (Grand Rapids: Eerdmans, 1976).

as servant, and between the church and the kingdom of God.[43] The point here, for purposes of this discussion, is that the church is broader than our common concept of the institutional church.

Moreover, the church does not exist in a vacuum. It is in the world. How then does the church relate to those outside the Christian community? While the people of God form a listening community, they must also function as a proclaiming community—proclaiming the good news to people outside the church. While they have been served by Jesus Christ, they must in turn become servants in the world by responding to the actual needs and suffering they find among those around them. While the people of God are to be a community shaped by the justice and mercy of God, so too they must endeavor to promote practices and structures that approximate God's standards of justice and righteousness, for as Jesus instructed in the Beatitudes, "Blessed are those who hunger and thirst for righteousness" (Mt 5:6).

The nature of the state. Another major principle associated with principled pluralism is the importance of institutions and their responsibilities. Politics is not simply about one's stances on particular issues; rather, it is largely about the exercise of governmental authority. For principled pluralists, the nature of the political realm is characterized by certain qualities: first, the state has limited powers; second, the state functions to secure justice—both individually and collectively—and finally, the state is an agent of common grace.

Limited powers. A central element of biblical teaching is that governments are limited in their powers, an understanding not unique to the principled pluralist perspective. For principled pluralists the authority of the state is not absolute but limited in two different senses of the term. First, it is limited because other legitimate structures of authority exist prior to and independent of the state. Even in a sinless world, the individual and the family (and whatever other private spheres may have developed naturally out of the "filling of the earth") would have had "their own special cultural duties to perform independently of the state."[44] Thus the state is not the only sovereign entity; there are many institutional spheres of authority within society that are also sovereign. The authority that these nonstate institutional entities (e.g., family, church) possess stem from God; they do not derive from the state. Each has "its own intrinsic authority that must be recognized and respected by government."[45]

---

[43]For a discussion of different models of the church, see Avery Dulles, *Models of the Church* (Garden City, N.Y.: Doubleday, 1974).

[44]Meeter, *Basic Ideas of Calvinism*, p. 81.

[45]Paul Marshall, *God and the Constitution: Christianity and American Politics* (Lanham, Md.: Rowman & Littlefield, 2002), p. 61.

Second, the power of government is limited in that Christians do not owe absolute obedience to the state's authority, even when it falls properly within that sphere of life where it is granted sovereignty. Christian citizens are called to submit to political authorities even though such political structures are corrupted by sin. (Likewise, children are to obey parental authority even though parental authority is corrupted by sin.) However, such submission to political authority is tempered by the fact that Christians may resist when political authorities compel them to behave in a way that would contradict God's law.

Some Christians interpret Romans 13 to suggest that Christians are to give total and unconditional obedience to the state: "Let every person be subject to the governing authorities; for there is no authority except from God, and those authorities that exist have been instituted by God" (Rom 13:1). However, a closer understanding of the text suggests our obedience to the state is not unquestioning in nature. A few verses later Paul adds that government is "God's servant for your good" (Rom 13:4). Thus in Romans 13 Paul recasts the prevailing understanding of the Roman political order by insisting that governments are *servants*—a fairly remarkable thing to argue at the time of the Roman Empire. Paul thereby relativized the Roman imperial order by refusing to accept the emperor as the ultimate authority and arguing that the emperor was under God—a servant with a particular task to do. Roman emperors (and government leaders more generally) were not gods, not lords, but servants; the emperor was not the only or the final sovereign entity.[46]

For principled pluralists, then, the state's authority rests squarely on God's delegation of authority, but this granted authority is limited in that God has assigned jurisdiction to other human agents as well and that our ultimate allegiance is owed to God, who holds supremacy over all of life. Governments do not have the prerogative to do anything they might please. As Jesus stated: "Give to the emperor the things that are the emperor's, and to God the things that are God's" (Mk 12:17). Clearly, then, Jesus' statement set limits on the things that Caesar could claim; some things lie outside Caesar's domain.[47]

Securing justice. Since the Fall, the state is, in part, an instrument to restrain evil, and its duties involve securing and administering justice. But justice involves more than just punishing wrongdoers and addressing the proximate causes of injustice. For principled pluralists it entails "just treatment . . . of all

---

[46]Luis Lugo, "Caesar's Coin and the Politics of the Kingdom: A Pluralist Perspective," in *Caesar's Coin Revisited: Christians and the Limits of Government*, ed. Michael Cromartie (Washington, D.C.: Ethics and Public Policy Center, 1996); Marshall, *God and the Constitution*, p. 52.
[47]Lugo, "Caesar's Coin"; Marshall, *God and the Constitution*, p. 51.

non-governmental institutions and relationships through which people constitute their lives."[48] In the principled pluralist perspective, when government acts against injustice or promotes justice, it must deal properly with both individuals as well as the many nongovernmental institutions and relationships that constitute our lives. Governmental authority, while limited, is nevertheless charged with "the responsibility for maintaining an overall order of justice in a territory."[49]

The government is meant to both insure that the various spheres of authority do not encroach on each other's domain and that the relationships between authorities (whether within one sphere or across different spheres) conform to a just order.[50] Justice does not simply relate to some protection and advancement of individual rights. Rather, justice "is more often about impartially adjudicating the interests of those making potentially conflicting rights claims."[51] In this endeavor the state may necessarily become involved in other institutions. But in so doing the state should not usurp their tasks nor place them under its domination. For example, the state is called to address the injustice of discrimination in society, but at the same time, the government must not undermine the legitimate ability of churches to choose who their members will be.

Government is charged with the pursuit of justice, but that is not equivalent to pursuing morality per se, except as it relates to justice.[52] The fact that an individual may be committing an immoral act is not in itself grounds for governmental action.[53] In fact, of the Ten Commandments given by God on Mount Sinai, only the sixth (murder) and the eighth (theft) are always considered wrong by the state and worthy of punishment. While engaging in an extramarital affair is immoral, it does not mean that the state should bring criminal charges against those who do so. Not all sins are crimes; as a result, the state cannot address or fix all wrongs evident in society.

The task of government is not to compel everything that is right or moral,

---

[48]Skillen, *Recharging the American Experiment*, p. 84.

[49]Marshall, *God and the Constitution*, p. 60.

[50]Ibid., p. 61.

[51]David Koyzis, *Political Visions and Illusions: A Survey and Christian Critique of Contemporary Ideologies* (Downers Grove, Ill.: InterVarsity Press, 2003), p. 259.

[52]Stephen Monsma, *Pursuing Justice in a Sinful World* (Grand Rapids: Eerdmans, 1984), p. 47.

[53]It should also be noted that government may choose to address a problem even though nothing immoral has occurred. For example, driving through an intersection is not immoral. But for purposes of safety and convenience, governments may choose to place a traffic light at an intersection, after which people are morally and legally obligated to stop when the light turns red. Only after a law has been passed and a traffic light placed at the intersection do such actions become matters of morality (Marshall, *God and the Constitution*, p. 141).

nor to punish everything that is wrong or immoral, but to enforce that particular part of morality we call justice. While governments may seek to deter certain behavior (e.g., killing one's neighbor) through laws threatening violators with imprisonment or even death, or may seek to encourage other kinds of behavior through various incentives, governments are far less able to control and shape human thoughts and desires. Governments might be able to stop an individual from acting out the hatred within one's heart, but this may not entail any moral improvement in the sight of God, as anyone who hates his or her neighbor has already committed murder in his or her heart (Mt 5:21-22). Because morality is a matter of the heart, no one can be forced to be moral. Rather, governments can deal only with outward actions, and "justice is a matter of overt acts, and that is what government can and should control."[54]

An agent of common grace. While God has given the state a separate sphere of authority, its responsibilities do not involve doing the work of the church. In other words, the state is not to be an agent for the propagation of religion or the securing of salvation. Rather, through God's graciousness to all people, he has granted the institution of the state to care for the common interests and general welfare of the people over which it has authority. Here the distinction between particular and common grace sharpens our understanding of the role of the state; it is an agency of common, not particular, grace. Government's role is the mitigation of evil in a fallen world, not the redemption of human sinful nature. Its task is not to redeem its citizens but to sustain the created order. The role of the state is specific and practical; it must maintain the law and uphold public justice.[55]

This principle is crucial for a Christian comprehension of the state, and several important implications flow from it. First, this understanding precludes any utopian view of politics. The state will not whither away with the passage of time, nor will governments eradicate all injustices or cure sin. Political activity and state action will never ultimately solve social evils, nor can they provide any hope of salvation. While Christians are called to participate in the task of reconciling, restoring and redeeming the created order, the kingdom of God will never be fully realized before Christ's return. In the present age, political and state activity may alleviate particular injustices (e.g., slavery and discrimination) and it may even ameliorate some of its root causes (e.g., racism). But political and state activity will never fully eradicate human pride or racism; only when Christ returns to earth will such redemp-

---

[54]Monsma, *Pursuing Justice*, p. 47.
[55]Alan Storkey, *A Christian Social Perspective* (Leicester, U.K.: Inter-Varsity Press, 1979), p. 299.

tion be fully and completely realized—when there will be a new heaven and a new earth (Rev 21:1).

A second important implication of this view is the need for patience. Reformed theology is amillennialist rather than premillennial or postmillennial in terms of its eschatology.[56] It neither holds that the world will grow increasingly corrupt and the church increasingly apostate prior to Christ's return, nor does it hold that the efforts of Christians, though working to more fully establish the kingdom of God on earth, can hasten the day of Christ's return. Premillennialism tends to weaken the foundation for Christian involvement in politics, while postmillennialism tends to encourage political efforts to separate the wheat from the tares prior to Christ's return.

Amillennialism, however, asserts that perfection is not ours to bring—it is ours to receive in God's good time. Our political work as Christians is therefore incremental in nature. As a result, we can support and work to implement laws that more fully, though perhaps not completely, embody Christian values (the "good") even though there may be other proposed laws that more fully reflect Christian values (the "perfect") but which have no chance of being enacted and implemented at the time. The need for patience and our trust that God holds the future require that the "perfect" should never be the enemy of the "good."

The call to political engagement. All of creation awaits redemption; the political sphere stands in need of redemption neither no more nor no less than any other sphere of human activity. Thus, because Christians are called to seek justice (Amos 5:15, 24), Christians are called to political engagement; they are not to refrain from politics because it is deemed to be a sphere of activity outside the domain of God's sovereignty. God instituted government for the welfare of humankind. It makes no sense then that God would not want his children to be involved in politics. Such an argument would contend that "there is a human institution or structure that God has established and that God intends for human good, but that it is so evil that God does not want his followers to be involved with it."[57]

---

[56]*Eschatology* relates to doctrines of "final things" or the "end times." Premillennialists argue that the millennium (a "thousand year" period of peace and tranquility in which "the lamb will lay down with the lion") will transpire only after Christ's triumphant second coming. Postmillennialists argue that the world will experience the millennium prior to Christ's triumphant second coming; for Jonathan Edwards, a postmillennialist, this millennium would be ushered in "through the preaching of the gospel and the use of the ordinary means of grace" (quoted in Timothy Weber, *Living in the Shadow of the Second Coming: American Premillennialism, 1875-1982* [Grand Rapids: Academie Books, 1983], p. 14).

[57]Stephen Monsma, "Christian Commitment and Political Life," in *In God We Trust? Religion and American Politics*, ed. Corwin Smidt (Grand Rapids: Baker Academic, 2001), p. 257.

Christians are called to political engagement. The belief that God's redemption is at work in this present world spurs Christians to engage in political activity. In submitting and contributing to the structure of public authority, Christians may bring Christ's renewing influence to bear on public life, furthering the cause of God's kingdom in this world in obedience to Scripture.[58]

Political modesty, toleration, cooperation and compromise. While the call to "political modesty, toleration, cooperation, and compromise" is not a "principle" that *distinctively* flows from principled pluralism, it is a call that seemingly develops from its theological underpinnings and one that is frequently expressed by the proponents of principled pluralism. Its foundation relates to the theological understanding of the present age—the time between the first and second advent of Jesus Christ—and to the doctrine of common grace. In terms of the present age, we see through a glass darkly (1 Cor 13:12). Thus, even with the generous gifts God has given us in this age to know him and to discern his will (e.g., the Bible and the Holy Spirit), we need to be cautious about claiming to speak for the Lord. As Skillen notes:

> We must constantly act with an attitude of true humility. We should undertake every civic duty, every political action . . . with the avowed understanding that they are not God's will but only our response to God's will. . . . This attitude of humility will lead us to be modest and self-critical in our claims and stated intentions.[59]

Accordingly, one can rightfully state that "modesty and provisionalism" in politics are not reflective of "weak-kneed accommodationism but are required by fidelity to the gospel."[60]

This call to modesty seeks to avoid each of two polar extremes that tend to plague contemporary Christian involvement in politics. The first is the position that Christians possess the truth and therefore that the laws of the land should reflect Christian values. Christians may know the Truth (Jesus Christ), but that does not mean they possess the truth when it comes to political issues and concerns.

Some might argue that such modesty leads to relativism and to indifference and toleration of moral wrongs. But, as their label suggests, principled pluralists are not relativists. First, tolerance is not indifference, since toleration is only present in relationship to those things we really care about. Genuine tol-

---

[58]For a discussion of the relationship between church and state from a principled pluralist perspective, see Monsma, *Positive Neutrality.*

[59]James Skillen, *Christians Organizing for Political Service* (Washington, D.C.: Association for Public Justice Education Fund, 1980), p. 23.

[60]Richard John Neuhaus, *The Naked Public Square* (Grand Rapids: Eerdmans, 1984), p. 123.

erance calls for peaceful coexistence despite the fact that there are areas in which real disagreements exist. Forbearance does not require us to celebrate our differences; nor does it demand us to hold that all views are equal. Genuine toleration means permitting others with whom we disagree to exist and, when appropriate, to persuade and engage others by word. In the present age, prior to the full establishment of the kingdom of God that will be inaugurated with the second coming of Jesus Christ, we must exercise genuine tolerance—an action that defends both truth and coexistence.[61]

But principled pluralists also address a second extreme that tends to plague contemporary Christian involvement in politics—the claim that Christians should not seek to implement Christian values in the form of public policy simply because it is wrong to impose our values on others. In fact, everyone (except perhaps anarchists) believes that some things should and others should not be compelled by the government. Laws always impose someone's values, because laws specify either directly or indirectly that certain forms of behavior are preferred over other forms. For example, because racial integration is preferred to racial segregation in public schools, busing to achieve school integration has been mandated and implemented in numerous school districts. Obviously, such a policy imposes certain behavior on segregationists—behavior that is inconsistent with their particular personal values. Therefore, the contention "that 'you can't impose your views on others' can be seen as, at most, a half-truth, and therefore, a distortion and manipulation."[62] All laws impose somebody's values.

The issue then is not whether Christians (or any other group, including even a majority of the electorate) are permitted to "impose their views" on others. Rather, the question is, what is the proper role of the state? Or stated somewhat differently, "in what areas of human life can the state properly impose or not impose views, and what kind of views can it impose?"[63]

Principled pluralists argue that the task of government is neither to compel everything that is right or moral, nor to punish everything that is wrong or immoral. Though we are called to love our neighbor, the state is unable to compel its citizens to do so; likewise, though it is immoral to tell untruths and lie to others, the state cannot punish all acts involving lying. Rather, what the state is called to do is to enforce that which we call justice.[64]

---

[61]Marshall, *God and the Constitution,* p. 121-23.
[62]Ibid., p. 147.
[63]Ibid.
[64]Monsma, *Pursuing Justice;* Marshall, *God and the Constitution.*

In this political effort to seek public justice, principled pluralists advocate the need for negotiation and compromise. First, principles must be applied to particular circumstances and changing contexts. Discerning what constitutes justice in these new and different circumstances may well require discussion and negotiation among different parties. Moreover, there may be varying principles that apply to the area of public policy that may well stand in tension with each other. Because, in such cases, emphasizing one fundamental principle diminishes another (e.g., in terms of American political values, a tension often exists between promoting freedom and equality simultaneously), negotiation and compromise may be necessary to seek a proper balance between the two principles involved.

Second, while evil pervades all of life, goodness is not necessarily absent even in the lives of the reprobate. As a result, Christians should not simply dismiss as unworthy the arguments or perspectives of those outside the faith. Governments are, according to the doctrine of common grace, agents of mercy for all. Public justice can be accomplished only when, through negotiation and compromise, the interests and concerns of all have been heard and addressed.

Third, the need for negotiation and compromise helps to avoid the theological error that the people of God (or Christians) should rule, and it stands in harmony with Christ's own mandate concerning leadership: "whoever wishes to become great among you must be your servant, and whoever wishes to be first among you must be slave of all" (Mk 10:43-44; see also Mt 20:26-27). Christians are not called to rule or "lord over" the people; rather, we are called to serve people.

Constructing just public policy requires debate and compromise, yet many Christians tend to believe that compromise is an evil thing and something to be avoided. Christians need to recognize that mutual concessions are a fundamental feature of human life (e.g., within a marriage, spouses frequently have to compromise with each other); it is not peculiar to the political realm.[65] But even as a political tactic, Christians have frequently been unwilling to practice give and take. Rather than constructing and pursuing a realistic agenda of incremental progress toward the achievement of one's policy goals, many Christians have expected too much too fast. In working to pass public policy that seeks to achieve public justice, the perfect should never become the enemy of the good. Thus one should not view taking incremental steps toward a desired policy goal as being unprincipled action.

---

[65]Marshall, *God and the Constitution*, p. 142.

Principled pluralism and public policy. But how does this perspective relate directly to specific issues of public policy? Some of these principles can serve to guide discussions related to issues of public policy; as a brief illustration, the matter of the Charitable Choice provision of the Welfare Reform Act of 1996 and the related faith-based initiative of President George W. Bush will be examined here. The Charitable Choice provision of the Welfare Reform Act of 1996 specifies that, when the government chooses to partner with community groups in addressing social welfare needs, no private agency is to be excluded from consideration simply because of its religious character. The specific nature of the program, rather than the agency, is to serve as the basis of assessment. All programs, whether "religious" or "secular," should be evaluated on the basis of how well they train the unemployed, care for children or heal drug addicts. The Faith-Based and Community Initiatives program goes beyond the Charitable Choice provision to allow governmental funding of nonwelfare-related services on a competitive basis, permitting religious organizations to pursue government funds to underwrite a whole range of social service related activities.[66]

The philosophical underpinnings of the principled pluralist position tend to be in accord with this approach in general, and principled pluralists as a whole are generally supportive of such legislative endeavors.[67] First, such a program implicitly recognizes that since individuals are social beings, a variety of voluntary organizations and associations form within society that exist outside the sphere of the state. While in a very restrictive sense of the term this associational life may be considered "private," due to its presence outside the realm of the state, associational life is both public and political in nature since it seeks "to address issues of the polis broadly conceived and to engage the

---

[66]John Bartkowski and Helen Regis, *Charitable Choices: Religion, Race, and Poverty in the Post-Welfare Era* (New York: New York University Press, 2001), p. 3.

[67]Though there may be individual exceptions to this support, those individuals who are most closely identified with the principled pluralist approach are generally supportive of such legislative endeavors. The Center for Public Justice (CPJ), headed by Jim Skillen, has played a major role in promoting the idea. In addition, Stanley Carlson-Theis left CPJ to join the White House Office of Faith-Based and Community Initiatives when it was formed by President Bush. And, finally, Stephen Monsma has engaged in major research endeavors that have examined the nature of church-state separation and public financing in different domains of public policy (Stephen Monsma, *When Sacred and Secular Mix: Religious Non-Profit Organizations and Public Money* [Lanham, Md.: Rowman & Littlefield, 1996]) as well as a study of faith-based and other types of welfare-to-work programs found in four major American cities and the implications of their receiving government funding (Stephen Monsma, *Putting Faith in Partnerships: Welfare-to-Work in Four Cities* [Ann Arbor: University of Michigan Press, 2004]).

broad interests and concerns of citizens."[68] Principled pluralists value associational life because it tends to reflect the deepest personal convictions and represent the most important civic activities of those so engaged. If these deep
convictions and civic activities are "deemed to be 'merely private,' then it is
not surprising that we are experiencing an atrophy of citizenship today."[69]

Second, principled pluralists tend to be supportive because such a program
implicitly recognizes the structural pluralism evident within God's created order. A host of nongovernmental agencies and programs exist that seek to address various social welfare needs of members of society. While the state is to
seek and administer justice, these various nongovernmental entities endeavor
to serve as agents of mercy and minister to basic human needs. Thus there are
both governmental and nongovernmental efforts that work to address the social welfare needs of Americans.

Third, efforts like Charitable Choice are favored by principled pluralists
based on their general view of separation of church and state in terms of neutrality rather than strict separation. The strict separationist view holds that the
establishment clause of the First Amendment prohibits any promotion of religion, even in a nonpreferential fashion, the consequence of which is that state
promotes nonreligion over religion. In contrast, the neutrality view contends
that the state can choose to promote religion, so long as it does so in a nonpreferential fashion. Without exploring the details and relative merits of these two
competing views of the establishment clause, suffice it to say that the neutrality interpretation holds that religion can

> receive recognition and material aid from the state in support of activities with
> public, this-world benefits to the broader society, provided the state does not dis-
> criminate among religious groups and provided the state gives recognition and
> material aid to secularly based groups with similar or parallel programs.[70]

Fourth, the fact that these programs recognize the confessional pluralism
evident within American society provides an additional basis for principled
pluralists to support such programs. Under President Bush's initiative, all religious and secular groups are eligible to compete for grants. Neither atheists
nor Christians, Jews nor Muslims, nor any other group can be excluded simply
because of their particular religious beliefs.

Finally, the support of principled pluralists derives from the acknowledge-

---

[68]Ronald Thiemann, *Religion in Public Life: A Dilemma for Democracy* (Washington, D.C.: Georgetown University Press, 1996), p. 132.
[69]Ibid.
[70]Monsma, *Positive Neutrality*, p. 188.

ment in these endeavors that poverty stems from multiple causes and that people are poor for different reasons. Since the root cause of poverty varies from individual to individual (e.g., poor education, lack of desired skills, poor health, addiction, laziness, slothfulness), welfare programs designed in terms of some nationally uniform, "one size fits all" endeavor are unable to help all people in need. Moreover, governmental programs, including programs that address matters of social welfare, operate within the constraints of limited resources and can provide only a limited amount of assistance. And finally, there are needy segments of society who fall through the cracks, failing to participate in governmental programs for which they are eligible, or who avoid participating in governmental programs because they are illegal immigrants within the country.

For all of these reasons there is increasing agreement that churches and parachurch organizations play an important role in helping the poor within American society. Beyond these particular considerations, however, it is also clear that, for some, poverty has a moral and personal root that public funding is unable to address. In such cases, distributing financial assistance may provide a short-term safety net for important material needs, but it cannot in itself provide a solution to the problem. Because humans are both material and spiritual beings, simply addressing material needs or seeking material causes may, at least on some occasions, be treating the symptom rather than addressing the root cause of the problem. In some cases the cause may be moral or spiritual in nature, and nongovernmental, faith-based service organizations are better (and more rightfully) equipped than governmental agencies to address these moral and spiritual facets.[71] As a result, faith-based programs may be able, at times, to accomplish results that government-run programs cannot achieve.

Conclusion

Principled pluralism recognizes and accepts the diversity evident in public life and the presence of different structures of authority operating within different spheres of social life. It affirms the state as a social structure possessing legitimate authority within a particular domain of life, but as only one among various structures to which God has delegated authority.

Given that humans are social beings by nature, principled pluralists stress

---

[71]It is not simply a matter of being better equipped than governmental agencies to address these moral or spiritual concerns. At least in theory it might be possible for governmental agencies to become better equipped than faith-based organizations to accomplish such tasks. Rather, for principled pluralists, governments are not given the authority by God to seek redemption of human sinful nature.

the intrinsic nature of associations and communities in society, and that these associations and communities make vital contributions to public life. While the state is limited in the powers that God has delegated to it, the state also plays an important role in God's created order: it is an agent of common grace, an instrument to secure and administer justice.

Christians are called to be engaged in public life; they are not to abandon the responsibilities they owe to their neighbors; nor are they to abdicate their political responsibilities. While the political domain, like all other domains of human life, is affected by the Fall, God remains sovereign over all of life and seeks to redeem all of the created order. Still, when Christians engage in political life, they are called to act with political modesty, to demonstrate tolerance for those with whom they disagree, to cooperate with others to achieve the public good, and to compromise in order that the endeavor to secure all desired political ends does not preclude the accomplishment of any one such goal.

Catholic Response

Clarke E. Cochran

The Reformed Protestant perspective that produces principled pluralism comes closest of all the essays to the Catholic position I describe. The differences between Corwin Smidt's and my accounts are principally tone, terminology and emphasis rather than fundamental differences of principle.[1] Here I highlight the principal similarities, while mentioning differences in emphasis. Finally, I point out two areas of divergence in perspective.

The theological basis for principled pluralism is, according to Smidt, the narrative of creation, Fall and redemption. This leads to an account of the natural, created purpose of the state nearly identical to the Catholic. This narrative justifies a cooperative dynamic between church and state, although Smidt does not use my four-part tensional model (though something like it seems implicit in his account). Similarly, the distortions of human life introduced by the Fall corrupt the action of the state and other institutions; therefore, the church must challenge it to return to its creation purposes.

Redemption is the ground of the *transformational* potential of the church with respect to all social institutions. My language, however, focuses on *transcendence* and the *sacramental* witness of the church and its institutions. Here there may be differences between us, though exploring them fully is impossible in this brief response. First, it is not clear to me how Smidt and the principled pluralists understand the transformation of nonchurch "spheres" to happen or how extensive it is. It also is not clear what specific role the church plays in facilitating this transformation. Second, the Catholic perspective emphasizes the sacramentality of social action and the transcendent witness of health care, social service and other Catholic institutions. Smidt's account is not explicitly sacramental, and it does not address extensively the role of church-related and church-operated institutions.

---

[1] In the interest of full disclosure, Corwin Smidt and I are friends, who have worked on various projects together and are active in the same political science organizations.

These may be differences of emphasis or terminology, but they could also reflect important differences of theology and philosophy. Discerning which is the case would require further dialogue.

Striking parallels (noted by Smidt) exist between Reformed sphere sovereignty and Catholic subsidiarity. Here I think that the Catholic tradition has much to learn from the Reformed since that tradition furnishes more adequate grounds for the proper appreciation of pluralism than the Catholic tradition.[2] Integrating sphere sovereignty into Catholic social theory will strengthen it considerably. Similarly, both the Reformed tradition, as developed by Abraham Kuyper, and the Catholic Church during the Second Vatican Council (1962-1965) came to a parallel (and somewhat late) appreciation of freedom of religion as a social principle and a constitutive part of the common good.

Another parallel lies in the theological anthropology of each tradition. According to Smidt, principled pluralism is rooted in the fundamentally social character of humanity. It is a theory that lies "between individualism and collectivism." Catholic social teaching makes the same commitment and the same claim.

These theological parallels mean that the two traditions have much in common in political practice, particularly commitment to a limited state with specific responsibilities for social justice. They share affirmation of the public responsibility of believers and a public role for religious institutions—but in modesty, tolerance and cooperation with others of similar or different faith commitments. With respect to the Faith-Based and Community Initiative and financial cooperation between government and religious institutions, the principled pluralist and the Catholic perspectives are in fundamental agreement. However, it is not clear from the sphere-sovereignty perspective why government and nongovernment entities *both* work to address social welfare needs. Are these needs a matter of public justice and therefore part of the government sphere, or are they a responsibility of other spheres? If spheres are "sovereign," what justifies crossing, and when is it justified to cross, boundaries in order to share responsibility?

There are topics where the Catholic perspective furnishes a fuller account of political life and its demands. They are topics that require a more complete description of the Reformed perspective. First, although principled pluralism has a fundamental commitment to social justice, it is not clear what role the

---

[2]My understanding and articulation of Catholic social theory in fact is indebted to my association with the Center for Public Justice (cited by Smidt) and its policy work from the perspective of principled pluralism and sphere sovereignty.

poor play in the demands of justice. This lack of clarity is related to the questions that conclude the preceding paragraph. The Catholic preferential option for the poor teaches that one of the primary tests for the presence or absence of social justice is the condition of society's least well-off. In Smidt's account, justice is principally about maintaining the proper boundaries, the proper order of responsibilities, among the institutions (spheres) of society. The Catholic tradition includes this responsibility as an integral part of the common good and of subsidiarity, but it also places responsibility on government to ensure that the least among us have their due—that is, their rights and their basic needs met.

Second, the Catholic tradition places important limits on private property. All property has a "social mortgage," meaning that its use must promote the common good as well as the owner's good. Government may place regulations on property to ensure such use and to protect the common good from abuse (air pollution regulations, for example). Principled pluralism may address such limits, but they are not discussed in Smidt's essay.

Finally, and most fundamentally, it is not clear what it means for the state to be an agent of common grace. Smidt describes common grace as the mitigation of evil, maintaining the law and upholding public justice. It is patient and nonutopian and does not aim at the redemption of citizens, which is the role of particular grace. It is not clear to me, however, how these tasks differ (if they do) from the responsibilities of the state with respect to its created purpose and with respect to its purpose of restraining the sin resulting from the Fall. That is, how is being an agent of common grace different from being a limited government dedicated to public justice, tasks Smidt also describes as flowing from creation and the Fall?

Classical Separation Response

Derek H. Davis

Corwin Smidt's chapter articulates impressively the principled pluralist position. This perspective, while not well known, is growing and now claims a sizable number of adherents in the United States and elsewhere. These adherents come mostly from the Calvinist theological tradition. This is somewhat odd, however, because it is a perspective that distances itself considerably from Calvin's political theology. But Smidt explains this well, noting that the adherents of principled pluralism rely more on the political theology of the nineteenth-century Dutch theologian and statesman Abraham Kuyper, who while remaining true to Calvin's basic theology, turned rather dramatically away from Calvin's "two-powers" view. Calvin's perspective, while granting to both church and state considerable independence from each other, nevertheless assigned the state essentially theological tasks such as battling heresy. Kuyper, as Smidt notes, sought to wrest this authority from the state and grant all religious groups considerably more religious freedom. He developed the "sphere sovereignty" theory, which granted to most societal groups a strong measure of sovereignty and independence from state oversight. Among these groups was a growing diversity of religions, both Christian and non-Christian, who, at least theoretically, were granted freedom by Kuyper from oppressive state oversight of their theological tenets and granted space to function in an environment of freedom.

I am not quite sure where the biblical permission to make this bold move to sphere sovereignty comes from. I think it is rationally derived, which is acceptable to me, but somewhat odd in a theological tradition so rooted in finding a biblical basis for everything. Applying reason to the formulation of church-state frameworks works for me because I think the Bible is not specific about this, and we therefore have the biblical justification to craft church-state frameworks that are workable in the modern context. If I were to cite my own biblical basis for taking political matters into our own hands, so to speak, I would

suggest that Christ taught that spiritual goals and political goals are not synonymous. In Matthew 22:21, Christ said that Christians are to "render to Caesar the things that are Caesar's, and to God the things that are God's" (ESV).
Christ here was affirming that spiritual commitments are to be distinguished
from political commitments.

I should add that I believe Christ modeled perfectly this distinction between spiritual and temporal ends. He never advocated the overthrow of the
Roman government, or even its adjustment, in favor of a more theocratic order. He never identified himself with any particular form of government, nor
did he even remotely suggest that it was the duty of human government to aid
his mission. Christ was amazingly unconcerned with much of what falls under
the rubric of politics. He preached against tyranny and oppression, of course,
but his main mission was to bring humans to himself, and it was apparently a
secondary matter to him what specific form of government (monarchy, communism, democracy, etc.) we live under. The temporal was for him far less important than the eternal; thus he focused on the spiritual rather than the physical aspects of kingdom building. The idea of a Christian or religious nation, it
seems, was foreign to him. He gave us room, so to speak, to frame political orders in keeping with a principle of justice.

I would hope not to be misunderstood here. I am not advocating indifference to politics. In their daily lives Christians are to be Christian *citizens*, not
merely Christians. But because the Bible does not require that political and
governmental affairs be Christian, those who are Christians are free to join
with non-Christians in our democratic form of government to make laws that
from the perspective of the American people as a whole, *not* from the perspective of their own interpretation of the Bible, best ensure the common good. In
this process, negotiation and compromise are not dirty words, and Christians
should be satisfied with laws that fall short of biblical standards as they understand them.

Biblical standards may dictate the contributions that Christians make toward
formation of laws, but Christians do not fail God if the negotiated product, even
laws on such controversial areas as abortion, school prayer and homosexuality,
do not meet their standards. The goal, even duty, of Christians should be to assist the government in the promotion of the welfare of *all* American citizens
based on a shared morality, not to set up a kingdom of God on earth.[1]

I think what I have said would ring true with most adherents of the princi-

---

[1]I elaborate more fully on these points in Derek H. Davis, "Christian Faith and Political Involvement in Today's Culture War," *Journal of Church and State* 38 (1996): 473-81.

pled pluralist position. The difference is that they are quite willing to breach the separation between church and state to implement programs that, for me, grant too much authority to religious institutions and compromise too much religious autonomy. I think this is because at heart they remain more Calvinistic than Kuyperian. Calvin and the Puritans who followed him are well known for building a political theology based on the Old Testament. They adopted theocratic notions at every turn on the theory that God is sovereign over all matters, including political matters. As Smidt states, "for Calvin, all human authority stands under the authority of God and his law." And in this worldview God is always about the task of redeeming every dimension of his fallen creation since, again in Smidt's words, "God sent Jesus Christ to redeem *all* things." Smidt continues:

> Christians have an obligation to facilitate this task of redemption. Certainly God is at work in saving his creation. Yet we who know God's salvation are saved not simply because God loves us, but in order to fulfill God's tasks for his people in the world—whether in farming, building, manufacturing, educating or engaging in political life. (p. 134)

Principled pluralists speak glowingly about the merits of the separation of church and state but then seem unreluctant to use Christian means to advance political causes. By doing so—as, for example, in their advocacy for Charitable Choice—they seek to frame, whether intentionally or unintentionally, the political order along theological lines. In this approach, they are true Calvinists. The Founding Fathers, however, specifically denied any notion of a religious state. In this respect, principled pluralists are not much different from members of the Christian Right who assume that government should advance Christianity or at least allow religion to have some supportive role in our national life. After all, they would say, Christianity represents the truth, and why shouldn't government be permitted to advance truth? The most commonly cited scriptural justification for this attitude is the theocratic order of Old Testament Israel. If Israel was under the direct rule of God, so the argument goes, and this model is the only political form of government endorsed in Scripture, then why should it not be modeled, if even in modified form, in our own day? If Israel was a godly nation under God's rule, then America should be a godly nation under God's rule. Principled pluralists do not go this far, but they are nevertheless about the task of building a religious state.

The full range of the biblical message, I believe, gives us a very different perspective on the appropriateness of framing modern governments in a way that encourages them to follow God's law. I think we learn that God's dealing with Old Testament Israel was unique. God established Israel under his rule primarily to create a people through whom he would do three things: (1) establish a messianic line; (2) offer to humankind (mostly through Hebrew instruments) holy writ, that is, the Scriptures, which we know as the Bible; and (3) demonstrate through the law (moral, ceremonial and civil components) his holiness and his requirements for personal and communal living. All of this, I believe, was a package—Israel's nationhood, the Mosaic Law and the way that all of it pointed toward its ultimate fulfillment in Christ's incarnation, life, death, resurrection and kingship in a kingdom yet future. I am oversimplifying, of course, but I think that Christ is the fulfillment of all of this ("Do not think that I have come to abolish the Law or the Prophets . . . but to fulfill them" [Mt 5:17 ESV]): Christ, in other words, is the true and final meaning of a mostly symbolic and typological Old Testament package. This means that we must be very careful about imposing Old Testament mandates on ourselves, except of course in those areas where the mandates are clearly not superseded (nine of the Ten Commandments, for example). In sum, I think that the theocratic order of the Old Testament is not binding on modern governments, or even recommended as a viable political order. It has been abrogated, set aside, by the coming of Christ.

If, as principled pluralists seem inclined to believe, we are somehow to be about the business of redeeming the political order in keeping with Scripture, which principles, which verses, do we use? Here even Smidt seems equivocal:

> Certainly, there are biblical instructions related to politics that remain true for contemporary political life. These political principles need to be discerned, as the particular context in which the principle is applied may color, but not necessarily negate, the principle itself. . . . Therefore, in the end, what can be drawn from biblical texts regarding political life are principles that should govern political life across time and space rather than detailed prescriptions about political institutional arrangements that transcend time and space. (p. 139-40)

But he never tells us which principles, which verses, are to be applied. Do we just pick and choose as we go? Don't we need some further guidelines if we are to open the door to constructing a church-state policy on biblical texts that "should govern political life"?

For me, the better way is to recognize that biblical texts are woefully inadequate for the task. I think the New Testament contains none at all. The better method is to approach the subject rationally since God has given us no binding prescriptions. If history has proven that giving government too much jurisdiction over religion and vice versa is dangerous, compromises religion, leads to persecution of religious nonadherents and frustrates religious freedom, then we are better off to follow these lessons of history. I believe this was the approach of our Founding Fathers. Steeped in the lessons of an inordinate mix of church and state, they removed religion from the public sphere and freed religion to be all it can be in citizens' lives without the coercive effects of government oversight.

Anabaptist Response

Ronald J. Sider

I agree with most of Corwin Smidt's lucid description of principled pluralism. Most of it flows from fundamental biblical teaching and careful historical analysis.

But why then does Smidt argue that "the principled pluralist perspective is ... derived largely from what might be called the Reformed tradition" (p. 126)? Or again, "The perspective largely arises out of a Reformed theological understanding" (p. 127)? Smidt's claim is one illustration of a rather more widespread tendency of some Reformed thinkers to state important biblical truths that many Christians of diverse traditions embrace and then claim they are uniquely Reformed ideas.

Consider a few examples. In his first citation that the unique character of the Reformed theology "provides the primary basis for the principled pluralist perspective," he cites as evidence the "great emphasis on the creation-fall-redemption' narrative" (p. 128). The last time I checked, major attention to the story of creation, fall and redemption is fairly widespread in Christian circles.

Smidt argues at some length that Reformed thinkers argued from their view of creation that government is a pre-Fall phenomenon. But so does Thomas Aquinas and the whole Catholic Thomist tradition. It is true that there are Christian traditions (e.g., Lutheranism) that see government as necessary only after the Fall. But there are other important Christian traditions (not least the Catholic one) that agree with Reformed thinkers. So it is astonishing (one might even say presumptuous) for Reformed thinkers to claim that the notion of government as pre-Fall is derived uniquely from Reformed theology.

One could say the same about the distinction between "particular grace" and "common grace." The terminology and nuances may vary some, but again the same basic ideas are central to Aquinas and Thomism. The same is true of the very important emphasis in principled pluralism on the social nature of human beings and the way that the biblical emphasis on both this truth and the dignity and worth of the individual enable us to avoid the extremes of individualism and collectivism. Aquinas and the vast majority of Christian thinkers from many different traditions agree. There is no justification for claiming this basic biblical insight as the result of the uniqueness of Reformed theology.

Finally, confessional pluralism. Genuine religious freedom for people of all religious belief is certainly a central part of principled pluralism. And one can be grateful that the wonderful Reformed leader Abraham Kuyper articulated this affirmation of religious freedom so clearly at the end of the nineteenth century. But the Anabaptists had clearly called for religious freedom and the end to the state's use of the sword to enforce particular religious beliefs and practices more than 350 years earlier. In fact, the Anabaptists got executed by their Reformed brothers for their defense of confessional pluralism. It is a bit strange to argue that confessional pluralism flows uniquely from Reformed theology.

Let me say again that I agree with most of Smidt's fine essay—because I think it flows from fundamental biblical teaching and a careful reading of history. But it would be both more historically accurate and less offensive to the rest of the Christian community if fundamental biblical truths were not labeled "uniquely Reformed."

Social Justice Response

J. Philip Wogaman

I cannot find much here with which to disagree, especially when I remember the late John Courtney Murray's dictum that genuine disagreement is a rare achievement.[1] Murray's point was, I take it, that we often talk past one another, sometimes defining key terms in different unacknowledged ways. Here and there, I suspect that Smidt and I would be in agreement if we could talk it through. This is possibly a point at which we can applaud his ready acceptance of compromise as a positive good and not only a necessary evil—acknowledging, of course, that there are both good and bad kinds of compromise.

There is, however, one point where we may simply be in disagreement. His several references to the second coming of Christ, such as his amillennialist view, appear to take this as a literal event in time, to be expected as a gift to be received "in God's good time" (p. 146). I am more inclined to take that eschatological expectation in symbolic rather than literal terms, although there is an even deeper sense in which we can refer to Christ's second coming as ongoing. When we are open to Christ, Christ is active in and through our faithful discipleship. The apostle Paul's brilliant metaphor, referring to the church as the body of Christ, is even suggestive of how Christ is *physically* present when the church is being his body in the world.[2]

While this may be a very different way of understanding Christian eschatology, I can agree with Smidt that this is God's gift, to which we respond. The problem I have with the more literal eschatology, in any of its traditional forms, is that it subtly transforms faith in the present power of God's love into belief in an external physical intervention. Physical power can thus easily tri-

---

[1]Murray writes that "disagreement is not an easy thing to reach. Rather, we move into confusion" (John Courtney Murray, *We Hold These Truths: Catholic Reflections on the American Proposition* [N.Y.: Sheed & Ward, 1960], p. 15).

[2]This is not exactly the same as C. H. Dodd's concept of "realized eschatology," which holds that Jesus was proclaiming the immediate presence of the kingdom of God as Jesus has ushered it in.

umph over the spiritual power of love in the faith of Christians. And since this is a future event, such a faith can even lead to a certain passivity among Christians. That postmillennial or premillennial or now amillennial Christians are instead often active in pursuit of what they take to be God's good in the world is a tribute to the power of grace alive wherever the body of Christ is truly faithful to its Lord.

Other points in Smidt's essay call more for elaboration than disagreement. For instance, he could very well note that the Reformed tradition has historically been a very important support for the kinds of democratic societies that he advocates. James Hastings Nichols observed half a century ago that Western democracy has flourished mainly in the Protestant countries most influenced by Calvinism.[3] We do not have to attribute democracy to Reformed theology, an attribution that would have surprised Socrates, but we can still ask what it is about that theological orientation that has helped foster it. Here, Smidt's own comments on the sovereignty of God and principled tolerance may be helpful, although we can put it more sharply. If God is truly sovereign, truly transcendent, the source of all, the Creator of all, from everlasting to everlasting—in a word, if God is truly God, then it behooves us to be restrained in absolutizing our views. Such restraint can even attend our limited human grasp of the fullness of God's revelation in Jesus Christ. We can and should have convictions, bearing witness to the truth as it is given to us. At the same time, we can expect God to be active in unexpected ways in the minds and actions of people who seem very different from us.[4] A democratic society is peculiarly open in this way; it provides critical settings in which ideas can be tested and a supporting environment in which all are encouraged to participate. This means that democratic pluralism really is *theologically principled!* Thus our support of religious liberty for all is not just a practical way of avoiding interreligious bloodshed, although that is no small matter. It is rather that by silencing others we may inadvertently be silencing God! The history of Christian mistakes, especially those reached with arrogant self-assurance, should give us pause.

---

[3]James Hastings Nichols, *Democracy and the Churches* (Philadelphia: Westminster, 1951).

[4]I developed this theme in one of my earliest books, *Protestant Faith and Religious Liberty* (Nashville: Abingdon, 1967). In that volume I observed that monotheistic faith can take two radically different directions. If I believe in the one God, then anybody who disagrees with me is by definition wrong. But on the other hand, if I believe in the one God, then that God is greater than I am and I cannot prejudge how God can be at work in the lives of others. The latter is not a relativism, at least not in the sense that all ideas are equally true. But it acknowledges God as the one absolute, to whom everything else is indeed relative. By faith, I affirm that God is revealed in the love of Jesus Christ, as I have written in my own essay in this volume.

In his discussion of government as an agent of common grace, Smidt has opened an important discussion that is worthy of further comment. While carefully avoiding any utopian idealism about what government can accomplish, he has rightly noted its responsibility "to care for the common interests and general welfare of the people over which it has authority" (p. 145). There can be a real grace here. I would put it this way: Government is the servant of the entire society when it acts as a whole through policy and law. As servant of the whole community, it must help to undergird the acceptance of all as participants. Thus government rightly abolished racial discrimination in law and sought to minimize its effects in custom and private institutions. Thus also government rightly helps undergird the economic basis for all people to participate meaningfully in society. American society has long since concluded that education of the young should be freely provided for all—even required for all, since education is so important a precondition for participation in society. I am among those who believe that basic levels of health care should be a responsibility of government, whether that means direct government provision of universal health care services or some other way of assuring access to adequate medical insurance for all. Medicaid was a fine step in that direction, and Medicare has been a boon for the elderly. But still, more than forty million Americans lack either health care insurance or access to direct government programs. When Michael Harrington wrote his prophetic book on poverty, aptly titled *The Other America,* he called attention to various categories of poverty. One of these was poverty among the elderly. There, he mentioned senior citizens huddled in inadequate rooms, eating dog food for survival. Poverty among the elderly has not entirely been eliminated, but the simple governmental act of increasing Social Security payments during the 1970s went a long way. That and a number of other specifically targeted governmental actions have been a kind of common grace—not the grace we experience through the love of God in Christ, but the grace of being affirmed by one's fellow citizens as accepted in the earthly community.

The liberation theologians used to speak of God's "preferential option for the poor." Whatever we might say about liberation theology as a whole, there is an important insight here. The poor and other marginalized people are the weakest links in the chain of community. If community is to be made whole, the weakest must be attended to especially. In its political and economic dimensions, Christians properly call the government of all the people to that task. We can add that Christians can well be called to such forms of government service as a God-given vocation—such as public school teachers, social workers, public health officials and so on.

I wish also to record my appreciation for Smidt's reminder that "human beings have the natural right to resist civil authority if obedience to the legal authority conflicts with God's law" (p. 135). Since "God's law," as Smidt has put it, also entails obedience to legal authority, we can say that that civil obedience is a presumptive obligation. That is, we presume the rightfulness of law unless it can be shown, beyond reasonable doubt, that it is in conflict with our more basic response to God. So the burden of proof must be borne by civil disobedience. Where possible, such disobedience should be accompanied by overall affirmation of the authority of civil law. In those extremely rare historical instances where out-and-out revolution seems necessary, it should be for the sake of establishing an acceptable new civil order.

I note, finally, that I appreciate Smidt's reminder that most social interactions do not involve government at all. We all have private lives that consume most of our time, resources and energy, and a healthy society is made up of a rich fabric of institutions. The government of all the people can help provide an overall climate of support for such institutions, but without attempting to control them. The exact terms of interaction will vary from time to time, for history itself presents an ongoing pageant of problems and possibilities, dangers and opportunities.

4 The Anabaptist Perspective

Ronald J. Sider

In the very early years of the Protestant Reformation, a rapidly expanding group of devout reformers emerged who argued that uncompromising fidelity to Jesus Christ and scriptural authority compelled them to reject Zwingli's and Luther's embrace of medieval Catholicism's Constantinian unity of church and state.[1] Soon to be called Anabaptists—and later Mennonites—these reformers accepted Luther's starting point, *sola gratia* and *sola scriptura*, and then concluded that the New Testament called for a believers' church of committed Christians who consciously chose to embrace and follow Jesus Christ. Since infants could not do that, they rejected infant baptism and baptized only those who as adults confessed faith in Christ. Arguing that the believing Christian community, not government, should govern the church, they rejected more than eleven hundred years of the union of church and state, demanding instead complete freedom from the state in all matters of religion. Believing that their Lord Jesus had taught that Christians should never kill, they rejected more than a millennium of Christian military participation, refusing to serve as soldiers or executioners. Believing that the evangelistic mandate still was binding, they spread rapidly across much of Europe, leading thousands into a vibrant personal faith in Christ.

It is hardly surprising that almost everyone else considered these passionate evangelists to be dangerous radicals who threatened the established order. Zwinglians, Lutherans, Catholics and Anglicans all urged their governments to execute the Anabaptists. An ancient law from the time of Augustine in the fourth century that stipulated the death penalty for heretics who rebaptized persons who had previously been baptized also provided the legal excuse to drown, shoot or burn at the stake these re-(ana)baptizers who, according to official theology, had no right to (re-)baptize as adults people who had already been baptized as infants. In just a few decades, thousands of

---

[1]For good overviews, see Cornelius J. Dyck, *Introduction to Mennonite History* (Scottdale, Penn.: Herald Press, 1993), and George H. Williams, *The Radical Reformation*, 3rd ed. (Kerksville, Mo.: Sixteenth Century Journal Publishers, 1992).

Anabaptists were slaughtered by their fellow Christians.

Slowly, however, the Anabaptists' radical call for religious freedom became common wisdom. Partially in Holland and England in the seventeenth century, then fully in the First Amendment to the federal Constitution in the United States in 1791, and finally (at least officially) in most countries of the world in the twentieth century, the Anabaptists' vision of a basic separation of church and state has prevailed. Persecution, however, decimated the earliest champions of religious freedom in the sixteenth century. Menno Simons, a Dutch convert to Anabaptism in the 1530s, managed to rally and organize scattered groups of Anabaptists who came to be called Mennonites. But for centuries persecution pushed Mennonites to the margins of society. Only in the last century have they fully enjoyed the religious freedom they championed so courageously four hundred years earlier.

What do contemporary Mennonites think about church, state and public justice? As in every other Christian tradition with a long heritage, there is no one answer to that question. There is a substantial "plain clothes," or Amish Mennonite, minority that largely ignores politics. There is a very tiny, theologically liberal circle of Mennonite intellectuals who tend to reduce Jesus' gospel to peace and justice activism. One recent poll discovered that 54 percent of Mennonites in the United States are Republicans; 19 percent, Democrats; 3 percent, Independents; and 23 percent have no affiliation.[2] What follows is, I hope, representative of mainstream Mennonite thought today, although I can only claim with certainty that it reflects the views of one evangelical Mennonite who is a convinced Anabaptist with Mennonite roots that stretch back to the sixteenth century.

Jesus Christ: The Center

At the center of all Anabaptist thinking about church, state and public justice stands Jesus: perfect man, Messiah, resurrected Lord and Savior, true God. From the first century, Christians have confessed that the carpenter from Nazareth is *now* King of kings, reigning Lord of the universe. The New Testament also taught that Christians should now live the way Jesus lived. "If any want to become my followers, let them deny themselves and take up their cross and follow me" (Mt 16:24). The New Testament explicitly summons Christians to follow Jesus' model of sacrificial self-giving everywhere, whether in their marriages (Eph 5:25), in the church (Phil 2:5-11) or in the marketplace (1 Pet 2:19-24).

---

[2]Keith Graber Miller, *Wise as Serpents, Innocent as Doves: American Mennonites Engage Washington* (Knoxville: University of Tennessee Press, 1996), p. 109.

Sadly, over the centuries Christians have found numerous rationalizations for abandoning Jesus' example and moral teaching[3]—sometimes implicitly, though sometimes explicitly, as in the case of Reinhold Niebuhr, who asserted bluntly that Jesus' way of radical love simply does not work in a fallen world.[4] But can we deny that Jesus' life is the norm for Christian living without denying the incarnation itself? Mennonite theologian John Howard Yoder has argued that to reject Jesus' life as moral norm is to fall either into the ancient Ebionite heresy (denial of Jesus' deity) or Gnostic heresy (denial of Jesus' humanity). "What becomes of the meaning of incarnation if Jesus is not normatively human? If he is human but not normative, is this not the ancient ebionitic heresy? If he be somehow authoritative but not in his humaneness, is this not a new gnosticism?"[5]

Understanding the gospel that Jesus proclaimed underlines the importance of living like Jesus. Most evangelicals—despite their central affirmation of scriptural authority—do not define the gospel the way Jesus did. In many places in Matthew, Mark and Luke it is clear that Jesus understands the gospel to be the "gospel of the kingdom." But what did he mean?[6]

Centuries before, when the prophets looked ahead to the time of the future Messiah, they foretold a new vertical relationship with God and a new set of horizontal relationships among people (Jer 31:31-34; Is 9:4, 6-7; 11:4). God will forgive our sins in a new way, and there will be peace and justice on the earth.

When Jesus comes announcing the arrival of the long-expected messianic kingdom, he explains how it brings both new vertical and new horizontal relationships. In parable after parable Jesus teaches that the only way to enter his arriving messianic kingdom is to believe that God longs to forgive wandering prodigals who repent. One enters Jesus' kingdom by sheer grace. But Jesus is not a lone ranger preaching to isolated hermits. He gathers a circle of disciples; he forms a new community of followers who begin to live the radical kingdom ethics he teaches. Jesus and his new community minister to the poor and chal-

---

[3]See John Howard Yoder, *Politics of Jesus: Vicit Agnus Noster*, 2nd ed. (Grand Rapids: Eerdmans, 1994), pp. 4-20. Glen H. Stassen and David Gushee write, "Christian churches across the theological and confessional spectrum, and Christian ethics as an academic discipline that serves the churches, are often guilty of evading Jesus. . . . Specifically, *the teachings and practices of Jesus*" (*Kingdom Ethics: Following Jesus in Contemporary Context* [Downers Grove, Ill.: InterVarsity Press, 2003], p. 11).

[4]For example, see *Reinhold Niebuhr on Politics*, ed. Harry R. Davis and Robert C. Good (New York: Scribner's Sons, 1960), pp. 139-51.

[5]Yoder, *Politics of Jesus*, p. 10.

[6]For a much longer discussion see chaps. 3-4 in Ronald J. Sider, *Good News and Good Works: A Theology for the Whole Gospel* (Grand Rapids: Baker, 1999).

lenge the rich, reject the way of the violent revolutionaries and love even their enemies. For those who meet and respond in faith to Jesus, salvation includes new economic relations with others, as Jesus explains in the encounter with Zaccheus (Lk 19:9).

Thus when Jesus proclaimed the gospel of the kingdom, he meant not only that God gladly forgives sinners who repent, but also that God is now creating a visible new community of Jesus' followers whose very life together is a little picture of what the kingdom will be like at his second coming, when he will complete the victory over all sin and evil.

The Church

The church is part of the gospel of the kingdom. The apostle Paul teaches that explicitly in Ephesians 2—3. In chapter 2, Paul shows how the cross ends the worst racial hostility in the ancient world. Jew and Gentile meet at the foot of the cross, where they are both accepted with God by sheer grace. But that new vertical relationship produces an equally radical new horizontal relationship: "In his flesh he has made both groups [Jew and Gentile] into one and has broken down the dividing wall. . . . [So] that he might create in himself one new humanity in place of the two, thus making peace" (Eph 2:14-15).

Then in Ephesians 3, Paul explains how this visible, new, multiethnic body of believers is part of the gospel. In verses 3 through 5 Paul speaks of the "mystery" of the gospel that he proclaims. Then in verse 6, he defines the mystery: "that is, the Gentiles have become fellow heirs, members of the same body, and sharers in the promise in Christ Jesus through the gospel." Part of the gospel Paul preaches, part of Jesus' gospel of the kingdom, is that right now there exists a new community, a new social order, where racial hostility is being overcome by the power of the risen Lord.

People looked at the early church and saw the rich sharing with the poor, Jews embracing Gentiles, masters accepting slaves and men welcoming women as dignified, gifted members of Christ's body. So radically different was this new, visibly redeemed social order that Paul could boast: "There is no longer Jew or Greek, there is no longer slave or free, there is no longer male and female; for all of you are one in Christ Jesus" (Gal 3:28). That is what Jesus' dawning messianic kingdom looked like.

The logic of New Testament church life is clear: now because the resurrected Jesus lives in believers' lives and rules the church; now because the Holy Spirit has been poured out upon all believers as a sign that the messianic kingdom is arriving; now, therefore, it is possible and obligatory for Christians to live the radical kingdom ethics that Jesus modeled and taught. Whether in the area of marriage and divorce, economic sharing, racial relations or response to enemies, Jesus' followers live as members of Jesus' new messianic community.

It is important to see that according to the New Testament, the church is a visible, public and, in some very real sense, political reality. It certainly is not something invisible, merely inward or "spiritual." The early church was a new, highly visible community whose public actions pointed people to the Lord they worshiped. The economic sharing and rejection of ethnic division was so visible and striking that it drew non-Christians to embrace Christ. In Acts the apostles responded to the legitimate complaints of the Greek-speaking minority that their widows were being neglected. They named seven new deacons—all from the minority community!—to correct this injustice. The result? "The word of God continued to spread; the number of the disciples increased greatly" (Acts 6:7).

Because Mennonites understand the church as Jesus' dawning messianic community, we emphasize the church as a countercultural community. The New Testament in fact sharply distinguishes the church and the world. Jesus bluntly warned that the world would hate his followers just as it hated him (Jn 15:18-20). One of the New Testament's images of the church is that of sojourners, strangers, aliens in a foreign land (Heb 11:13; 1 Pet 1:1; 2:11). Again and again throughout Mennonite history, repeated persecution has confirmed the truth that to faithfully follow Jesus demands a forthright countercultural stance.

That, however, in no way means an anticultural stance. It in no way justifies H. Richard Niebuhr's label "Christ against culture."[7] Culture is the Creator's good idea, and we are placed as stewards to shape cultures and civilizations of great beauty. In fact, throughout our history Mennonites have delighted in and been gifted shapers of culture in many areas, including agriculture and music. But biblical faith teaches that sin has profoundly twisted all culture. As kingdom Christians, therefore—precisely because we love the culture intended by the Creator—we must live contrary to the pervasive sin that has invaded culture. A church that is not against the world where it is in rebellion against God fundamentally undermines everything it says to the world.[8] Precisely as the church is countercultural in that sense, it affirms culture by point-

---

[7]H. Richard Niebuhr, *Christ and Culture* (New York: Harper Torchbooks, 1956). See John Howard Yoder's brilliant, devastating critique of Niebuhr's *Christ and Culture* in Glen H. Stassen, D. M. Yeager and John Howard Yoder, *Authentic Transformation: A New Vision of Christ and Culture* (Nashville: Abingdon, 1996), pp. 31-90.

[8]See further John Howard Yoder, *Body Politics: Five Practices of the Christian Community Before the Watching World* (Scottdale, Penn.: Herald Press, 1992), p. 78.

ing through its common life to a new model of transformed, redeemed culture.

Because the Christian's highest loyalty is always Jesus Christ and his body, the church, Christian faith relativizes all other loyalties. "Strive first for the kingdom of God and his righteousness" (Mt 6:33) is Jesus' command to his followers. Other group loyalties—of nation, race or family—must take a back seat to and be judged by Jesus and his kingdom. Few things tame the deadly dangers of rampaging nationalism more effectively than a clear understanding that one's loyalty to Christ and his one global body of believers is a higher loyalty than any commitment or obligation to fellow citizens of one's nation.[9]

It is the understanding of the church as Jesus' new messianic community—which, in the power of the Spirit, is now beginning to model Jesus' kingdom values in the face of widespread cultural brokenness—that explains the Mennonite insistence that the first and most basic way that Christians shape the larger society is simply by being the church. When the church truly lives out Jesus' and the New Testament's radical call to care for the poor, share economically, overcome the dividing walls of ethnic hostility, live in sexual purity and marital fidelity, and affirm the full dignity of women, the very life of the church is a radical challenge to the larger society. The visible integrity and goodness of Jesus' new community encourages the surrounding society to improve.

John Howard Yoder (citing his teacher Karl Barth) often argued that there is an important analogy between what the church community and the larger society should do. Both are human, historical, social and public communities. Although the world does not recognize it, both have the same Lord. "Because the risen Messiah is at once head of the church and *kyrios* of the *kosmos*, sovereign of the universe, what is given to the church through him is in substance no different from what is offered to the world. The believing community is the new world on the way."[10]

Yoder often cites at least five marks of the early church that ought to be imitated by the larger society.[11] Sin prevents that from happening fully, of course. It is only by faith in Christ that anyone can truly live like Jesus. But everyone ought to live the way the Creator intends, and to some extent it is possible even

---

[9]Hence Duane Friesen's insistence in his book *Christian Peacemaking and International Conflict* that his first identity is as a member of the church, second as a world citizen before being an American, and third with the poor (*Christian Peacemaking and International Conflict: A Realist Pacifist Perspective* [Scottdale, Penn.: Herald Press, 1986], p. 46).

[10]John Howard Yoder, *For the Nations: Essays Evangelical and Public* (Grand Rapids: Eerdmans, 1997), p. 50.

[11]See Yoder, *Body Politics*; see also Yoder, *For the Nations*, pp. 27-33, 39-50, and Duane K. Friesen, *Artists, Citizens, Philosophers Seeking the Peace of the City: An Anabaptist Theology of Culture* (Scottdale, Penn.: Herald Press, 2000), pp. 224ff.

for those outside the church to imperfectly imitate wholesome Christian practice. "The church is the part of the world that confesses the renewal to which all the world is called."[12]

1. Jesus and the New Testament call the church to be a community of "binding and loosing" (Mt 18:15-20), where differences are resolved not by force but by reconciling dialogue. "To be human is to have differences; to be human wholesomely is to process those differences, not by building up conflicting power claims but by reconciling dialogue."[13]

2. Jesus and the early church engaged in sweeping economic sharing. The early Christians ate together, inviting rich and poor to the common table (1 Cor 11:17-34).

3. By grace the early church became a new, inclusive community, breaking down and transcending the sinful human barriers of ethnicity, race, class and gender.

4. In early Christian worship all could speak (1 Cor 14:26-33). Every voice was important. Every person had special gifts from the Holy Spirit needed by the body (1 Cor 12:4-26).

5. Forgiveness rather than retaliation is the way to reconciliation. The early church sought to live Jesus' command to forgive each other as God has forgiven us.

All of these practices were visible, observable activities of a living, thriving community. Outsiders could observe them—and in part, imitate them. To the extent that the world resolves differences by reconciling dialogue rather than destructive violence, the world is a better place. To the extent that the world shares generously with the poor in empowering ways, society improves. To the extent that the world respects and affirms all people regardless of race, class and gender, building communities of inclusion, the social order is more wholesome. To the extent that every person's gift and voice is heard, affirming freedom of speech and democratic decision making, society is better. To the extent that forgiveness replaces vengeance, the social order's deadly cycles of escalating violence are broken.

To argue for an analogy between what the church and the world are called to do is not to suggest that unbelieving sinners can do all they ought. But sin has not obliterated all knowledge of truth and goodness; nor has it destroyed all human ability to mimic the good, however imperfectly. Therefore the

---

[12]Yoder, *Body Politics*, p. 78.
[13]Ibid., p. 5.

church serves the larger society first by living a faithful model of Jesus' new messianic community—inviting the larger society to imitate what it can and offering the gospel of Christ and his kingdom to make possible what it cannot.

Government, Society and the Sword

Mennonites have a great deal in common with other Christians in their thinking about government. Government is a good gift ordained by God. Its ultimate source of authority is God. Its purpose is to restrain evil and promote the good. Both because of the prevalence of sin and also because the Creator designed every person to be a free, creative being, government must be limited. Although government must be limited, its role is significant. The two key Hebrew words for justice and righteousness show that God wills government to shape both fair legal systems and just economic structures.[14] All this and much more Mennonites share with other Christians.

But what about the sword?

Virtually every government known in history has used state-of-the-art technology to devise lethal weapons to enforce its demands and protect its borders. Most people conclude that government and killing are inseparable. How then, since Anabaptists refuse to kill others, can they participate in government?

To answer that question, we must first explore more carefully why Anabaptists reject lethal violence and then explore the logic of Anabaptist political engagement.

We believe that Jesus the carpenter, true God and true man, clearly taught his disciples not to kill. In fact, for the first three hundred years, every single one of the many extant Christian writings dealing with this issue indicates that Jesus said Christians should never kill other persons. For that reason, the early Christians rejected abortion, capital punishment and killing in war.[15]

The biblical argument. For much of the three hundred years preceding Jesus' birth, cruel foreign conquerors ruled Palestine. First Greeks and then Romans demanded heavy taxation and imposed pagan values. The Jewish response was intense messianic longing and widespread expectation for a conquering military Messiah who would overthrow the foreign rulers. When Herod the Great died just after Jesus' birth, three different messianic pretend-

---

[14]Ronald J. Sider and Diane Knippers, eds., *Toward an Evangelical Public Policy: Political Strategies for the Health of the Nation* (Grand Rapids: Baker, 2005), pp. 163-93.

[15]See Michael J. Gorman, *Abortion and the Early Church* (Downers Grove, Ill.: InterVarsity Press, 1982).

ers provoked armed rebellion. One of the popular political options of Jesus' day was a movement of violent, devoutly religious Jewish nationalists who believed the Messiah would come if the Jewish nation would rise up in armed rebellion.

Jesus lived and taught a different way. When Jesus chose to make a clear public messianic claim in his triumphal entry into Jerusalem, he chose to fulfill Zechariah's vision of a humble, peaceful Messiah riding on a donkey, not a war horse (Mt 21:5; Jn 12:15; Zech 9:9-10). At his arrest Jesus rebuked Peter's attempt to defend him with the sword: "All who take the sword will perish by the sword" (Mt 26:52).[16]

Matthew 5:38-48, of course, is the most important text in Jesus' nonviolent teaching.

> You have heard that it was said, "An eye for an eye and a tooth for a tooth." But I say to you, Do not resist an evildoer. But if anyone strikes you on the right cheek, turn the other also; and if anyone wants to sue you and take your coat, give your cloak as well; and if anyone forces you to go one mile, go also the second mile. Give to everyone who begs from you, and do not refuse anyone who wants to borrow from you.
>
> You have heard that it was said, "You shall love your neighbor and hate your enemy." But I say to you, Love your enemies and pray for those who persecute you, so that you may be children of your Father in heaven; for he makes his sun rise on the evil and on the good, and sends rain on the righteous and on the unrighteous. For if you love those who love you, what reward do you have? Do not even the tax collectors do the same? And if you greet only your brothers and sisters, what more are you doing than others? Do not even the Gentiles do the same? Be perfect, therefore, as your heavenly Father is perfect.

To a people so oppressed by foreign conquerors that over the previous two centuries they had repeatedly resorted to violent rebellion, Jesus gave the unprecedented command: "Love your enemies." New Testament scholar Martin Hengel believes that Jesus formulated this command in conscious contrast to the teaching and practice of the Zealots.[17] Thus Jesus rejected one currently popular political method in favor of a radically different approach.

Jesus' command to love one's enemies contrasts sharply with widespread views that Jesus summarizes in verse 43: "You have heard that it was said, 'You shall love your neighbor and hate your enemy.'" The first part of this verse is a

---

[16]The following is an abbreviation of the argument in Ronald J. Sider and Richard K. Taylor, *Nuclear Holocaust and Christian Hope* (Downers Grove, Ill.: InterVarsity Press, 1982), pp. 95-158. Full citation of sources is available there.

[17]Martin Hengel, *Victory Over Violence* (London: SPCK, 1975), p. 76.

direct quotation from Leviticus 19:18: "You shall love your neighbor as your-self." But who is one's neighbor? The first part of Leviticus 19:18 indicates that the neighbor is "any of your people." This was the normal Jewish viewpoint. New Testament scholar John Piper, in his extensive study of pre-Christian thinking about love for neighbor, shows that in Jewish thought the neighbor that one was obligated to love was normally understood to be a fellow Israel-ite.[18] Thus love for neighbor had clear ethnic, religious limitations. A different attitude toward Gentiles was expected. Seldom, however, did the Old Testa-ment command or sanction hatred of foreigners or enemies. But Jewish con-temporaries of Jesus did. The Zealots believed that "slaying the godless enemy out of zeal for God's cause was a fundamental commandment, true to the rab-binic maxim: 'Whoever spills the blood of one of the godless is like one who of-fers a sacrifice.' " And the Qumran community's *Manual of Discipline* urged people to "love all the sons of light . . . and . . . hate all the sons of darkness."

Jesus' way was radically different. Loving those who love you (Mt 5:46), Jesus says, is relatively easy; even great sinners such as tax collectors can do that. In fact even the pagan Gentiles act kindly toward the people in their own ethnic group. Jesus totally rejects that kind of ethnic or religious limitation on love.

For the members of Jesus' messianic kingdom, "neighbor love" must ex-tend beyond the limited circle of the people of Israel, beyond the limited circle of the new people of God. This text says explicitly what the parable of the good Samaritan (Lk 10:29-37) suggests: all people everywhere are neighbors to Jesus' followers and therefore are to be actively loved. And that includes ene-mies—even violent, oppressive, foreign conquerors!

The difficulty of actually implementing this command has led to many at-tempts to weaken its radical demand. Martin Luther did that with his two-kingdom analysis. He restricted the application of these verses on love of ene-mies to the personal sphere and denied their application to the Christian in public life. Luther went so far as to tell Christians that in their roles as public officials "you do not have to ask Christ about your duty."[19] The emperor sup-plies the ethic for public life. Exegetically, however, that seems highly ques-tionable. New Testament scholar Eduard Schweizer says in his commentary on Matthew, "There is not the slightest hint of any realm where the disciple is not bound by the words of Jesus."[20] The context demonstrates clearly that

[18]John Piper, *Love Your Enemies* (Cambridge: Cambridge University Press, 1979), pp. 21-48.
[19]Quoted in John Stott, *Christian Counter-Culture* (Downers Grove, Ill.: InterVarsity Press, 1978), p. 113.
[20]Edward Schweizer, *The Good News According to Matthew* (Atlanta: John Knox, 1975), p. 194.

Jesus intends the command to apply to the public sphere. In Matthew 5:39-41 Jesus discusses issues that clearly pertain to the public sphere of the legal system and the authorized demands of the Roman rulers.

When Jesus rejects the principle of "an eye for an eye," he is not merely offering some admonitions for private, interpersonal relationships, but rather is transcending a basic legal principle of the Mosaic and other near-Eastern legal systems (e.g., Ex 23:24). Instead of demanding what the law permitted, namely, full retaliation, Jesus commanded a loving response governed by the needs of the other person. One should even submit to further damage and suffering rather than exact equal pain or loss from the unfair, guilty aggressor. In no way should we allow the other person's response to govern our action. Verse 40 ("if anyone wants to sue you and take your coat, give your cloak as well") also clearly speaks of how one should respond in the public arena of the judicial system.

Matthew 5:41 ("if anyone forces you to go one mile, go also the second mile") deals with how to respond to Roman rulers who demand forced labor. From Josephus we know that the verb translated as "force" is a technical term used to refer to the perfectly legal requisition of services by Roman civil and military authorities.[21] It is hardly surprising that the revolutionaries of Jesus' day urged Jews to refuse this kind of forced labor. Jesus, on the other hand, condemns their violent, angry response, even to the Romans' unjust demands.

Nonresistance or nonviolence? But this raises a pressing problem. Is Jesus forbidding all forms of resistance to evil? It seems some forms of coercion are fully compatible with love and respect for the other person as a free moral agent while others are not. In the home with children, in the church in disciplining brothers and sisters, and in the marketplace with economic boycotts, coercion can be applied that still respects the other person's freedom to say no and accept the consequences. Lethal violence is different. When one engages in lethal violence, one cannot lovingly appeal to the other person as a free moral agent responsible to God to choose to repent and change.

Jesus' own actions demonstrate that he did not intend to forbid all forms of resistance. Jesus constantly opposed evil persons in a forthright, vigorous fashion. He unleashed a blistering attack on the Pharisees (Mt 23:13-33). When Jesus cleansed the temple, he resisted the evil of the moneychangers in a dramatic act of nonviolent resistance. At his trial when a soldier unjustly struck him on the cheek (Jn 18:19-24), he protested!

What then does Matthew 5:39 mean? It means four very radical things:

---

[21]W. F. Albright and C. S. Mann, *Matthew*, Anchor Bible (New York: Doubleday, 1971), p. 69.

1. We should not respond to an evil person by placing him or her in the category of enemy.

2. We should not retaliate but rather respond according to the needs of the offending person, regardless of his offensive attitude or action.

3. Regardless of the offending person's response, we must continue to love because love does not depend on reciprocity.

4. We should act in these ways even at great personal cost.

Jesus' command not to resist evil must be understood in light of the preceding verse. To exact an eye for an eye was the accepted norm. Its fundamental principle was retaliation—limited, to be sure, by the nature of the offense. But Jesus rejected all retaliation. Instead of hating or retaliating, Jesus' followers are to respond lovingly in light of the need of the other person. And that love is to be so clear and costly and so single-mindedly focused on the needs of the other that it will even accept additional insult and injury from the aggressor—even a blow with the back of the hand, the most insulting of all physical blows in Jesus' day. But that does not mean that we cannot offer any form of resistance to the evil person. That would contradict Jesus' own actions. Rather it means costly, aggressive love, controlled by the genuine needs of the other person. The members of Jesus' new messianic kingdom are to love opponents, even oppressive, persecuting enemies, so deeply that they can wholeheartedly pray for their well-being and actively demonstrate their love in actions that exceed unjust demands.

Weakening Jesus' costly call. Until Emperor Constantine adopted Christianity in the fourth century, all Christian writings on the topic reflect the belief that Jesus clearly and explicitly forbids Christians to participate in war and capital punishment. Since that time, however, many Christians have thought otherwise.

Some version of ethical dualism lies behind almost all these post-Constantinian arguments. In the Middle Ages many distinguished between the commands that apply to all Christians and the counsels of perfection (e.g., "Love your enemies") that apply only to the particularly devout, such as monks and nuns. In Luther's view of the two kingdoms, the love ethic of Jesus applies to the inner disposition of the heart of the individual believer, who never kills in his role as a member of the kingdom of Christ. But in his role as public official in the kingdom of the world, he rightly kills via capital punishment and war. Some dispensationalists relegate the application of the Sermon on the Mount to the future millennium. Reinhold Niebuhr, who acknowledged that Jesus himself rejected all violence, considered Jesus' teaching an impossible ideal in a sinful world.

Especially common is the dualistic distinction between the personal and public roles of the Christian. In his or her personal role, it is argued, the Christian must always refuse to retaliate or kill. But the same person acting in the public role of judge or soldier rightly does both. Jesus then was not forbidding capital punishment or war on the part of duly authorized Christian executioners and soldiers. He was merely forbidding private retaliation on the part of individuals who want to take the law into their own hands.

I think all these versions of ethical dualism are misguided. I do not believe God has a double ethic. I do not believe that God ordains a higher ethic for especially devout folk and a lower ethic for the masses. I do not believe that God intends Christians to wait until the millennium to obey the Sermon on the Mount.

Nor do I believe that Christ urges the individual Christian in a personal role to love his enemies but then authorizes that same person as public official to kill them. This thesis ignores the historical context of Jesus' teaching. It overlooks the most natural meaning of the text. It also relies on pragmatism. Historically, it has led to very bad consequences. Finally, it neglects the first three centuries of Christian teaching.

In his historical context Jesus came as the Messiah of Israel with a plan and an ethic for the entire Jewish people. He advocated love toward (political!) enemies as his specific political response to centuries of violence. His radical nonviolence was a conscious alternative to the contemporary religious revolutionaries' call for violent revolution to usher in the messianic kingdom. There is no hint that Jesus' reason for objecting to the violent revolutionaries was that they were unauthorized individuals whose violent sword would have been legitimate if the Sanhedrin had only given the order. On the contrary, his point was that this whole approach to enemies, even unjust, oppressive Roman conquerors, was fundamentally wrong. The revolutionaries offered one political approach; Jesus offered another. But both appealed to the entire Jewish nation.

Second, the personal-public distinction also seems to go against the most natural, literal meaning of the text. There is no hint whatsoever in the text of such a distinction. In fact, the text is full of references to *public* life. "Do not resist an evildoer" applies, Jesus says, when people take you to court (Mt 5:40) and when foreign rulers legally demand forced labor (Mt 5:41). Indeed, the basic norm Jesus transcends (an eye for an eye) was a fundamental principle of the legal system. We can safely assume that members of the Sanhedrin and other officials heard Jesus' words. Jesus claimed to be the Messiah for the whole Jewish people. He wanted the whole nation, indeed the whole world, to implement his kingdom ethics because he said the messianic kingdom was breaking into history in his person and movement. The most natural conclusion is that Jesus intended his words to be normative, not just in private but also in public life. The burden of proof would seem to rest on those who want to argue that Jesus was speaking only of the way the individual should act in his private role.

Third, an essentially pragmatic presupposition often underlies the argument that Jesus could not have meant his followers to never use lethal violence. In a sinful world that often tramples on gentle, loving persons, it is argued, violence is necessary to defend oneself and others. Love will simply not work. The factual claim may or may not be right. What is surely most important for Christians, however, is the essential pragmatism of the argument. Surely the *pragmatic* question of whether Jesus' ethic works—that is, whether it enables us and others to avoid suffering and resist aggressors—dare not be decisive in our analysis of what Jesus actually meant.

Fourth, the consequences of this dualistic distinction have often been disastrous. Christian soldiers have justified their participation in terrible evil on the pretext that it is not appropriate for them to challenge official orders. The failure of most German Protestants to oppose Hitler's atrocities is often attributed in part to Luther's two-kingdom ethic. In 1933 German Christians argued that "the church is obliged to obey the state in every earthly matter." And they concluded that "unconditional allegiance" to the Nazi state was fully compatible with allegiance to Christ.

Finally, the first three centuries of the Christian church offer weighty evidence against the personal-public distinction. Every one of the many Christian writers who discussed the problem of war and capital punishment thought that Jesus' teaching explicitly forbade Christians from participation in both. Repeatedly they rejected the view that Christians could kill people in the public role of soldier or executioner. The only adequate explanation for the vigorous rejection of Christian participation in state-authorized lethal violence by the early Christians is that Christ himself commanded it.

The foundation of Christian nonviolence lies not in some calculation of effectiveness. It rests in the cross. The ultimate ground of biblical opposition to taking life is the nature of God, revealed first in Jesus' teaching and life and then most fully in his death.

God's love for enemies. There is one central aspect of Matthew 5:38-48 that we have not yet explored. What, according to Jesus, is the theological foundation of his call for costly, nonretaliatory love, even for enemies? Jesus did not say that one should practice loving nonviolence because it would always transform vicious enemies into bosom friends. The cross stands as a harsh reminder that love for enemies does not always work—at least not in the short run. Jesus grounds his call to love enemies, not in the hope of reciprocity but rather in the very nature of God. "Love your enemies and pray for those who persecute you, *so that* you may be children of your Father in heaven; for he makes his sun rise on the evil and on the good, and sends rain on the righteous and on the unrighteous" (Mt 5:44-45, emphasis added). Jesus said a similar thing in the Beatitudes: "Blessed are the peacemakers, for they will be called children of God" (Mt 5:9). God loves his enemies. Instead of promptly destroying sinners, he continues to shower the good gifts of creation upon them. Since that is the way God acts, those who want to be his sons and daughters must do likewise. Conversely, the text implies that those who do not love their enemies are not the children of God. "Be perfect, therefore, as your heavenly Father is perfect" (Mt 5:48). One fundamental aspect of the holiness and perfection of God is that he loves his enemies. Those who by his grace seek to reflect his holiness will likewise love their enemies—even when it involves a cross.

Jesus' conception of the suffering Messiah who goes to the cross as a ransom for sinners takes us still further in our understanding of God's way of dealing with enemies. At the Last Supper, Jesus stated unequivocally that he was going to die as a sacrifice for others. The One who had claimed divine authority (blasphemously, his enemies charged) to forgive sinners now dies for others at the demand of those very enemies. The One who taught his followers to imitate God's love for enemies now dies with a forgiving prayer on his lips for the enemies who nail him to the cross (Lk 23:34).

That the cross is the ultimate demonstration that God deals with his enemies through suffering love receives its clearest theological expression in Paul. "God proves his love for us in that while we still were *sinners* Christ died for us. . . . [W]hile we were *enemies,* we were reconciled to God through the death of his Son" (Rom 5:8, 10, emphasis added). Jesus' vicarious cross for sinners is the foundation and deepest expression of Jesus' command to love one's enemies. As the substitutionary view of the atonement indicates, we are enemies in the double sense that sinful persons are hostile to God and that the just, holy Creator hates sin (Rom 1:18). For those who know the law, failure to obey it results in a divine curse. But Christ redeemed us from that curse by becoming a curse for us (Gal 3:10-14). Jesus' blood on the cross was an expiation (Rom 5:18) for us sinful enemies of God because the One who knew no sin was made sin for us on the cross (2 Cor 5:21).

Nothing discloses the horror of sin as fully as the cross. The cross is no cheap declaration of "indulgent amnesty." Sin is an outrageous affront to God's holiness. It would be a horrible, intolerable world if sin, evil and injustice could continue to rampage and destroy, forever unpunished. The cross demonstrates that the holy Sovereign of the universe will not tolerate that. Sin's penalty must be paid.

But the cross is not the sacrifice of a human victim on the altar of an angry, hostile deity. That would deny the doctrines of the incarnation and the Trinity. God himself suffers; God himself bears the penalty of sin.

Jesus' vicarious death for sinful enemies of God leads to nonviolence. It was because the incarnate One knew that God is loving and merciful, even toward the worst of sinners, that he associated with sinners, forgave their sins and completed his messianic mission by dying for the sins of the world. Precisely this same understanding of God prompted him to command his followers to love their enemies.

At the cross God himself suffered for his enemies. Certainly we can never fathom all the mystery there. But it is precisely because the One hanging limp on the middle cross was the Word who became flesh that we are absolutely sure of two interrelated things: first, that a just God mercifully accepts sinful enemies, and second, that he wants us to go and treat all our enemies in the same merciful, self-sacrificial way.

If the cross were the last word about the carpenter from Nazareth with the radical call to love even enemies, then rejecting his way would make sense. He may have had good intentions, his vision may be noble, but it does not work in this violent world. But Christians know that the last word about Jesus is resurrection. On the third day God raised him from the tomb, conquering the powers of evil and demonstrating that this teacher of nonviolence is God incarnate, King of kings and Lord of lords. The resurrection shows that Jesus' messianic kingdom has dawned, that Jesus' way is God's will for us. The resurrection—with its promise that in God's time, every knee shall bow—is the ultimate foundation for biblical nonviolence.

That is not to forget the cross. Christians who follow Jesus, who value Jesus' powerful concern to reconcile adversaries more than claiming justice for themselves, who are willing to let go of legitimate goals when they cannot be attained by legitimate means, will experience the cross. But they know that will not be the last word. Sometimes the mighty power that raised Jesus will do astonishing, even miraculous things to overcome vicious enemies even now. Sometimes, in his wisdom, he will allow evil to triumph—temporarily. But the last word for those who participate in the triumphant suffering of the Lamb will be resurrection.[22] The resurrection both makes possible and demands obedience to Jesus' nonviolent way.

---

[22]See Yoder, *Politics of Jesus,* esp. pp. 238-40.

The Logic of Anabaptist Political Engagement

Since Anabaptists reject all killing, and since all contemporary states use lethal violence in their armies and police, some conclude that Anabaptists have no consistent foundation for political engagement. Some even argue that a pacifist cannot even articulate a logically consistent political philosophy. Both claims are wrong.

First, a vast amount of political activity and debate does not deal directly at all with the issue of lethal violence. John Howard Yoder is right that "most of what a public order (i.e., government) does is not violent."[23] A great deal of what contemporary governments do consists of coordinating and organizing nonviolent communal activity to promote the common good. Government provides health insurance, education, roads, Social Security and assistance to the poor and needy. Mennonites can participate fully in political debates about the wisdom of such policies and even partner with government agencies funding private organizations to carry out social programs approved by legislatures without in any way violating their opposition to all killing.

It is true that behind every law and every collection of taxes to fund social programs stands an implicit threat to use lethal violence. But in day-to-day practice the types of government programs being discussed here involve no use of lethal violence. Furthermore, Mennonites do not give moral approval to the implicit threat of lethal violence merely by endorsing and participating in good social programs that operate day to day in completely nonviolent ways.

Second, Mennonites can and do use a wide variety of nonviolent forms of power to shape the political process. It is empirically false to claim that the gun is the only source of power.[24] In our complex world, there are many sources of power that shape politics: truth, ideas, well-argued viewpoints, persuasive dialogue, education, economic decisions (including boycotts), local, national and global nongovernmental advocacy groups, and so forth. Political scientist Karl Deutsch underlines the importance of people power; simply by accepting or refusing to cooperate with government, the masses wield enormous nonviolent power. "The voluntary or habitual compliance of the mass of the population," Deutsch argues, "is the invisible but very real basis of the power of every government."[25]

Modern history demonstrates that a willingness to defy governmental

---

[23]Yoder, *For the Nations*, p. 36.

[24]See, for example, Jonathan Schell, *The Unconquerable World: Power, Nonviolence and the Will of the People* (New York: Henry Holt, 2003).

[25]Karl Deutsch, *The Analysis of International Relations*, 2nd ed. (Englewood Cliffs, N.J.: Prentice Hall, 1978), pp. 17-18, quoted in Friesen, *Christian Peacemaking*, p. 38.

power nonviolently and endure suffering for an alternative vision can have enormous political impact. Not just Mohandas Gandhi and Martin Luther King Jr. but also the vast crowds defying Marcos' dictatorship in the Philippines and communist totalitarianism in Poland and East Germany won stunning victories. As Yoder says, "That suffering is powerful and that weakness wins is true not only in heaven but on earth."[26]

Third, it is entirely consistent for an Anabaptist who rejects all killing to conduct political debate within the framework of a traditional just-war framework, challenging nonpacifists to live up to their own just-war norms, including criteria like "last resort" and so on. For example, running a detailed argument that a proposed military invasion of a dangerous neighboring country is unwarranted because the just-war tradition demands that war must be a last resort and all viable nonviolent alternatives have not yet been tried is entirely consistent with also opposing all war. The same is true of arguing that less expenditure on arms and more on economic development would be in the long-term interest of one's nation. Seeking to shape public opinion on such issues and lobbying elected officials, using arguments that fit within a just-war framework, are quite consistent for Mennonites.

The same standard applies to voting for the lesser evil among two or more candidates for office. Voting for, and otherwise promoting the election of, a specific politician in no way means accepting or endorsing all of that person's ideas and actions. It only means that one thinks this candidate's platform and likely activities will be a little less destructive than those of the other candidates.

One can state this third point in a broader way. Virtually all governments and political leaders claim to do good and act for the well-being of their people and the world. Without accepting every part of their vision of justice or their means to achieve it, Anabaptists can challenge governments and politicians to live up to what is good in the ideals they themselves claim to embrace.

It is true that an Anabaptist could probably not get elected to any major office. Honesty would demand that an Anabaptist politician tell voters that he or she opposes all use of lethal violence. If a majority still chose to elect such a person as, say, a senator, then that Anabaptist senator would regularly vote against military expenditures. But the fact that a person running on such a platform would hardly ever be elected does not mean at all that Anabaptists cannot be consistently engaged in political activity and debate using arguments grounded in premises that the majority share even when one does not embrace those premises.

---

[26]Yoder, *For the Nations*, p. 35.

One of the many effective ways Mennonites have worked in a broadly political fashion challenging just-war persons to live up to their own criteria has been
to develop new nonviolent ways to deal with violent situations. Christian Peacemaker Teams is a recent, growing Anabaptist movement to train Christian citizens to intervene nonviolently in situations of great conflict (e.g., the West
Bank).[27] One does not need to be a pacifist to recognize that during the last century, nonviolent resistance to oppression, dictatorship and violence has achieved
many stunning successes—not just with Gandhi and King but also in numerous
other instances.[28] Since war must always be a last resort, further concrete demonstration of the effective use of nonviolent intervention by groups like Christian
Peacemaker Teams will encourage just-war people to extend the area where they
expect nonviolence to be a better approach than the use of lethal violence.

In an analogous way, Anabaptists have developed a successful alternative
to incarceration called the Victim Offender Reconciliation Program (VORP).[29]
VORP offers an alternative to prison in which the guilty person in a crime develops a relationship with the victim and seeks to partly compensate the victim. Genuine reconciliation is the ultimate goal.

One need not think that all societal conflict can be handled through nonviolent approaches to agree both that wherever possible we ought to use
nonviolence rather than violence and also that today we resolve many
things nonviolently that earlier societies settled through fighting. Only a
few centuries ago gentlemen often solved disputes with a duel in which one
party frequently was killed. Today, we settle those disputes nonviolently
through the legal process.[30] We cannot eradicate human selfishness and evil,
but history demonstrates that some forms of that evil (e.g., slavery, dueling)
can end.

Does God want government to use the sword? That is not at all the same
question as, does God use lethal governmental action to accomplish good
things? The answer to the second question is obviously yes. Regularly armies
and police use lethal violence in a way that ends some oppression, restrains
evil and eliminates vicious dictators like Hitler. But it might be the case that if
people had the courage and obedience, there would be (better) nonviolent

---

[27]For many news stories, contact Christian Peacemaker Teams online at cpt@igc.org or by
phone at (773) 277-0253.

[28]See the dozens of examples in Ronald J. Sider, *Nonviolence: The Invincible Weapon?* (Dallas:
Word, 1989).

[29]For more information on this successful program, see their website <http://vorp.org>. For
its Mennonite origins, see David Cayley, *The Expanding Prison* (Toronto: House of Anansi,
1998), pp. 215-37.

[30]Friesen, *Christian Peacemaking*, p. 183.

ways to accomplish those goals and that although God permits and uses lethal violence, it is never his desire.

Historically, Mennonites have adopted two different positions on whether government ought to use lethal force. Some have said yes, Christians should not kill, but government is outside the perfection of Christ, and God intends that government should use the sword.[31] Such a position, however, leads to the strange conclusion that God does not want all to become Christians because if they did, there would be no one to perform the proper governmental use of the sword.

Other Mennonites, including myself, reject that kind of ethical dualism. We believe that although God regularly uses lethal violence for some good outcomes, God has revealed his will for human beings most fully in Jesus, God become flesh, and that human use of lethal violence is never God's will.

Frequently in Christian history Christians have used Romans 13:1 to argue that God wills whatever governments decide and therefore Christians must obey all demands of government. But that is not what Paul means. Paul certainly believes that all "rulers or powers" were originally part of God's good creation (Col 1:16), and that includes governmental power. But Paul is equally clear that the powers have rebelled against God and now often do what God does not want. Therefore the mere fact that Paul says God has ordained government does not mean that God also decided that government must use lethal violence.

In Romans 13:4, Paul says government uses the sword as a servant of God to "execute wrath on the wrongdoer." Obviously God uses lethal actions by governments to punish evil and protect good. But not even verse 4 requires the interpretation that God *wants* governments to punish evil and protect good through killing. In the Old Testament, God clearly used pagan empires to punish Israel and Judah for their sin. Isaiah 10 describes the way God used pagan Assyria as "the rod of my anger" (Is 10:5), but that does not mean God approved of the vicious ways that Assyria wreaked havoc. Isaiah 45:1 calls the pagan Cyrus God's "Messiah" (i.e., "anointed" one) because God used Cyrus to accomplish a divine purpose. But again that does not mean God approved all of Cyrus's methods.

I would argue that it is always God's will that human beings use nonviolent rather than lethally violent methods to restrain evil. No society has ever tried

---

[31]To some extent, Ted Koontz offers a sophisticated contemporary version of this position. See Koontz, "Mennonites and the State," in *Essays on Peace Theology and Witness*, ed. Williard M. Swartley (Elkhart: Institute of Mennonite Studies, 1988), pp. 35-60.

it consistently over a long period of time, so it is impossible to point to historical evidence, but I would argue that if whole societies would abandon the
sword, the result would be less killing than we now experience. We do have
evidence that with some frequency nonviolence is stunningly successful. Al-
geria used lethal violence in its ten-year campaign for independence, and one
of every ten Algerians died. Gandhi's India used nonviolence in its own struggle, and only one in 400,000 Indians died in the struggle.[32] I am not suggesting
that sin or murder would disappear. Selfishness would persist. But human sinfulness does not need to take the form of dueling and slavery; maybe it need
not take the form of governmental killing.

Obviously, if any society truly chose nonviolence, it would suffer. Outsiders
would take advantage of it. The nonviolent society would have to share its
goods, respond to evil with love and forgive attackers. Many thousands, perhaps millions would die. But just-war theorists consider World War II a great
success even though tens of millions died. Not until whole societies dare to
live out Jesus' call to love even enemies will we have substantial empirical evidence for or against my claim that the way of nonviolence would actually result in less killing than the way of war.

Anabaptists like myself—who think that although governments regularly
do use lethal violence, they should not—nonetheless have a perfectly consistent framework for political engagement in our present context. We can work
to persuade public opinion and elected politicians to try more nonviolent alternatives, by both arguing that their own just-war framework demands nonviolence whenever that is workable and articulating the much more radical
claim that killing is always wrong. And most of the time, for most political discussions, the explicit issue of lethal violence is not even on the agenda.

Separating Church and State and "Legislating Morality"

Anabaptists obviously believe strongly that the state should not use its power
to establish or endorse any particular religion. What the Bible tells us about
human freedom, the nature of the church and the purpose of the state all lead
to the kind of religious freedom that Americans thankfully enjoy.

That does not mean endorsement of the liberal Lockean tradition, which
dictates that religion should be relegated to some personal, private sphere. Religious beliefs profoundly shape our political views. Hence a genuine respect
for religious freedom grants full rein for religious people to publicly articulate
the implications of their beliefs for public policy.

---

[32]Sider, *Nonviolence*, p. 76.

Immediately, of course, this leads to one of the most complicated of contemporary problems. Our vision of church and state demands that government remain neutral on religious beliefs. But every act of government and every legislative decision in Congress is grounded finally in a political philosophy that is itself in turn grounded in a set of ultimate philosophical/religious beliefs. So how does a highly pluralistic society committed to religious freedom for everyone decide what to legislate?

If, as Catholic thought has often argued, every rational person has access to the natural law embedded in everyone's mind and conscience by the Creator, then perhaps we could develop a common set of principles, derived from natural law, which all citizens, no matter what their belief, could accept as the foundation of public discourse about what to legislate. But the Fall has obscured human moral insight too much for this approach to work adequately.

I prefer an approach that recognizes that religious belief inescapably shapes everybody's political views and also that contemporary America is enormously pluralistic; therefore the only fair approach is to encourage every person and group of whatever religious belief to articulate a concrete vision for public life, including specific legislation, that flows from their deepest beliefs about the world and persons. Only those specific proposals that a majority endorse in the course of open debate and democratic process will become law.

Obviously, there must be clear constitutional protections of religious freedom and the rights of minorities. Other things being equal, a majority should not use government to coerce minorities to adopt the lifestyle of the majority. (For example, Anabaptists believe divorce, homosexual practice and racist attitudes are all sinful, but Anabaptists should not try to use the law to prohibit all divorce, private homosexual acts or personal racist attitudes.) Normally, individual citizens should be free to harm themselves—and, to some extent, their families—without the government intervening. On the other hand, when private acts harm entire classes of people, then legislation is often appropriate— for example, laws against racial discrimination in the renting or sale of housing.

The present debate about the legal definition of marriage illustrates the problem. Gay activists claim that anything short of defining marriage to include gay couples constitutes an inappropriate legislation of traditional Christian (and Jewish, Muslim, etc.) religious beliefs about marriage. Others, including myself, think that public law should uphold the long tradition stretching over many millennia in almost every human civilization that marriage is a relationship between a man and a woman, intended for a lifetime and open to procreation. A commitment to the common good and to the well-being of all children, not a specific religious belief, compels us to insist that public law should retain the traditional legal definition of marriage.

Anabaptists have a strong concern for the poor. We believe that government, as well as all the other institutions in society, has a proper role in creating economic justice, especially for the most disadvantaged.[33] Does that mean that Anabaptists should support President George W. Bush's faith-based initiative?

Evaluating the Faith-Based Initiative

The recent discussion, especially during the 2000 presidential election campaign and after President Bush established the new White House Office on Faith-Based and Community Initiatives in early 2001, offers a significant, current church-state issue to discuss from an Anabaptist perspective.[34]

While the debate has been most intense since 2000, President Clinton actually signed four specific pieces of legislation with Charitable Choice language beginning in 1996. Since Charitable Choice—and especially its stipulation that religious nonprofits who receive government funds retain their right to hire staff who share their faith commitments—has become the most debated aspect of the broader faith-based initiative, I will focus on Charitable Choice.

Religious nonprofits may not use government funds for "inherently religious" activities—defined in the Charitable Choice provision as "sectarian worship, instruction, or proselytization." Religious nonprofits, however, may raise money from nongovernmental sources to cover the costs of such religious activities. Religious nonprofits are free to hire only staff who share their religious perspective. A "secular" option for the same services through another agency must always be available, if requested, and participants in faith-based programs must be free to decline to participate in specifically religious activities.

One of the most obvious places to look for possible reasons to reject or question the Charitable Choice provision is in the historic theological arguments

---

[33]See Ronald J. Sider, *Rich Christians in an Age of Hunger,* 5th ed. (Dallas: Word, 2005); see also Ronald J. Sider, *Just Generosity: A New Vision for Overcoming Poverty in America,* 2nd ed. (Grand Rapids: Baker, 2007).

[34]The following discussion is a summary of Ronald J. Sider and Heidi Rolland Unruh, "An (Ana)Baptist Theological Perspective on Church-State Cooperation: Evaluating Charitable Choice," in *Welfare Reform and Faith-Based Organizations,* ed. Derek Davis and Barry Hankins (Waco, Tex.: J. M. Dawson Institute of Church-State Studies, 1999), pp. 89-138. More complete documentation is available there. See also Ronald J. Sider and Heidi Rolland Unruh, "Evangelism and Church-State Partnerships," *Journal of Church and State* 43 (2001): 267-95; Ronald J. Sider and Heidi Rolland Unruh, "'No Aid to Religion?' Charitable Choice and the First Amendment," in *What's God Got to Do with the American Experiment?* ed. E. J. Dionne Jr. and John J. DiIulio Jr. (Washington, D.C.: Brookings Institution Press, 2000), pp. 128-37; and Heidi Rolland Unruh and Ronald J. Sider, *Saving Souls, Serving Society: Understanding the Faith Factor in Church-Based Social Ministry* (New York: Oxford University Press, 2005).

that state and church should be separate—surely one of the greatest contributions of Anabaptist thought to the American experiment.

Sixteenth-century Anabaptists often argued that the very nature of God compels us to reject the union of church and state. The nature of persons strengthens the argument. God created persons in the divine image, granting them freedom as a central characteristic of human beings.

A proper understanding of faith also demands full religious freedom. Faith is genuine only if it is a voluntary response to God's grace, given by someone old enough to understand what they are doing.

Our understanding of the church leads to the same conclusion. Anabaptists rejected the notion of a territorial church where every child born in the country was baptized as an infant and thus incorporated into the church. Instead, they believed that the church should be a believers' church, composed only of persons old enough to respond personally in faith to God's gift of salvation. Only such genuine believers are competent to make decisions for the church, and they must govern the church, not with the power of the sword but with the truth of God's revealed Word.

These arguments clearly lead both to the nonestablishment of any religion by the state and the avoidance of any state infringement on the free exercise of religion. But does Charitable Choice violate these principles in any way?

As long as participants in faith-based programs freely choose those programs, always have the option of choosing a "secular" provider and may choose not to participate in particular religious activities within the program, no one is coerced to participate in religious activity, and freedom of religion is preserved. As long as government is equally open to funding programs rooted in any religious perspective, whether Islam, Christianity, philosophical naturalism or "no explicit faith perspective," government is not in any way establishing or providing preferential benefits to any specific religion or to religion in general. As long as the religious institutions maintain autonomy over such crucial areas as program content and staffing, the integrity of the church's separate identity is maintained. As long as government funds are exclusively designated for activities that are not inherently religious, no taxpayer need fear that taxes are paying for religious activity. Charitable Choice respects the innate religious liberty of persons, the freedom of religious worship and the separate authority and identity of church and state. It is true that Charitable Choice may have the effect of increasing the level of interactions between government and religious institutions, but these interactions do not in themselves violate religious liberty. Charitable Choice is designed precisely to discourage such interactions from leading to impermissible entanglement or establishment of religion. I do not see how any of the traditional arguments for religious freedom require that we reject Charitable Choice. Our history, to be sure, suggests that we should be cautious. But that is a call for prudential judgment about pragmatic advantages and disadvantages, not a theological veto against Charitable Choice.

Three other issues are important. Historically, Anabaptists have placed special emphasis on personal conversion, developed an understanding of the church as a countercultural community radically different from the world and stressed the communal character of the church. How, if at all, do these theological concerns bear on the evaluation of Charitable Choice?

Conversion. The historic Anabaptist emphasis on personal conversion is rooted in the biblical understanding that persons are more than just complex socioeconomic machines. Each person is a body-soul unity made for community. Conversion involves more than soul salvation; it means making a commitment to following Christ with one's whole life, which often leads to changes in one's social condition. That means that no amount of activity directed exclusively at the physical, material, economic side of people will be sufficient by itself to solve many fundamental social problems (e.g., drug addiction, high rates of single parenthood, etc.) that contemporary government programs seek to alleviate. If the biblical view of persons is correct, then these problems cannot be resolved through programs that only adjust socioeconomic incentives.

On the other hand, programs that work at both the spiritual and the material side of human beings at the same time are, other things being equal, more likely to succeed. Such holistic programs are also far more faithful to the Anabaptist understanding that evangelism and social ministry are inseparable elements of the mission of the church.

What does all this mean for our question about Charitable Choice? As long as people freely choose to participate in a government-funded faith-based program—whether because they are drawn to the faith perspective or because the program has been demonstrated to be effective—then the agency should be free to incorporate an emphasis on spiritual conversion and discipleship, if these are considered important to the overall effectiveness of the program. Great care should be taken to avoid coercion of any form, but faith-based agencies should be free to present their religious beliefs and lead persons who so choose into active faith.[35] Charitable Choice offers a way that is consistent with the First

---

[35]The current government policy—which stipulates that when faith-based agencies receive *direct* government funding, they must separate in space or time the privately funded specifically religious activities from the government-funded other activities—is an acceptable, workable approach.

Amendment to allow government funds to flow to faith-based holistic programs (which combine the best techniques of contemporary medical and social sciences with specifically spiritual components such as prayer) in such a way that these holistic programs use these funds to further the government's desire and criteria for specific public goods (e.g., a certain rate of job placements).

Second, Anabaptists understand the church—at least their theology suggests they ought to—as a countercultural community dramatically different from the world. But does that mean, as some have thought, that Christians therefore should have little interaction or cooperation with broader societal structures?

Not at all. Jesus' gospel of the kingdom does not mean that we should withdraw from the world, but that it is possible now, in the power of the Spirit, to live Jesus' way in the midst of this fallen world. Certainly our understanding of sin, the world and the church warns us against any utopian expectation that we can build a near perfect social order here and now. But that should not lead Christians to abandon efforts to transform the social order now. The fact that we must reject any idolatrous commitment to "American civilization" that would lead us to neglect evangelism or blur the distinction between Jesus' church and America does not mean that we should neglect the task of treasuring and strengthening what is good in our culture. And if holistic programs (e.g., to prevent single parenthood or reduce long-term welfare dependency) work as well as or perhaps much better than exclusively "secular" programs, then there is no reason why Christians should not use Charitable Choice to help fund those parts of holistic social programs that are not specifically religious.

Third, is there any connection between Charitable Choice and the strong Anabaptist emphasis on the church as a community? Historically, the Anabaptist understanding of the church has emphasized the importance of mutual accountability, support and church discipline. Christians are not spiritual lone rangers. They need the loving, challenging support of other members of Christ's body to live as they should. The reality of strong communal support is essential to the transformation of some of society's most broken people. Many people who have adopted habitual, destructive patterns will only be changed if other people walk with them over an extensive period of time, holding them accountable, challenging them when they stumble and nurturing them into new patterns of behavior.

A holistic, inner-city community center run by a religious nonprofit has unusual access to all the necessary components for transformation. The program's excellent health care center or job training program may provide the initial point of entry. Personal faith in Christ may offer a new orientation and inner power. But the center's dedicated staff (in addition to volunteer mentors, perhaps from local churches) are also essential to walk with broken people over the period of months and years needed to develop a radically reshaped set of values and habits. Charitable Choice guarantees that religious non-profits receiving government funds have the right to maintain autonomy in their hiring decisions so that they may select staff who not only have the right social work skills but also share a belief in God's transforming grace.

I am not calling for government funding of churches or of conversion. All I am suggesting is that faith-based community centers working with the most broken in society can add essential resources that will likely enable them to expand their success in rehabilitating broken people. Government should only provide funding via Charitable Choice for program components that are not inherently religious. And government funds should flow to any nonprofit, religious or otherwise, that demonstrates significant effectiveness in helping people. This policy is not only pragmatically beneficial to the nation, but it is consistent with the central teachings of Anabaptist theology.

Funding all effective programs, including deeply religious ones, is the only way for government to fairly implement the First Amendment.

Funding only "secular" programs offers preferential benefits to a particular quasi-religious perspective. In the current context of extensive government funding for a wide array of social services, a policy that limited government funds to allegedly secular governmental or nongovernmental programs would actually have the effect of giving preference to one specific religious worldview. In the current American context in which government funding of social services is so widespread, if government funds only secular programs, it puts all significantly faith-based programs at a government-created disadvantage.

There is also a second problem. Allegedly secular programs are not really as neutral as it is often claimed. It is true that there is no explicit teaching in these programs that philosophical naturalism is true and that nothing exists except the natural order. But *implicitly,* these programs support such a worldview. Implicitly, purely "secular" programs convey the message that all that is needed to address social problems such as drug addiction, low job skills, single parenthood and the like is nonreligious technical knowledge and skills. Implicitly, such programs teach that persons are such that social problems can be solved solely through technical, materialistic, naturalistic procedures, with no reference to any spiritual dimension. Such a claim involves beliefs about the ultimate nature of reality and human existence. Instead of being religiously neutral, this belief system actually serves the same function as religion.

Whether it is advanced explicitly or implicitly, it thus represents one particular, contemporary religious worldview. In a context where government funds a vast array of social services, if government monies go only to allegedly secular programs, which in fact implicitly teach that religious faith is unnecessary to solve our social problems, government ends up massively biased in favor of one particular quasi-religious perspective—namely, philosophical naturalism.

In our kind of society, it is simply not possible for government to carry out the "no aid to religion" principle. If the state ever tried to implement that principle consistently today in the funding of social services, it would end up offering aid almost exclusively to the quasi-religion of philosophical naturalism, even though that worldview would often be communicated in a nonverbal, implicit way. Charitable Choice offers a better alternative that is fair to every religious perspective. Via Charitable Choice, government offers equal benefits to any faith-based nonprofit as long as the money is not used for inherently religious activities and as long as the nonprofit successfully provides the social benefits desired by government.

We still must ask, can faith-based nonprofits accept government funding without compromising their God-given mission and identity?

Any church-state interaction has potential dangers and problems. Witness, for example, the ongoing problems that result from tax deductions for donations to religious institutions. But the fact that problems are inevitable does not mean that we should seek totally to separate church and state and abandon every interaction and cooperative effort. In fact, that would be impossible, since the state is finally responsible for public justice in a given territory, and the mission of the church demands that Christians let Christ be Lord of their activity to promote justice.

What we need is vigilance to avoid the clear dangers. Three are especially important.

1. *Pressures to secularize.* Religious agencies must be aware that pressures to secularize their programs will continue even after implementation of Charitable Choice, and they must carefully seek ways to resist.

2. *Loss of prophetic critique.* Will religious agencies that accept federal funds become passive agents of the government, reluctant to speak out against political injustice? Not necessarily, but we must be crystal clear about this danger.

3. *Loss of religious vitality.* It is true that Christianity has declined in Europe, where the church has a long history of state establishment, which, at least nominally, still continues in some places. I doubt that the alleged analogy

with Europe is helpful, however, because the situations are substantially different. Charitable Choice does not establish a state church because government works with any nonprofit provider (religious or otherwise) that successfully provides certain public benefits. It does not, as in Germany, have the government collect the money to run the church; government merely funds the secular activities of specific programs that promote social goods.

Because of the dangers, we will need to watch carefully and protest loudly if subtle forms of pressure emerge to water down the privately funded religious components of faith-based programs. We will need to continue to nurture Christian leaders who have the courage to engage in vigorous prophetic critique of their society. We will need to figure out how to prevent spiritual stagnation in publicly funded faith-based agencies, and how to reverse the long thirty-year decline in per-member congregational giving. We will need to develop a more sophisticated understanding of the risks and establish internal standards and review procedures for agencies receiving funding. But we should also keep in mind that *not* to allow church-state cooperation via Charitable Choice also involves dangers: lost opportunity to offer what may be the best hope for the most desperate in our society, the establishment of a bias against religion in the courts, the secularization of social services and the potential of the church's becoming socially irrelevant because of the fear of getting involved.

I find no substantive Anabaptist objection to Charitable Choice.[36] Most criticisms of Charitable Choice finally amount either to the unconvincing claim that it violates the First Amendment or to a warning that our long struggle for the separation of church and state should make us cautious. I disagree with the first claim and accept the second. But a warning to be cautious does not mean that we should not proceed if the apparent benefits seem to outweigh the dangers. In this case, I think they do. By expanding the possibilities for the right kind of cooperation between church and state, Charitable Choice offers society a rich resource for meeting critical social needs.

---

[36]My support of Charitable Choice and, more generally, President Bush's faith-based initiatives, does not in any way involve an endorsement of other Bush policy initiatives. For my persistent denunciation of President Bush's tax cuts, see Ronald J. Sider, "Compassionate Conservatism or Blatant Injustice? Evaluating the New Bush Tax Proposals," *Prism*, March-April, 2003, p. 36; Ronald J. Sider, "Evangelical Leaders Not in Support of Tax Cut," *Philadelphia Inquirer*, May 13, 2001, A.E5; Ronald J. Sider, "At a Time of Growing Poverty, New Tax Cut Plan Is an Outrage," *Philadelphia Inquirer*, February 12, 2003, C.A23.

Catholic Response

Clarke E. Cochran

In its picture of the church, its pacifism and its countercultural stance, the Anabaptist perspective drawn by Ron Sider differs most among the essays in this volume from the Catholic perspective. Nevertheless, there are vital points of contact and much to be learned by Catholics from the Anabaptist tradition.[1] I highlight differences in this response, but also point to fruitful convergences.

The most obvious and important difference is that Sider's position is more Christ-focused, Scripture-based and cross-centered than the Catholic position that I lay out in my essay. Jesus—fully human and fully divine—is the heart of Anabaptist theology and ethics; therefore, imitating Christ and following his normative example in all areas of life take center stage in Sider's political theory. The authoritative statement of what following Christ entails is found in Scripture. The frequency and the effectiveness of Sider's citation of the Bible are one of the first features one notices. The countercultural stance of the Mennonite tradition is validated by the cross. One cannot live the disciple's life without going to the cross. Christian life is too much at odds with the ways of politics and culture to escape unscathed.

These three features of the Anabaptist perspective create a vivid picture of the church as a community of believers dedicated to following their Savior, publicly witnessing to their faith in action, engaging with culture and politics, and paying the price for this way of life. These features are nowhere more evident than in the strict pacifism of the Mennonite tradition—its rejection of violence in all forms, especially war, capital punishment and abortion. Sider's essay thus devotes a very long section to testimony against war. The pacifist position stands on its own as a key element of Anabaptist political theory; it

---

[1] In the interest of full disclosure, I am happy to admit to calling Ron Sider a friend. We have worked on various public-policy projects together. His work at Evangelicals for Social Action and especially in the Crossroads program has been a model of active ecumenical cooperation and mutual learning.

also stands as an exemplar of a range of countercultural positions.

What struck me as I read Sider's essay is that this Christ-focused, Scripture-based and cross-centered approach is also at the heart of Catholic faith. These features, however, are found most prominently in Catholic devotional life, worship and systematic theology. They are not prominent in Catholic political theory. The imitation of Christ (witness the classic devotional text by that name) is central to Catholic personal piety. Indeed, in Catholic popular devotion there has appeared at times a "cult" of suffering and the cross. The cross, with the suffering body of Christ, is prominent in Catholic homes, churches and institutions. In Catholic worship, the entire Bible is read in the three-year cycle of Sunday lectionary texts; Scripture-study groups enrich parish life, and Catholic scholars have been among the most prominent twentieth-century students of the Bible.

Yet, there is the evident paradox that these central features of Catholic life have not been vital in its political theory, which has been more natural-law oriented. This is not the place to unpack the paradox, but only to observe two things. First, the Catholic tradition can and should learn from the Anabaptist tradition in these regards. Second, this learning is already taking place. The life of Christ and the text of Scripture have become far more pronounced in Catholic social teaching during the last three decades, as is evident in the political and social writings of Pope John Paul II and Pope Benedict XVI.

These strengths of Sider's account of Mennonite political thinking, however, generate corresponding weaknesses. He paints a robust and clear picture of the church, but only a fuzzy and vague picture of the state. This receives only a short paragraph or two as prelude to the long discussion of the non-violent commitment of the Anabaptist tradition. Thus, it is difficult to know what that tradition makes of the state. Sider argues that God "uses" government, even government's sword-bearing (although God does not intend or approve government violence). But what about government itself? For what purpose (if any) does government exist, either in the order of creation or the order of grace?

In the Catholic tradition, government's purposes are multiple: to order the political community and its many units (reflecting subsidiarity), to restrain sin and its effects (reflecting the consequences of the Fall), to pursue justice and the common good (reflecting the social nature of the human person and the requirements of collective action for the good of all), and to protect and defend human rights and dignity. The social justice duty of the state characteristic of the Catholic tradition is neglected in Sider's account of political life, though his other writings have strongly challenged evangelical Christians with the duty to do justice, particularly to the poor of the world. In these regards, I think, the Catholic position is more complete and full than the Anabaptist and is closer to the Reformed tradition described by Corwin Smidt.

Given the absence of a theory of the state, Sider has difficulty justifying Christian political engagement with a state whose instruments are often violent and to whose culture the church should be counter. Here the notion of tension between different dynamics would strengthen Sider's argument against "ethical dualism." Sider does reasonably well in justifying engagement, but his case would be stronger with a more complete state theory. To put this in terms of my own essay, the challenge and transcendence elements of the Anabaptist tradition are strong, especially its rejection of violence and its picture of the church as a witness to culture. The competition dynamic does not find a home in Sider's account. The cooperative dynamic is reflected dimly in the notion of engagement with plural religious perspectives on public life. In short, Sider's account of Christian political engagement is compatible with the Catholic account, but rests on a weaker foundation. Living in the tension between cooperation, competition, challenge and transcendence is, I believe, a more comprehensive account of the demands of Christian political engagement, while avoiding ethical dualism.

In this regard, more attention to the *institutional* and *sacramental* character of the church would strengthen the Mennonite position. The lack of emphasis on institutions, however, does reflect the relatively smaller and more local institutions characteristic of that tradition. Catholics tend to create larger, more complex and more widespread institutional presences, especially in health care and social services.

Finally, I want to address briefly the rejection of killing central to Sider's essay. The convergence and divergence of the Catholic and Anabaptist perspectives on war is too large a topic for this brief response. Let me simply state a few points. First, Catholic social teaching strongly opposes the violence inherent in abortion and capital punishment, although its rejection of capital punishment is a recent development of the last twenty years and is not complete. Catholic teaching recognizes extremely rare instances in which the death penalty might be justified. Second, just-war theory is Catholic social teaching's most prominent approach to war. This position is founded on the most difficult question for pacifism: Why is force not a legitimate means to respond to an attack on one's own life or on the life of others, if nonlethal means are not available or effective? Particularly, why should force be unavailable to Christians or non-Christians who are not persuaded by pacifism? Sider does attempt to answer this question, but the mainstream Catholic tradition finds his answers unpersuasive. There are, it believes, frequent conditions in this fallen world where lethal force is justified (police work, for example), and less frequent conditions where, as a last resort and in accordance with strict moral norms, even war's relatively unlimited lethal force can be justified. Just-war theory describes the conditions and the limits of such violence. Third, over the last fifty years Catholic social theory has come to both appreciate and honor Catholics who adopt a pacifist position identical to the Mennonite and to doubt seriously the actual presence in modern global life of conditions that justify warfare. At present, there are a wide variety of Catholic voices debating just-war theory; however, the hierarchy in the United States, in Europe and at the Vatican has come increasingly to regard war as an unjust option except under the most strictly limited circumstances. Wars of preemption, such as the American invasion of Iraq in 2003, could not be approved under most versions of Catholic just-war theory.

Classical Separation Response

Derek H. Davis

I have the greatest respect for Ron Sider. I have always admired his integrity, his collegiality, his compassion for helping those on the margins, his commitment to historic Christianity and his scholarship. He is a model for all persons who try to make a difference for good in the world.

After reading Ron's contribution to this book, my respect was renewed, even enhanced. He makes a strong and passionate case for historic Anabaptist approaches to the relationship between religion and government, which supposedly are grounded in a strong principle of the separation of church and state. But, frankly, he is inconsistent in that his arguments—for pacifism and Charitable Choice—do not measure up to traditional Anabaptist arguments for church-state separation. For example, he makes a good argument for pacifism based on the nonviolence ethic modeled by Christ, but notes that there is no reason to inhibit Christians from putting into practice their pacifist principles in the public sphere, the ultimate result of which would be, if successful, a Bible-based government advocacy of pacifism. This would make the United States a religious state, since it would be implementing theologically based justifications for its policies. The Constitution prohibits this, since it is based on a secular state model not hostile to any theological worldviews but expressly prohibited by the Establishment Clause from adopting any. I am guessing that he would say in this hypothetical scenario that the pacifist position of the United States occurred informally due to the fact that it developed out of the convictions of government officials rather than because the nation is formally a religious state. This is a distinction without a difference. The result would be a government policy built on the religious outlook of officials who "won" the right, probably because they represented the majority viewpoint, to implement their theology in the public sphere. Grounding public policy in any kind of religious worldview is something the Establishment Clause prohibits and the Supreme Court would not hesitate for a second to say so. In other words, Sider wants a soft separation of church and state, one with rather uncertain boundaries.

I think he repeats the same error when he argues that the Bush faith-based initiative, or at least the Charitable Choice aspects of it, illustrates the proper interaction between church and state. I will comment more extensively on this topic.[1] Sider proposes that government be permitted to fund religious organizations, provided it funds programs that are not excessively religious in orientation (secularity principle) and provided all religious organizations are entitled to receive funding alongside their secular counterparts (nondiscrimination principle). In theory, this should be permissible because government is acting "neutrally" toward all groups, religious or nonreligious.

As to the secularity principle, I would suggest that few programs administered by religious groups are not excessively religious, which is as it should be. The reason that religious groups operate these programs, in most cases, is based on theological reasons. They typically believe they are called to carry out in the world a mission of rendering aid to the poor and deprived in our society. They do not look upon their programs as "secular" but rather as an extension of their religious mission. Yet, in order to receive government funding, they are compelled to accept the government rhetoric that only "secular" programs can be funded. These programs cannot be both secular and nonsecular. If religious motivations undergird the funded projects, the government is essentially a religious state, advancing religious aims and programs to achieve its interests. This is not what the Constitution permits, or at least this was what the constitutional prohibition on funding "pervasively sectarian" organizations was intended to prohibit prior to the Bush years. Thus, the secularity principle in Sider's argument pays inadequate respect to the separation of church and state.

Sider's position also violates the nondiscrimination principle he claims that Charitable Choice upholds. Ironically, it is debatable whether the alterations to the American church-state structure demanded by the Charitable Choice concept will achieve their stated objective—the elimination of discrimination against religious groups. In fact, it can be strongly argued that the greatest flaw in Charitable Choice programs is that they simply miss their stated target. Rather than eliminating discrimination against religious groups, they merely rearrange the nature of discrimination, often in favor of majority religions or

---

[1]Much of the argument presented here follows part of Derek H. Davis, "The U.S. Supreme Court as Moral Physician: *Mitchell v. Helms* and the Constitutional Revolution to Reduce Restrictions on Governmental Aid to Religion," *Journal of Church and State* 43 (2001): 213-33.

those groups predisposed to receiving government subsidy. Consider the case of the Jehovah's Witnesses. The Witnesses' denial of the legitimacy of the state and their prohibitions on the involvement of their membership in government activities generally restrict their participation in programs that would be permitted under a neutrality principle. Advocates of neutrality, like Sider, might argue that such exclusions are rare, self-imposed and result from uncoerced acts of conviction. Nevertheless, these arguments simply do not hold.

Under the Charitable Choice scheme, a broad range of social services inevitably will be opened up to potential church-state ventures under the neutrality principle. Religious groups that would fall on the "high participation" end of the continuum likely would include the Eastern Orthodox and Roman Catholic churches, while mainline Protestants and certain minority faiths like the Jehovah's Witnesses would be placed on the "low participation" end. Certain evangelical Christian groups that have moved away from their separationist traditions would fall somewhere in the middle of this hypothetical continuum. Churches undoubtedly will pick and choose to participate in those government programs that are consistent with their beliefs and practices. Roman Catholics would participate heavily in aid to religious education programs but might reject participation in a program that provides funding to churches to provide certain family-planning services. Jehovah's Witnesses and Seventh-day Adventists likely would reject all government aid programs. Some evangelical groups might accept funding to support the operation of soup kitchens while rejecting aid to support child-care centers for working moms. Every religious group in the country would fall somewhere on this continuum of participation under any neutrality scheme, and where those religious institutions fall on this continuum would determine the level of government subsidization of the services they provide. Churches whose doctrine permits extensive participation in government programs have at the very least a financial advantage over those whose faith communities deny such participation.

The point of this construct is to illustrate that participation in the system of government subsidization of religion under the auspices of the neutrality principle is heavily conditioned by the traditions of participant faiths and is likely to result in a very definite and ordered system of discrimination.

There might appear to be no coercion in this pattern of discrimination, but in fact there is. All institutions in the United States, including religious ones, have a strong interest in their own survival. Programs distributing aid under the neutrality principle offer financial inducements for religious groups to participate in certain programs that government desires for the nation and that may or may not conflict with certain tenets of the nation's faith communities. These programs easily can be seen to tempt religious groups to go against their basic principles in order to secure government funding and receive the same benefits of other faith traditions. The key here is that not all issues addressed by such programs will fall into the black and white categories that might be associated with abortion or similar issues. It will be those programs that center on social issues more "in the gray" respecting a faith community's belief system that will begin the erosion, or perhaps more accurately the assimilation, of our nation's religious traditions.

Consider the evangelical community that falls in the middle of this hypothetical continuum of participation and believes that a woman's role is in the home and not in the workplace; therefore, it rejects participation in the childcare program for working moms. However, this community is not impervious to the larger society, and its leaders recognize that there are working mothers among its membership. The community also recognizes that many other churches do participate in this program and receive government subsidies for their participation. Doesn't the very existence of the government aid program for working mothers provide a financial incentive to this evangelical community to drift away from its doctrinal position on the role of women in the family? If it buckles to popular pressure and the government-supplied financial incentive and chooses to participate, after many years of involvement in this program will the members of the community even remember the original position of their tradition regarding this issue?

Consider the possibility of dozens, perhaps hundreds, of government-aid-to-religion programs involving many of the nation's faith traditions projected out over a few decades. One might easily predict the homogenization of America's diverse faith traditions into a form of civil religion that encourages a malleability of doctrine shaped by the designs of government programs. Funding faith communities might appear as a societal good, but in fact it will have the long-term effect of denigrating religion and causing religion to lose its autonomy and identity.

Public resources inevitably will flow to those programs that are popularly affirmed by a majority of the nation to the exclusion of minority faiths. The public never will accept the "nondiscriminatory" allocation of funds to some groups, such as a "Branch Davidian Child Abuse Center" or a program to aid the development of Buddhist missions in the inner cities. It will be the causes that tend toward the center, are noncontroversial and that receive the greatest popular support that will obtain the lion's share of funding from government agencies. Lost in the shuffle will be social issues of importance to minority religions and that have little popular appeal. The result will be substantial funding of programs that attract participation by "acceptable" religions with minority groups left out, an inherently discriminatory situation. The funding of various faith-based programs by the Bush administration bore this out; almost no non-Christian groups ever received any funding. America is better off with a solid commitment to separating government and religious institutions.[2]

[2]I am grateful to Chuck McDaniel, Baylor University, for assistance in preparation of this essay.

Principled Pluralist Response

Corwin Smidt

Rather than repeating certain preliminary points that I wish to make about each of the Christian perspectives examined in this volume, I would urge the reader to read first my opening paragraph of response to the classical separationist perspective (see p. 117). What was said in that paragraph applies also to the Anabaptist perspective.

The Anabaptist perspective is rooted primarily in its particular theological interpretations. While principled pluralists share many theological perspectives with adherents of the Anabaptist perspective, they diverge in their theological perspectives in certain other matters. In terms of the argument presented in the chapter, the primary features of the Anabaptist perspective are those of (1) radical discipleship, (2) the church as counterculture and (3) pacifism. Consequently, each of these features will be addressed in light of the principled pluralist perspective.

As fellow Christians the principled pluralist perspective would agree with the Anabaptists that Christians are called to be disciples of Christ and that the church constitutes an alternative polis or culture. Where differences emerge in these matters tend to be primarily in terms of the "radicalness" of these differences and the issue of what is normative for Christians today. Consider, for example, the matter of congregational life in America today. Like Anabaptists, principled pluralists acknowledge that Jesus and the early church engaged in sweeping economic sharing. Likewise, principled pluralists also acknowledge that any local congregation of believers in Christ is called on to be generous in aiding those in need within their faith community (as well as their neighbors in need who live outside their congregation). But where the two perspectives likely begin to diverge is on the question, what should be the norm for Christians today in terms of their sharing of resources? Are the economic practices of the early church necessarily normative for the practices of the church today? While principled pluralists would hold that our earnings and resources are gifts from God and do not simply belong to us solely as individuals, they are less likely to emphasize living in community and communal sharing of resources as a normative ideal for Christian living today.

Principled pluralists would also agree with Anabaptists that the church constitutes (or should be) a counterculture. However, just what this may involve or represent for principled pluralists may be somewhat different than what it involves or represents for Anabaptists. Certainly, principled pluralists acknowledge, at a minimum, that Christian worship is in essence a political act. Our worship of Jesus Christ as Lord and Savior is a declaration that our ultimate sovereign resides in someone other than the duly selected head of government or state. Our loyalty is given to a different sovereign, a different kingdom, a different people. In worship we gather to be formed as an alternative polis: the people of God. And in worship we proclaim that a new political order is present, though not fully yet realized—namely, the kingdom of God that will someday come in fullness, a fullness to which all kingdoms and republics will submit.

Where the two perspectives are more likely to diverge is on the strategy of cultural and political engagement. Anabaptists insist that "the first and most basic way that Christians shape the larger society is simply by being the church" (p. 174) and that "the church serves the larger society first by living a faithful model of Jesus' new messianic community" (p. 176). It would be incorrect to assert that this perspective reflects an act of "withdrawal" from temporal matters by focusing instead on spiritual matters. After all, Anabaptists do seek to engage society; they simply seek to do so through creating an alternative community. Nevertheless, this act of creating an alternative community does tend to move Christians toward that particular alternative community and away from the larger culture, whereas the principled pluralists are more likely to insist that, after coming together in its countercultural act of worship of our sovereign God, Christians shape the larger society by moving out from congregational worship into service and cultural transformation through Christian vocations, as we seek to serve our Lord and be faithful servants in our various professions and activities within the larger society and culture.

Moreover, because principled pluralists emphasize the creation-fall-redemption narrative, they see all of creation awaiting redemption. The political sphere stands in need of redemption neither no more nor no less than any other sphere of human activity. And it is the belief that God's redemption is at work in this present world that spurs Christians to engage in political activity. God's work in the world is not limited to the confessing church; it is the fact that he is active both within and outside the church that allows principled pluralists to move out from the church into the world in order that they may bring Christ's renewing influence to bear on public life.

But it is with regard to the pacifism, the third characteristic of the Anabaptist perspective, where the greatest differences between principled pluralists and Anabaptists emerge. In some ways, this may be surprising in that nothing discussed in the chapter on principled pluralism directly touches on pacifism. Consequently, the logic of principled pluralism would seemingly allow for pacifism, as there appears to be nothing inherent to principled pluralism that would preclude its adherents from articulating a position of pacifism. Nevertheless, most well-known advocates of principled pluralism today would likely be classified as advocates of the just-war tradition, arguing that governments may use lethal force for just cause (e.g., upholding public security, protecting the innocent), when used only as a means of last resort and when the success of such retributive action appears probable. Just why this may be the case takes us well beyond what can be addressed here. But whatever the reasons, historically these two perspectives have diverged on what may constitute the rightful and just use of force on the part of the state.

Finally, it should also be noted that, while different Christian perspectives may diverge in some very important respects, they may converge, despite such differences, on their approach to particular pieces of legislation. This is a function of several factors. First, while there may be a variety of different Christian perspectives on politics, we are confronted in much of political life with simply a twofold choice—namely, a decision either to favor or oppose a particular piece of legislation or a decision to vote for either candidate A or candidate B (this latter point is particularly true in a two-party system as found in the American context). In the abstract there may be many different positions that Christians might take with regard to addressing an issue of public policy. But when it comes to legislation, such ideas must be translated in a particular bill or proposed law. In that bill may be a variety of provisions, some facets of which one might favor, others one might oppose. But as legislators (and indirectly as voters), one is called on either to pass or defeat such legislation. It is this fact that different kinds of people, advocating different kinds of positions, can come to support (or oppose) together the same piece of legislation that has led to the saying "Politics makes strange bedfellows."

Thus, despite various differences in political perspectives, it is possible for principled pluralists and Anabaptists to stand together politically on many policy proposals, including the favoring of faith-based initiative legislation.

Social Justice Response

J. Philip Wogaman

Ronald Sider has been a significant intellectual force in the evangelical Christian community, and I have long respected his contributions, even at the points of our disagreement. The present article is typical of his work. The heart of this essay is affirmation of the centrality of Jesus Christ for Christians. I would not express this exactly as he has done, but I'm sure we would be in agreement that if you want to understand God, the clearest revelation is in this one person. Jesus' teaching, fully exemplified in his own life, is "radical love." Radical love is therefore what defines the Christian life. That love of Christ is so basic, so radical, that Christians have a terrible time understanding, much less living, it. Who could disagree with Sider that "over the centuries, Christians have found numerous rationalizations for abandoning Jesus' example and moral teaching" (p. 171)? That is sadly true.

The difficulty I have with the Anabaptist position, as expressed here, is in its excessive self-assurance about what radical love means. Sider may be right in criticizing Reinhold Niebuhr for asserting that such love does not work in a fallen world. You could make that case on the basis of Niebuhr's distinction between ideal love and a tolerable justice. But with a little closer attention to definition, couldn't Niebuhr respond that, for the Christian in this fallen world, achieving that tolerable justice is the best way of expressing radical love? Here we have to grapple with the pacifist position of such Anabaptists as Sider and John Howard Yoder. Surely that position has much to commend it, not least including the Sermon on the Mount and Jesus' own obedience to death on the cross as an alternative to violent self-defense or artful escape. Even Niebuhr commends pacifism, although a bit patronizingly, as an important witness about the evils of violence. Niebuhr's view was that while neither church nor state can be fully pacifist, the presence of a few pacifists is a good reminder. I agree with that, although with slightly more respect than Niebuhr could summon.

The true alternative to pacifism, for Christians, is not to treat war or other forms of violence as intrinsically good as the medieval crusades tended to do. The real alternative is the just-war tradition, the very heart of which is *to treat violence as evil, not good.*[1] In that moral tradition we may find military force to be the most loving among the nasty alternatives—or, better put, it may be the least unloving. But responsible Christians place the burden of proof against it. The just-war tradition has developed several difficult tests that violence must meet to pass muster. To speak of this as a possible expression of radical love is to invoke Luther's "strange love." It is, as Paul Tillich writes, following Luther, "the strange work of love to destroy what is against love."[2] As a concrete example, might it possibly have been a work of love for the international community to have intervened militarily in Rwanda and Burundi to stop the Hutu genocide of hundreds of thousands of Tutsis? Sider himself acknowledges that this is a fallen world and that "government is a good gift ordained by God" (p. 176) and that its purpose includes the restraint of evil. He would, however, restrict that function of government to nonviolent forms of incentive and coercion. And, of course, consistent users of the just-war approach always affirm that violence should be a last resort, after every positive method has failed.

I do appreciate that Sider is not approaching this problem as a biblical literalist. If he were to do so, he would have to take the violence of Armageddon in Revelation into account—not to mention the almost genocidal conflicts touched on in the Old Testament. I join Sider in seeking a grounding for Christian ethics that is deeper than biblical literalism. Whether consciously or unconsciously, every Christian who takes the Bible seriously must determine which parts are more basic than others. I find my own sense of that rather close to Sider's, although I probably make more use of the epistles of Paul than does Sider. Even with Paul's indispensable presentations of our shared faith, we must distinguish between what is deep and timeless and what is a response to particular problems of the first century, partly written also on the basis of first-century perceptions of factual reality. We can all differ as we sort this out, but it is very important for Christians of our time to ground ourselves in the deeper faith perspectives as we seek to address a quite different factual situation.

With that in mind, I cannot quite agree with Sider on his brief comments on gay marriage. That issue has proved to be as divisive in the churches, includ-

---

[1] Many ethicists who identify with the just-war tradition prefer to speak of it as the "justified war" tradition. The word *just* suggests there is something positively good about war, while *justified* conveys that under extremely limited circumstances war may be the most acceptable alternative.

[2] See Paul Tillich, *Love, Power, and Justice* (New York: Oxford University Press, 1954), p. 49.

ing the mainline denominations and secular society. When Sider appeals to long tradition on this issue, some of us may find ourselves more counter-cultural than him! In part, this may come down to the not-yet-fully resolved question of why some people are homosexual rather than heterosexual in orientation. This is one of those points where facts matter, even though there continues to be disagreement about the facts, although there seems to be increasing evidence that sexual orientation really is not often a matter of choice. In any event, given the fact that there are and will continue to be numbers of gay and lesbian people, isn't it better to encourage them to be in committed monogamous relationships than to practice a promiscuous lifestyle? I didn't always hold such views, but becoming acquainted with numbers of gay and lesbian persons in long-standing committed relationships of this kind has forced me to revise my thinking. Today, both within and beyond the churches, there is a certain stigma attached to gay and lesbian people, and I am reminded that our Lord did not hesitate to associate himself with stigmatized people.

There is much in the Anabaptist ecclesiology that I find attractive. It seeks to foster a thoroughly Christian community as a beautiful example to the rest of the world of how Christian faith and life is a huge improvement over so much in the rest of culture. Insofar as communities in the Anabaptist tradition truly live this out, we can only respect them. I have noted questions about some of the views associated with this, but any community of faith formed by the grace of Jesus Christ and witnessing to that in a broken world is authentically Christian. I do not sense in Sider's portrayal of this tradition that he judges other views of the church as un-Christian. In Ernst Troeltsch's classic *Social Teachings of the Christian Churches*, the German scholar distinguishes between what he called the "church-type" and the "sect-type."[3] The former is an ideal state in which the church is inclusive of the whole civilization—best exemplified, perhaps, in medieval Christianity. The sect type is based on withdrawal from the world by true, believing Christians whose life is in total contrast with the fallen world. There is no perfect example of either, but these are tendencies in the different ways we view the church. Sider would fall more on the sect type side, although I don't find in his writing a total rejection of the world outside the church.

That said, however, the risk in the Anabaptist tradition is that one will overstate the faithfulness of Christians in the believing community—which contin-

---

[3]Ernst Troeltsch, *The Social Teaching of the Christian Churches,* trans. Olive Wyon (New York: Macmillan, 1931). This two-volume work is now published in English by Westminster John Knox Press.

ues to be made up of sinners, while understating the extent to which God is at work in the world beyond the church. Take Gandhi, for instance. He continued to be a Hindu until his death, but he was deeply influenced by his reading of the New Testament and, indirectly, by nineteenth-century New England Quakers. His views on violence were virtually indistinguishable from those Sider has outlined. A sectarian conception of the church risks being too judgmental, just as Troeltsch's "church type" risks diluting the gospel with too much world.

Troeltsch's insight was to show that our conception of society as a whole is already contained in our view of the church. If society outside the church is simply evil, then the sectarian approach makes sense. Otherwise, we can be more affirmative about the larger society—including the world society—of which the church is a part. The mainline churches and most evangelicals tend toward the latter. So, actually, does Sider as he writes positively about the role of government. The state, of which government is chief institution, includes all of us. We all have a real stake in its being democratic in constitution and practice. We recognize our responsibility, as citizens, to participate in political decisions that are compatible with God's loving purposes for the world. And we respect the rights of people who disagree with us.

5   The Social Justice Perspective

J. Philip Wogaman

I have been asked to interpret the attitude, typical of mainline churches and councils of churches, that social justice should be promoted by churches in and through public policy. I undertake this task cheerfully, since I have been studying and participating in this form of ministry for most of my adult life. Nevertheless, we must be wary of stereotypes and generalizations. The different church bodies present a great diversity of viewpoints. Often particular issues give rise to heated controversy within and among denominations, and there are many within each of the mainline churches who consider public policy to be none of the church's business. Even the term *mainline* is highly problematical, particularly insofar as that it is taken as a value judgment that some churches are more acceptable or respectable in our society than others. For present purposes I use the term only to refer to most of the churches currently belonging to the National Council of Churches or World Council of Churches, such as United Methodist, Presbyterian Church (U.S.A.), Episcopalian, Disciples, American Baptist, National Baptist, United Church of Christ, Evangelical Lutheran Church of American and Reformed Church of America. While not a member of either the National or World councils of churches, the Roman Catholic Church would certainly have to be included among the mainline churches, which are broadly committed to the social justice model.

I must also acknowledge at the outset that my interpretation of this model might not be shared by many who find the model appealing but understand it differently. Still, I hope this interpretation will lead others to think about the subject more deeply, even if they have reservations about my way of dealing with it.

The State as Expressing the Community as a Whole

Since the social justice model advocates a large role for the state, we need to understand what the state is. Elsewhere, I have sought to define the state as "society acting as a whole."[1] That does not mean that everything that happens within a given society is an expression of the state, for most of the time society is not "acting as a whole." Nor does it mean that everybody within a society concurs in actions of state. The point is that everybody is a participant in actions of the state whether they like it or not. I can find things to agree with and to disagree with in the federal budget, and yet my tax dollars are used even for activities I find reprehensible. I recently wrote an article seriously questioning an expensive U.S. military venture (on the basis of my understanding of the Christian just-war tradition), and yet my tax dollars (including a small payment I received for writing the article) helped to finance that very undertaking. To be sure, I didn't like it, but for good or ill the military action went ahead, and like it or not, I was included in supporting it. That would have been true even if my income was so low I didn't have to pay taxes. Why? Because anything I do that adds to the national economy strengthens the resource base for actions taken by the state. That may even be true in a noneconomic sense: anything I do that helps to sustain the nation's institutions, including its churches, contributes to the sociocultural fabric of the society and, at least indirectly, to the effectiveness of actions taken by the nation.

The broad implication of this understanding of the state, for Christians, is that there is no privileged zone of innocence into which one can retreat to avoid participation in what we perceive to be the evils of the state. We're all there already, like it or not. I can think of only two exceptions to this: either by leaving the country or by going to jail (or otherwise becoming a ward of the state).

So, for most of us, it may come down to whether we will be passive participants in what the state is doing or actively seeking to shape the directions of its policies toward ends we consider to be in harmony with Christian conscience. The beauty of a democratic country is that, whatever its flaws, it affords opportunity to be a participating citizen and not simply a passive subject.[2] What are Christians and their churches to make of that opportunity?

---

[1]J. Philip Wogaman, *Christian Perspectives on Politics*, rev. ed. (Louisville: Westminster John Knox Press, 2000), p. 15. To this I added the phrase "with the ultimate power to compel compliance within its own jurisdiction." Many thinkers, including Martin Luther and the social theorist Max Weber, emphasize the state's monopoly on the use of force. We should, however, be cautious in regarding the use of force as what finally defines the state. The possible use of force is always implicit in the state, but no state could long exist without some measure of voluntary compliance with law.

[2]The tragedy of a totalitarian state is that people are doing what the state is doing, but without having a voice or a vote. Still, I find it interesting that even in a totalitarian dictatorship the tyrant or elite at the top must cultivate at least *some* degree of public support. That is generally assured by an artful mixture of fear and favors.

Values and Public Policy Formation

Do values make a difference in public policy formation? Obviously they do, but the point must be understood more carefully. Except for sheer accidents, the actions of state express purposes that, in turn, reflect the values of decision makers. Sometimes a given policy or action represents a convergence of very different values, held by different people, all of which may be advanced by the policy or action. Political power flows from the appeal of the values held by people.[3]

No less a thinker than Niccolò Machiavelli made the point. In *The Prince*, Machiavelli counsels that a political leader must of all things *appear* to be *religious*. Machiavelli was cynical enough not to take religion too seriously, and he counsels the prince to be prepared to set religion aside when needful. But why would he want to mention religion in the first place? Clearly it is because the people care about it, and if you want to influence the people, you had best give at least lip service to *their* values! Sometimes political theorists hold that most political behavior is determined by economics, with people, for example, always voting their pocketbooks regardless of their purported ideals. Machiavelli, whose reputation for cynicism seems well earned, at least understood that people can be influenced by values other than material self-interest, even by their religious faith.

The political truth I wish to underscore is that *anything that is actually valued by people is potentially a source of influence and therefore of political power*. Thus, a typical American presidential campaign will have components aimed at particular segments of the public—business, labor, farmers, veterans, educators, ethnic minorities, the elderly and so on. Some of this involves appeal to the economic self-interest of the different segments, but not all. For instance, those who are most deeply concerned about the abortion issue—either from the prolife or prochoice perspective—will be influenced by where a candidate or political party seems to stand on that issue, quite apart from considerations of economic self-interest. Those who are most influenced by the National Rifle Association make the point quite well indeed, while reminding us that a single-issue group can be passionate in its support of a very limited range of values.[4]

---

[3]See also the discussion of political power as influence over the will of people in Franz Neumann, *The Democratic and the Authoritarian State* (New York: Free Press, 1957), p. 3.
[4]I had an excellent opportunity to observe firsthand how presidential campaigns "target" particular audiences during the campaign of 1968. As one of the managers of the "religion" component of the Humphrey-Muskie campaign that year, my desk was surrounded by similar desks of other, very different, segments of the campaign, including farmers, labor, business and veterans. While not an active participant in subsequent presidential campaigns, I have observed that this is typical of all of the Republican and Democratic Party campaigns.

How then are we to relate this understanding of political power (as appeal to the values held by people) to our understanding of the state as society acting as a whole? I believe it is through another very important political concept, that of *legitimacy*. When the state is accepted by its people as *legitimate*—basically in accord with their overall system of values and beliefs—they will go along with its specific actions, even when they do not agree with them. I have already written about my opposition to a recent American military action, but notwithstanding that, I accept the overall legitimacy of the democratic state of which I am a citizen. The concept of legitimacy is tested more rigorously in oppressive countries where most of the people *do not* accept the moral values represented by the state. Even there, the values of safety and harmony can supersede everything else. People will go along because they feel the consequences of not doing so are just too grim. That is a very fragile kind of legitimacy, but it can be enough to sustain a "society acting as a whole" for a limited period of time.

Conceptions of legitimacy have varied widely over the two millennia of Christian history. Thomas Aquinas or Martin Luther could not conceive of anything other than authoritarian rule by a king or prince, nor would the common people of the medieval world have given a second thought to a democratic alternative. The king was king by the grace of God, thank you, and obedience to God implied obedience to the king. The king was also subject to God's rule, of course, and his exercise of power would be accountable to the awful judgment of God. But that did not set aside the legitimacy of his rule. Only in some of the writings of John Calvin do we begin to get a hint that an oppressive prince could possibly be removed from power. But, largely in countries influenced by Calvinism, more democratic conceptions of legitimacy began to flourish.[5]

The Theological Basis for Social Justice
Aristotle famously spoke of justice as "rendering to each his due." That simple definition begs the question, of course, since it doesn't tell us what *is* due to each person. Retributive theories of justice provide the simplest answers: people should get what they deserve. The biblical (Old Testament) conception of "eye for eye" and "tooth for tooth" (Ex 21:23-24) conveys the idea. If you destroy somebody else's eye, you deserve to lose the sight of your own eye—similarly with a tooth or, in the case of murder, with a life. If you murder some-

---

[5]See James Hastings Nichols, *Democracy and the Churches* (Philadelphia: Westminster Press, 1951).

body else, you deserve to die.[6] When victims of crimes (including surviving loved ones) insist on justice, that is what they generally mean. We can understand that theory of justice perfectly well, even though Christians then have to come to terms with Jesus' own response: "You have heard that it was said, 'An eye for an eye and a tooth for a tooth.' But I say to you, Do not resist an evildoer" (Mt 5:38-39). While speaking of that, Jesus also seems to modify the idea that people should simply get what they deserve by reminding us that God's sunshine and rain are given to the righteous and the unrighteous alike.

Economic attitudes are also greatly shaped by the notion of deserving. From the time of John Locke, property has often been understood as what people have because they made it or were given it by those who made it. In his *Second Treatise on Civil Government,* Locke speaks of property as rightfully belonging to those who have created something by mixing their labor with the state of nature, thus withdrawing some product from its natural state. Greatly influenced by the experience of English colonists in seventeenth-century North America, Locke could envision the hard physical labor of a colonist in creating a farm by clearing the land. The farm should be his, by right, since he made it. And it should be his to sell or to pass on to his heirs, who then rightfully own it. Economic libertarians, such as Ayn Rand and Robert Nozick, are essentially relying on this theory of economic justice. They believe that government has no right to take (steal) the property of people who have earned it in order to give it (e.g., through welfare programs) to people who have not earned it. Practically speaking, of course, it is increasingly difficult to trace out who has made what under the conditions of modern invention and production. Even Locke's illustration of the North American wilderness breaks down, at least to some extent, if one remembers that the forests were "owned" by the Native Americans for use in hunting, fishing and simple agriculture. Most modern production is so thoroughly social in character, with complex divisions of labor, organized worldwide, that the primitive "right" of property, in accordance with Locke's theory, is extremely elusive. Even intellectual or artistic property can be highly dependent on unacknowledged sources and influences.

But the deeper challenge to these simple understandings of justice is theological. What is "due" to everyone in Christian theological perspective? Given the biblical understanding that we are all sinners, the answer to that question

---

[6]The philosopher Walter Berns puts it bluntly: "A just society is one where everyone gets what he deserves, and the wicked deserve to be punished—they deserve 'many sorrows,' as the Psalmist says" (*For Capital Punishment: Crime and the Morality of the Death Penalty* [New York: Basic Books, 1979], p. 147).

may well be that we all *deserve* divine retribution! The apostle Paul is most conscious of that—he who persecuted Christians, even participating in the assassination of Stephen. Yet he, sinner though he was, received a full measure of God's grace. Did he "deserve" it? Hardly. But it was God's will to bring him, through Christ, into right relationship with God and other people. That was *grace* at work.

Jesus' little story of the hiring practice of the owner of a vineyard can be taken as a kind of parable about grace. In the parable (Mt 20:1-16), the owner hired different workers at different times during the day. But despite the fact that some worked all day and some for only an hour, he gave them all exactly the same wage. The parable was possibly intended to illustrate how Gentiles, despite their much later entry into God's covenant than the Jews, still were to be included in the same way. But that was God's grace at work, not a theology based on deserving.

Is this relevant to a theory of social justice?

In a certain basic sense it clearly is. What is "due" to every person, by God's own undeserved gift, is to be included in God's intended community of the covenant. To be *included*, to *belong*. We can readily understand this in family terms. When we are "family," we are accepted by others, and the conditions enabling us to belong are attended to. Something of that is suggested by Robert Frost's famous comment that "home is where, when you have to go there, they have to take you in." Is it like that in God's intended community?

A possible objection is that since we are sinners, alienated from God by the reality of original sin, we cannot be accepted until we accept God—that is, until we repent and seek the forgiveness and grace that will then be freely given. Thus, it can be argued, it is premature to think of everybody's being a member of a divinely established community or "family" of humankind since there are people who have not themselves accepted either God or that community. It is, after all, not unheard of for people to become alienated from ordinary human families. Home may be where they have to take you in, but first you've got to want to go there!

But then there is a whole lot of scriptural emphasis on God taking the initiative. Jesus persistently refers to God as "Father," suggesting that such an intimate, caring relationship is the underlying reality. We can run away from it, *but God does not run away from it!* The parable of the prodigal son conveys that God has never ceased to love the wayward, even before the prodigal has come to his senses. Similarly, the parable of the lost sheep depicts a love so great that God will not cease to go after that one-in-a-hundred sheep until it is found and restored. I do not think such teachings of Jesus, and Paul's emphasis upon grace, leaves much room for a limited view of God's love. We are given the freedom to reject God, but like the "hound of heaven," we can expect God to pursue us relentlessly.

These theological points do not settle all the difficult questions of social justice, but they put those questions in deeper perspective. Social justice is not a merely "sociological" concept. If it is anything at all, it is based on the very fundamentals of our faith.

Social Justice as Participation

Does *justice*, for Christians, have to be preceded by the adjective *social?* Is there any difference between justice and social justice?

Perhaps not. But since justice is so often taken in the narrower, more individualistic sense of giving people what they earn or deserve, the adjective *social* is a reminder that justice is about community. It is a constant reminder to us that we are not just individuals engaged in a constant competition for power, wealth and prestige; we truly belong to one another because we first belong to God. Aristotle was right in referring to human beings as "social" or "political" animals, an insight that to be only an isolated individual is not to be fully human. It can be added, and Aristotle's whole philosophy assumes this, that to be social is also to be fully an individual. We are both individual and social by nature. If our individuality is reduced to our only being a unit of a social whole, then that means we are not even, in a real sense, social at all. Similarly, if society is treated only as a collection of individualistic monads, then we are not fully individual persons either. Thus, to be a real person is to be both individual and social. I believe that is implied by Aristotle's writings on ethics and society, and if it is not, it should be! It is a pity he did not yet understand all of this in deeper theological terms.

Nevertheless, to grasp that we are social by nature can help us see what it really means to speak of justice as rendering to each of us what is our "due." What is due to each person is for it to be possible to be, fully and actively, a social being, a member of the community. In an insightful 1986 pastoral letter, the National Conference of Catholic Bishops phrased the matter in this way: "Social justice implies that persons have an obligation to be active and productive participants in the life of society and that society has a duty to enable them to participate this way."[7] Underscoring the point, the bishops add:

Basic justice demands the establishment of minimum levels of participation in

---

[7]*Economic Justice for All: Pastoral Letter on Catholic Social Teaching and the U.S. Economy* (Washington, D.C.: National Conference of Catholic Bishops, 1986), p. 36.

the life of the human community for all persons. The ultimate injustice is for a person or group to be treated actively or abandoned passively as if they were nonmembers of the human race. To treat people this way is effectively to say that they simply do not count as human beings. This can take many forms, all of which can be described as varieties of marginalization, or exclusion from social life. This exclusion can occur in the political sphere: restriction of free speech, concentration of power in the hands of a few, or outright repression by the state. It can also take economic forms that are equally harmful. . . . The poor, the disabled, and the unemployed too often are simply left behind.[8]

Much of the social justice model, as articulated by denominations and councils of churches, is based on this kind of understanding.

One of the more interesting formulations of this was by the First Assembly of the World Council of Churches (Amsterdam, 1948). That assembly included some of the most formidable theologians of the twentieth century, such as Karl Barth, Reinhold Niebuhr, M. M. Thomas and Hendrik Kraemer. In its message to the churches of the world, the assembly declared that

We have to remind ourselves and all men that God has put down the mighty from their seats and exalted the humble and meek. We have to learn afresh together to speak boldly in Christ's name both to those in power and to the people, to oppose terror, cruelty and race discrimination, to stand by the outcast, the prisoner and the refugee. We have to make of the Church in every place a voice for those who have no voice, and a home where every man will be at home. . . . We have to ask God to teach us together to say No and to say Yes in truth. No to all that flouts the love of Christ, to every system, every programme and every person that treats any man as though he were an irresponsible thing or a means of profit, to the defenders of injustice in the name of order, to those who sow the seeds of war or urge war as inevitable; Yes, to all that conforms to the love of Christ, to all who seek for justice, to the peacemakers, to all who hope, fight and suffer for the cause of man, to all who—even without knowing it—look for new heavens and a new earth wherein dwelleth righteousness.[9]

In concluding the message, the assembly makes clear that in this fallen world in which "it is not in man's power to banish sin and death" we cannot expect perfect justice and righteousness. Nevertheless, God "has given us at

---

[8]Ibid., p. 39.
[9]World Council of Churches, *Man's Disorder and God's Design: The Amsterdam Assembly Series* (New York: Harper & Brothers, 1948), the unnumbered "Message" is at the end of this volume. Typical of writings in that period, generic male pronouns refer to persons of both genders.

Easter the certainty that His purpose will be accomplished" and "by our acts of obedience and faith, we can on earth set up signs which point to the coming victory." The eloquent call to the churches to be "a voice for those who have no voice, and a home where every man will be at home" is a reminder that one does not have to choose between advocacy on behalf of social justice and efforts by the churches to provide direct aid. It is also an early reminder that marginalized people should not be patronized by the church but treated with human dignity and respect. They should be affirmed in their God-given rightful place of participation in the human community.

Social Justice, Liberation Theology and Marxism

For a decade or two, commencing in the late 1960s, various forms of liberation theology captivated the attention of many in the mainline churches and ecumenical movements who were attentive to social justice issues. The movement was mostly Latin American in origin,[10] but the liberation motif was quickly associated with various forms of black theology (as illustrated by the writings of James Cone) and feminist theology (whose principal theological voice was probably Rosemary Radford Ruether). In various ways the liberation theme made use of the biblical Exodus as a metaphor for God's engagement with humanity in liberating the captives and the oppressed from inhuman systems of dominance. In Latin America, this was from forms of economic peonage, while in the United States it was liberation of African Americans from the continued realities of racial oppression and of women from sociocultural systems of male dominance.

While liberation theology has undoubtedly had some influence in the mainline churches and ecumenical movements, it was never (in my judgment) the dominant theological framework out of which the churches taught and acted. In a general sense the churches have emphasized the urgency of liberating the oppressed—including the economically exploited, the racially oppressed and those who have been "put down" and exploited by male dominance. More recently, churches have begun to pay attention to the sociocultural constraints arising from sexual orientation.

But with the passage of time, mainstream churches have come to perceive

---

[10]Gustavo Gutiérrez's *A Theology of Liberation: History, Politics and Salvation* (Maryknoll, N.Y.: Orbis, 1973) was arguably the most formative of the movement's early writings, with books by other Latin American theologians such as Juan Luis Segundo, José Miguez Bonino and Hugo Assmann also making important contributions. Persistent economic and political oppression in many of the Latin American countries provided a seedbed for the radical sociopolitical analysis represented by these theologians.

some of the blind spots of the more radical versions of liberation theology. For instance, when sin and evil are portrayed exclusively as institutional problems and liberation is understood entirely as overcoming oppressive structures, it is easy to forget that sin is also, even primarily, a spiritual condition. The flaw in much individualistic pietism has been to overlook corporate evils, but there can be a corresponding flaw on the other side when the sinfulness of the human heart is forgotten. Ironically, the two contrasting flaws can be mutually reinforcing. Institutional evils can have spiritual effects, but personal sinfulness can complicate efforts at social reform.

Thus liberation theologies, with flourishes of revolutionary rhetoric, could so easily overlook the sinfulness of the revolutionaries themselves. So the question has to be posed, after the revolution, after the liberation, who is going to rule? Can it be assumed that the liberators are incapable, despite their own sinfulness, of becoming oppressors themselves? Earlier writings by Gustavo Gutiérrez and José Miguez Bonino neglected such questions. A number of liberation theologians sought to expose the hypocrisies of democratic institutions, considering democracy to be a façade for selfish economic interests. But, of course, revolutions can also be a façade for the power interests of their own elites—Joseph Stalin is one especially egregious illustration of that danger. A chastened liberation theology needed to face more directly the question how a postliberation world would be structured. The neglect of such a question has its roots in an inadequate understanding of human sinfulness. Later writings by Gutiérrez and Miguez Bonino came to terms with these questions much more directly.

Sometimes the churches, in their efforts at social reform, have been characterized as Marxist or socialist. Indeed, some church leaders have obviously been influenced by aspects of socialist theory. But it would not be accurate to describe mainstream church social action as being committed to socialism. More often, economic pronouncements presuppose a largely capitalist economic order while insisting on governmental actions to regulate business and industry and to tax part of the wealth created by the market system for social goods (like schools, parks, highways, etc.) and to assist people who have been left behind. That is not full-blown socialism, and it is certainly not Marxism. On the whole, churches and the ecumenical movement have distanced themselves from Marxism, both because of its atheism and its inadequate understanding of the roots of evil.

In balance, liberation theology has increased Christian awareness of the importance of overcoming oppressive systems and institutions but without being seen as the all-encompassing basis for Christian thought on issues of social justice.[11] Other theological tendencies, including thought about the doctrine of creation, have also played an important role.

Social Justice and the Doctrine of Creation

One of the persisting conundrums in Christian social teaching is how to treat the externals, such as laws and institutions and material goods. Often such teaching implies that these externals are ultimate in their significance, but this gives rise to the criticism that the spiritual gospel has been replaced by some form or other of materialism. Insofar as the externals are given ultimate status, that is a fair criticism. Indirectly, at least, it has become a form of idolatry—making a god out of something that is less than God.

On the other hand, it has long been recognized by theologians and the churches that the gospel is not just "spiritual." Indeed, such spiritualism was one of the first teachings to be regarded as heresy. In its early form that heresy was to regard Jesus Christ as only appearing to be a real, live, physically present human being who was actually born, lived, suffered and died. In that early form, docetism taught that Christ only appeared to be physical, as the etymology of the Greek root of *docetism* suggests. Early forms of this spiritualism even suggested that the whole physical world was not created by the "God and Father of our Lord Jesus Christ" but by some alien demiurge. Thus the material world is itself the source of sin and a faithful response to Christ is to detach ourselves from this world. Some scriptural rhetoric may have conveyed that impression to those, like the second-century Marcion, who thought of the world in such radically negative terms, although this impression is surely a misinterpretation. Upon reflection, Christians were not about to jettison the book of Genesis, nor to reject the words of Psalm 24:1 that "the earth is the LORD's and all that is in it, / the world, and those who live in it."

Two twentieth-century theologians have been especially helpful in resolving the problem of how to relate the spiritual to the physical. The first of these, Karl Barth, explored the Christian doctrine of creation in the massive volume four of his *Church Dogmatics*. Referring to *creation* as everything tangible that has its ultimate origin from God and *covenant* as the relationship we have with God, Barth put it this way:

> Creation is the external—and only the external—basis of the covenant. It can be said that it makes it technically possible; that it prepares and establishes the sphere in which the institution and history of the covenant takes place; that it

---

[11]I have dealt with liberation theology and Marxism more extensively in a number of my other writings. See especially J. Philip Wogaman, *Christian Perspectives on Politics*, pp. 79-101.

makes possible the subject which is to be God's partner in this history, in short the nature which the grace of God is to adopt and to which it is to turn in this history.[12]

In a pithy summary of his whole doctrine of creation, Barth speaks of "creation as the external basis of the covenant" and "covenant as the internal basis of creation." All of those tangible aspects of existence that we understand to be God's creation are good, but their goodness is a means to an end, not an end in themselves. The intrinsic good, which is served by the externals of creation, is the covenant. Material or institutional realities *serve* the ultimate good; they are not themselves ultimate.

The other theologian whose work helps us to see this is Dietrich Bonhoeffer. His *Ethics*, largely formulated in prison before his execution by the Nazis, refers to the relationship between the "ultimate" and the "penultimate." He writes:

> What is this penultimate? It is everything that precedes the ultimate, everything that precedes the justification of the sinner by grace alone, everything which is to be regarded as leading up to the last thing when the last thing has been found. . . . For the sake of the ultimate the penultimate must be preserved. Any arbitrary destruction of the penultimate will do serious injury to the ultimate. If, for example, a human life is deprived of the conditions which are proper to it, then the justification of such a life by grace and faith, if it is not rendered impossible, is at least seriously impeded. . . .
>
> The hungry man needs bread, and the homeless man needs a roof; the dispossessed need justice and the lonely need fellowship; the undisciplined need order and the slave needs freedom. To allow the hungry man to remain hungry would be blasphemy against God and one's neighbour.[13]

Both of these thinkers thus help us see why material questions are terribly important. They can either facilitate life as God has intended it or they can get in the way—they can help or hinder. It is not as though the creation or manipulation of external circumstances will cause the life of the spirit to flourish. Even under the best of conditions, people can continue to reject God and remain as mean as ever, while under highly unfavorable conditions it can still be possible for heroic spirits to keep the faith, both to God and to fellow humanity. Still, the external conditions can make a difference, and many of the churches' teachings on social justice seek to illuminate their implications.

---

[12]Karl Barth, *Church Dogmatics*, 3/I (Edinburgh: T & T Clark, 1957), p. 97.
[13]Dietrich Bonhoeffer, *Ethics* (New York: Macmillan, 1955), pp. 134, 137.

The Relationship Between Moral Teachings and Factual Realities

Before turning to some actual church teaching concerning social justice, I wish to clarify one other often-misunderstood relationship. Sometimes it is alleged, against such teaching, that it substitutes sociology or some other science for the gospel. That is always possible, of course, when some science is taken to provide the ultimate values by which we live, thus usurping the place of religion. Such a use of science has been labeled "scientism," transforming the legitimate quest for ordered knowledge about factual realities into an overarching theory of what is ultimately good and true. In the history of ethics that is an instance of what G. E. Moore described as the "naturalistic fallacy,"[14] which is the fallacy of assuming that things that exist are necessarily good. Social practices or institutions, faithfully and accurately described by the social sciences, may be bad and not good. There can really be a difference between the "normative" of what is good and right and the "empirical" of what exists factually. Isn't the gulf between what is and what ought to be quite routinely encountered in human life on this planet?

But that does not mean that normative thinking can dispense with empirical sources of knowledge. If the gospel has anything to do with the real world, it cannot ignore what can be known about the world. Our sources of knowledge are many and varied, some gained through personal experience, some through the gathered wisdom of the ages, passed down from generation to generation, and some through systematic study. The sciences, when not engaged in the pretenses of scientism, are in the latter category. They are systematic examinations of available data. Through science, we know much more about the cosmos than our forebears did, including that this is not a flat earth and that there are hundreds of trillions of stars. We also know more about matter and energy, enough to know that there is much more that we do not know. Our grasp of nonhuman life forms and of the genetic building blocks of all life provides both insight and a profound sense of wonder. The social sciences—sociology, anthropology, economics, social psychology—provide greater insight into how people characteristically behave. It is not that these sciences diminish our sense of freedom and the miracle of transcendent human consciousness; it is that we better understand the social and material context in which we live and act as human beings.

An illustration: For decades, even after the American Civil War, many well-

---

[14]G. E. Moore, *Principia Ethica* (Cambridge: Cambridge University Press, 1902). I have written of this more extensively in J. Philip Wogaman, *Christian Moral Judgment* (Louisville: Westminster John Knox Press, 1989), esp. pp. 11-17.

meaning Christians thought of "the Negro" as intellectually inferior to white people. They should be loved and cared for, it was thought, but it was no favor to them to have equal expectations about them, for they were not equally endowed. It was probably in their best interests, it was thought, for them to be segregated socially, even for their own good. I recall reading the words of a highly respected Methodist theologian to a 1936 conference that God had created the races separate and intended that they be kept separate. I also read the words of a Methodist bishop, in a private letter during that period, in which he wrote that he had always thought of "the Negro" as being "pre-Adamic"— the chilling thought that while white people were created by God with Adam, the colored races were part of the evolution of nonhuman life forms preceding the creation of real human beings. Admittedly, his was an extreme form of principled racism, but it illustrates the point that for a very long time even respected leaders regarded persons of other races as inescapably inferior.

But such racist notions, notwithstanding their long histories, were blown apart by careful social and biological studies during the first half of the twentieth century. Genetic studies and systematic examination of cultural influences made clear that unequal treatment is what creates the perceptions of intellectual inequality. Deprived of educational equality, people will not function as educational equals! Most interesting, the biological analysis of genetics has shown beyond dispute that even the concept of race itself has little biological support. Race is a social construct, based on socially designated physical features, but the genetic background of those selected features does not correlate with any other genetic properties. For instance, many people native to the Indian subcontinent have darker skin color than many Africans, but they also vary genetically in other ways. Such studies—and many more— mean that it is no longer possible to think of race in the way our forebears did, and that has immense ethical consequences.

Another illustration: the social psychologist Solomon Asch was interested in why people tend to conform to their groups in decision making. So he structured experiments in which everybody except the hapless subject of the experiment arranged to give the same wrong answer to a question—such as the length of a stick. The subject would squirm nervously but, in the end, usually agree with that wrong answer. However, if just one other person in the group gave the right answer, the subject was free to do the same.[15] That kind of socio-

---

[15]Solomon E. Asch, "Effects of Group Pressure upon the Modification and Distortion of Judgments," in *Readings in Social Psychology*, ed. Eleanor E. Maccoby et. al., 3rd ed. (New York: Henry Holt, 1958).

logical research does not mean that people lack the freedom to dissent, but it helps us understand the immense pressure we feel when we see things differently from those whose acceptance and approval we value. And it helps us understand the importance of "speaking out" as a way of freeing up others who may actually agree with us but who are afraid to express themselves without some visible human support.

To repeat: empirical studies, including the sciences, do not provide the ultimate values by which we live, but they do help to illuminate the factual world in which we live out the implications of the gospel. Thus church teachings about social justice have to attend to such sources of information, even though those teachings are grounded theologically.

Who Speaks for the Church?

In *Who Speaks for the Church?* ethicist Paul Ramsey criticized the World Council of Churches for issuing specific ethical teachings at the World Conference on Church and Society, Geneva, 1966.[16] While largely exercised by that conference's opposition to the war in Vietnam, Ramsey raised serious questions about the constitution of church bodies making pronouncements (who is and is not present to deliberate and issue the statements) and about the propriety of a church body advocating or condemning particular policies of governmental decision makers. Ramsey was not opposed to all such church statements; he decried their frequent lack of awareness of the moral dilemmas faced by decision makers, their ignoring of alternative options and the fact that persons with relevant practical expertise were so often not invited to participate in their formulation.

Such points are not unimportant. Insofar as declarations speak about what are taken to be social justice issues, their factual basis must be accurate and the connections between the factual situation and Christian faith must be clearly drawn. Moreover, Ramsey's point about the church's need to include persons with relevant practical expertise is well-taken. Large denominations and their councils of churches have, within their membership, many such persons with practical expertise on any imaginable question.

Of course, the fact that a church member has great practical competence does not necessarily mean that he or she is making the connections between practical experience and Christian faith. People are quite capable of compartmentalizing their church life and their secular experience, consciously or un-

---

[16]Paul Ramsey, *Who Speaks for the Church? A Critique of the 1966 Geneva Conference on Church and Society* (Nashville: Abingdon, 1967).

consciously keeping the two separate. Just as a theologian cannot legitimately address a social issue solely on theological grounds that ignore the facts, so a factual expert cannot relevantly offer a Christian moral judgment solely on the basis of fact and without consideration of the faith. It can be a wonderful thing when the two are deeply harmonized.[17]

When it is alleged that church leaders are not speaking for the church on an issue where many if not most church members are thought to hold different views, it is sometimes forgotten that church members (at the grass roots) do not always think about such things on the basis of the faith they profess. Most of the mainline Protestant denominations have largely democratic procedures for choosing church leaders and spokespersons. But always there lurks in the background the question of how faithfully such leaders represent and articulate the deep faith of the church. Nobody is perfect in that regard, and all are also subject to secular viewpoints and cultural prejudices of the times. But those who have been chosen to represent the church cannot exercise that responsibility simply by taking superficial opinion polls of church membership. They are not only representing the church membership; in a more fundamental sense they seek to represent the mind of Christ, the will of God. The fact that this cannot always or even generally be done perfectly does not mean that it is not their responsibility to try. Most human endeavors, even by the most faithful of Christians, fall short of the mark. But trusting in the grace of God and the correcting work of God through successive generations in the church, it is possible to proceed.

Learning from failure. Over time the church even learns from its failures. A notable example of this may well be the Prohibition movement. The advocacy by several Protestant denominations of a constitutional amendment and laws prohibiting the sale of alcoholic beverages was an outgrowth of real experience in frontier America. The churches were facing up to the tragedies of lives broken by alcoholism, families neglected and brutalized by drunkenness, violence in and about saloons, and so on. The desire to be rid of these evils once and for all was thus borne out of real human compassion for people caught up in immense tragedies. In retrospect it is easy to see how alcoholism was as

---

[17]An illustration of this occurred at the World Methodist Council in Nairobi, Kenya, in 1989. That year the council addressed the realities of South African racial apartheid, formulating a careful statement advocating international economic sanctions to bring pressures on the South African government to abandon its racist policies. A leading official of an American company with heavy investments in South Africa not only refrained from speaking against the proposed statement, but he actually voted for it. Explaining his vote later, this Christian layman and company official declared that "I didn't come here as a representative of the ___ Corporation."

much a symptom of personal and social malaise as their cause—although substance abuse in our time is no less a problem than it was under frontier conditions. The movement was a stunning political success, with passage of the Eighteenth Amendment to the U.S. Constitution and appropriate implementing legislation. But it was also a stunning social failure, leading to widespread law violations, organized crime and contributing to disrespect for the law—and disrespect for the churches that were behind Prohibition. These churches themselves lost sight of the moral impulses that had led to their movement in their zeal to seek enforcement of the law. What had begun as a moral cause degenerated into a largely legalistic crusade. By the time the Eighteenth Amendment was repealed (with the Twenty-first Amendment), Prohibition had probably done more harm than good.[18]

Those American Christians in the prolife movement who have sought to criminalize abortion procedures might do well to reflect on such illustrations. Absent a broad public consensus of support for this cause, might its success lead to bitterness and disillusionment among millions of citizens who believe that abortion can sometimes be a morally responsible choice? Sometimes in our enthusiasm we neglect to distinguish between the morality of an action and the morality of laws intended to prohibit the action. Often there is and ought to be a close relationship between law and morality, but law is not always the best way to deal with perceived moral evils. Sometimes it is better to try to influence the culture and the behavior of individuals in other ways.

Celebrating success. Still, there have been important social justice issues that Christians have sought to address through public advocacy, sometimes with enduring success. The antislavery movement of the eighteenth and nineteenth centuries may be the most notable of these. Few people today would dispute the evil of chattel slavery. It is a terrible blight on American history, creating a tragic legacy that even today distorts our culture. The abolitionist movement was directed toward ending slavery through law, *requiring* (not just inviting) slave owners to free their slaves. I suppose it can be dis-

---

[18]Paul A. Carter makes a persuasive case that the human insensitivity and moralism of the Prohibition movement after its victories had much to do with the increasing secularism of American culture in the 1920s and 1930s. See Paul A. Carter, *The Decline and Revival of the Social Gospel: Social and Political Liberalism in American Protestant Churches* (Ithaca, N.Y.: Cornell University Press, 1954). Carter also attributes the secularism between the two world wars, in part, to the insensitivity of American churches to the vast carnage of World War I. Uncritical pulpit support for that conflict had joined enthusiastically in demonizing the enemy and painting the war effort as a great crusade to stamp out evil. Thoughtful but disillusioned cultural leaders were increasingly turned off by the churches.

puted whether a civil war—with its own awesome evils and tragedies—was finally necessary to preserve the Union and bring slavery to an end, or whether other alternatives could have succeeded within a reasonable time frame. There can be no dispute that slavery itself was evil in its essence and that it blighted vast numbers of lives, including, paradoxically, the slave owners themselves. Nor can it be disputed that sooner or later—preferably sooner than later—slavery had to be made illegal. In retrospect the arguments of Christian abolitionists were theologically convincing while those of their opponents were contrived and unconvincing. It is a good thing that many Christians sought to end slavery and that their efforts were ultimately crowned with success.

Similar things could be said about the Civil Rights movement. Intended to replace laws requiring racial discrimination with laws prohibiting it, this movement was hugely controversial within and beyond the churches. When it is said that Southern churches opposed the movement, it is forgotten that while that was generally true of Southern *white* churches, their African American counterparts were either actively engaged or quietly supportive in fearful silence. Such movement organizations as the NAACP, the Southern Christian Leadership Conference and the Congress of Racial Equality had substantial Christian and Jewish participation. During the 1960s the legislative advocacy aspect of the movement centered in the Leadership Conference on Civil Rights, with significant participation by the social action agencies of a number of denominations and the National Council of Churches. Such participation was significant politically, but it also helped keep the movement focused on nonviolence and racial reconciliation. The top leaders of the movement, especially Dr. Martin Luther King Jr., Dr. Ralph Abernathy and Rev. Andrew Young, were Protestant ministers. In some respects the key moment in the civil rights struggle was the Selma, Alabama, campaign, which came to focus in March 1955. This was especially important because it precipitated passage of the Voting Rights Act, and the right of suffrage helped to assure all other rights.

In the early years of the twentieth century, church bodies, inspired by what came to be called the Social Gospel movement, helped draw attention to the exploitation of child labor and the need for recognition of labor unions. Like the Civil Rights movement, the push for fairness in economic relations required churches to be realistic about political power. The churches were not always successful, and they may not always have been wise, but on the whole they helped make this country a land of greater social justice.

Issues Claiming the Churches' Attention

The *Book of Resolutions of the United Methodist Church* 2000,[19] a volume of some 850 pages, is a particularly good illustration of the tendency of contemporary mainline denominations to speak on a very wide range of social issues. The 338 statements and resolutions in this volume reflect varying degrees of factual knowledge, political astuteness and theological wisdom. Clearly they were not all written by the same person or group of persons, and it is inconceivable that all of the delegates to the general conferences adopting them could have devoted careful consideration to such a massive body of material. Still, most of these statements are thoughtfully developed, and collectively they represent an effort to make the church relevant to the issues of our time. This essay obviously could not analyze all of the resolutions and statements adopted even by this one denomination, but a sampling here may help illustrate the viewpoints and style included in this very large collection.

A resolution on child labor begins with the scriptural note that "in the Gospels, the disciples' attitude toward God was measured by their attitude toward children and their ability to 'become as a little child,' " continuing with the assertion that "the protection of childhood and the nurture of children are, therefore, among our most sacred human responsibilities." The resolution continues with factual observations about inhumanities faced by children in many countries and by their "being forced into labor under abusive and destructive conditions." It proceeds then to call for "ratification and enforcement of international labor conventions regarding child labor" and support for "legislative and administrative measure to enforce bans against the international trafficking in goods made by child labor." It includes a call "to support unilateral and multilateral aid and development policies that attack the root causes of child labor, such a lack of basic education, gender and caste prejudice, and unbalanced development schemes that disadvantage certain populations."[20]

A resolution on voting representation for the people of the District of Columbia calls attention to the fact that "no provision for voting representation in the Federal Legislature for residents of this Federal District was made in the Constitution or has been made at any time since." Considering this to be "an egregious moral wrong," the resolution affirms that "district citizens are entitled to political rights equal to those of other Americans, including voting rep-

---

[19]*Book of Resolutions of the United Methodist Church* (Nashville: United Methodist Publishing House, 2000). This volume contains the "Social Principles" of the United Methodist Church and official declarations by the church's General Conference, a body that meets once every four years.

[20]Ibid., pp. 179-80.

resentation in both houses of Congress," and it calls on the president and Congress to take action to provide such representation "by whatever means they should find suitable and appropriate."[21] In arguing for this position the resolution appeals to both national tradition and such practical considerations as the contributions the people of the District of Columbia make to the well-being of the nation. While there is little specifically theological argumentation in the resolution, it refers to the broader statements contained in the United Methodist Social Principles concerning democracy.

The abortion question has been especially challenging to churches along with the rest of American society. Reflecting the conflicted state of public opinion on this issue, the United Methodist Social Principles statement on abortion weaves its way uncertainly between recognizing that abortion can be justified under some circumstances and should be permitted by law. But at the same time, "our belief in the sanctity of unborn human life makes us reluctant to approve abortion."[22]

The church's position on the equally controversial issue of capital punishment is more direct: "The United Methodist church declares its opposition to the retention and use of capital punishment and urges its abolition." The position is argued partly on the basis of empirical studies that "have overwhelmingly failed to support the thesis that capital punishment deters homicide more effectively than does imprisonment."[23] But at a more basic theological level the statement asserts that "the death penalty . . . denies Christ's power to transform and restore all human beings." Christ, we are reminded, "came among us and suffered death. Christ also rose to new life for the sake of all. His suffering, death, and resurrection brought a new dimension to human life, the possibility of reconciliation with God through repentance. This gift is offered to all without exception."[24] The resolution emphasizes that "the United Methodist Church cannot accept retribution or social vengeance as a reason for taking human life [because] it violates our deepest belief in God as the Creator and Redeemer of humankind." The statement concludes with a call for action to United Methodists to "work in collaboration with other ecumenical and abolitionist groups for the abolition of the death penalty" and to "speak out against the death penalty to state governors, state and federal representatives."

---

[21]Ibid., p. 646.

[22]Ibid., p. 44.

[23]Ibid., p. 595.

[24]Ibid., p. 594. Astonishingly (in view of majority support for the death penalty in opinion polls of Americans), the United Methodist position was reaffirmed by a margin of 98 percent to 2 percent at the 2000 General Conference.

The homosexuality issue has been singularly divisive among the mainline churches. In that respect the United Methodist Church is quite typical. For thirty years the denomination has asserted among its Social Principles that "we do not condone the practice of homosexuality and consider this practice incompatible with Christian teaching."[25] In 1984 the General Conference applied this to ministry by prohibiting the ordination or appointment of "self-avowed practicing homosexuals," and in 1996 clergy were prohibited from presiding over ceremonies of homosexual union. Still, the church has emphasized the importance of ministry to gay and lesbian persons, and their inclusion in the life of the church. Most recently that point was underscored with the following declaration: "We implore families and churches not to reject or condemn their lesbian and gay members and friends." In relation to public policy the church's Social Principles includes a sweeping affirmation of "basic human rights and civil liberties" that should apply to all, regardless of sexual orientation. The church considers it to be "a clear issue of simple justice" that the basic rights of homosexual persons should be protected, including "their rightful claims where they have shared material resources, pensions, guardian relationships, mutual powers of attorney and other such lawful claims typically attendant to contractual relationships that involve shared contributions, responsibilities and liabilities, and equal protection before the law."[26] This lengthy list strikingly resembles the legal status of marital relationships, although the church elsewhere defines marriage as the relationship between a man and a woman. In a further resolution the church flatly declared that "the U.S. military should not exclude persons from service solely on the basis of sexual orientation."[27]

Issues of war and peace, and related problems concerning military service by Christians, have also received much attention in the mainline churches. Some of the mainline denominations are broadly pacifist in orientation, others fall more within the Christian just-war tradition and still others include both. It is fair to say that all churches consider war to be a problem for Christian conscience, and it would be difficult to find any statements by church bodies glorifying war as a positive good. United Methodism includes people of different persuasions. This church is not to be numbered among the peace churches (like Mennonites or Friends), but it has taken pains to support those of its members who choose to be conscientious objectors. Prior to the 2000 General

---

[25]Ibid., p. 43.
[26]Ibid., p. 49. This language was adopted by the General Conference in 1992.
[27]Ibid., p. 160.

Conference, the church's rhetoric could have been described as semipacifist, with the flat declaration that "war is incompatible with the teachings and example of Christ," but also with support for those who are conscientious participants. The 2000 General Conference modified its language in a more nuanced statement including reference to both the pacifist and just-war perspectives. It begins by saying that "we deplore war and urge the peaceful settlement of all disputes among nations," noting that Christians have long "struggled with the harsh realities of violence and war, for these evils clearly frustrate God's loving purposes for humankind." It then includes both of the basic Christian views by saying that "some of us believe that war and other acts of violence, are never acceptable to Christians" while most other Christians "regretfully realize that, when peaceful alternatives have failed, the force of arms may be preferable to unchecked aggression, tyranny and genocide."[28]

This sampling of positions taken by one rather typical denomination may help introduce the reader to the complexity of church witness for social justice in recent years. These statements, and the hundreds of others that could be exhibited alongside them, do illustrate the commitment by the church to bear witness to the implications of the faith in the arenas of public decision making. Invariably, the statements reflect multiple authorship and sometimes transparent efforts to accommodate contrasting views. That may not be all bad, for none of us can claim to have the last word on the issues facing humankind. Perhaps the voice of God can best be heard through the faithful, thoughtful and prayerful struggle of many persons to understand it.

How Effective Is the Church's Witness for Social Justice?
It is also evident from these samples that the church is not content to teach without also acting. Typically, the various resolutions and declarations call on Christians, churches and public officials to take suggested actions. Does that really happen?

Sometimes, surprisingly enough, it *does!* We've already seen how the churches contributed to the Civil Rights revolution and, before that, to the Prohibition movement. In my years in Washington, D.C., I have been aware of a number of other instances where church representatives have influenced public policy. Even when public officials pay no attention at all to the thousands of statements of the various denominations at national and local levels, the resolutions do serve one salutary purpose. They provide the occasion for serious debate within the church bodies, stimulating everybody to *think* more clearly

---

[28]Ibid., pp. 62-63.

about the relevance of the gospel to the world. Even heated exchanges can serve that function, although it is a sad thing when Christians lose sight of all they have in common.

I believe the churches could be even more effective and more faithful to the gospel if they spent more time developing public statements. Some church documents are carefully elaborated, with serious attention given to biblical and theological foundations and to responsible research on factual questions. Such documents are usually longer. Often they take more time to develop and involve more people. By contrast, some church statements—possibly even most of them—are written too quickly and seem to be content with stated conclusions. I do not consider that to be a reason for abandoning social witness, but we certainly can improve the way we do it.

Catholic Response

Clarke E. Cochran

Although the perspective Philip Wogaman articulates is most associated with mainline Protestantism, his account is highly ecumenical and draws frequently on Roman Catholic sources. This means that there is much in common with the Catholic perspective of my chapter. This ecumenical orientation of the social justice perspective is a key strength; however, its narrow focus on one theme furnishes a more fragile foundation than the comprehensive Anabaptist, Reformed and Catholic perspectives in this volume.

Similar to the Catholic account, and owing to the same natural-law foundation tracing to Aristotle, Wogaman describes the role of the state as acting and speaking for the entire community, particularly in its responsibility for social justice. Moreover, he describes social justice in quasi-natural-law terms with reference to Aristotle's definition of rendering to each his or her due. The theological modification of this natural purpose is that, under God, all are due retribution; in his mercy and justice, however, God opens the door of community to all.

Justice, therefore, includes everyone in community, which Wogaman interprets as participation in the life of society. His examples of the successes of the social justice perspective point in the same direction. The abolition and Civil Rights movements aimed at and produced the participation of African Americans and other excluded groups as full members of American community. Two of Wogaman's examples of specific issues also focus on participation and inclusion: voting representation for the District of Columbia and inclusion of homosexuals in the rights and responsibilities of citizenship.

These positions resonate deeply with Catholic social teaching. That teaching embraces Wogaman's community orientation as implicitly accepting a social account of the human person. It agrees that government has a natural basis and a fundamental role in promoting social justice. Catholic theology defends as well his specific examples of inclusion. Moreover, Wogaman's creation account stresses the same incarnational grounding of Christian life as the Catholic view, and his description of God's interest in the material conditions of life echoes the sacramental theme in Catholic social teaching. Finally, Wogaman's welcome and refreshing account of the importance of empirical knowledge in the social sciences and of experience in ministry (for example, Catholic or Methodist hospitals) echoes natural law, rationality and institutional themes within Catholicism.

Given all this, can there be any Catholic objection to the social justice perspective Wogaman advocates? In fact, there is, and at both theoretical and policy levels.

At the theoretical level, despite its attractiveness, the idea of government and social justice derived from citizen participation in articulating the fundamental and legitimate values of the community is too narrow. In Wogaman's account the state works when it reflects and acts legitimately on the fundamental values held by the people. This account is open to the objection that sin distorts popular values and distorts them in different ways in different times. Slavery was once legitimate; now it is not so. His footnote 18 on the churches' mistaken uncritical support of xenophobic attitudes during World War I illustrates how popular values, legitimately expressed, can go badly wrong for society and church. Ultimately, an account of social justice and government grounded on values and participation is a *process* account. Although legitimate process is indeed a foundational component of social justice, process can lead in unjust directions when divorced from substantive standards such as common good, defense of human life and dignity, and the preferential option for the poor. The more objective moral and political standards endorsed by the Catholic tradition can effectively criticize, challenge and transcend popular values because they are not essentially dependent on them.[1] Wogaman's social justice perspective is deficient on precisely this theoretical basis.

Some of his practical policy examples are equally troubling, and for two reasons: they move in the wrong direction or they are vague and noncommittal. For example, Wogaman's mild critique of the prolife movement for attempting to bring morality and law too close together would not sit well with Catholic social teaching's commitment to the defense of innocent life—a substantive moral principle that extends to life in the womb. Although the Catholic tradition agrees with Wogaman's general point that not all morality should be legally enforced, its commitment to a robust defense of life and to

---

[1]This is not to say that the Catholic Church has always done so or done so successfully; only that it possesses the theoretical and theological resources for this task.

the foundational importance of the right to life to all other rights points to law's vital role in protecting unborn life.

The Catholic Church joined with the mainline social justice churches early in the twentieth century in attacking child labor and laws that impaired the right of workers to organize and join labor unions. These two religious traditions joined later in the century to support the Civil Rights movement. They join now in opposition to capital punishment. Given these clear moral stands, it is difficult for Catholics to understand how a social justice commitment can, in Wogaman's description, "weave its way uncertainly" on abortion.

The same noncommittal stance seems to characterize Wogaman's summary of the Methodist positions on homosexuality and war and peace. Although the Catholic stance on war, summarized in my response to Sider's essay, shares some of the same ambivalence that I read in Wogaman's essay, I wanted to hear him speak more decisively on these questions in his own voice as a proponent of the social justice perspective. Finally, I wanted Wogaman to describe a social justice position on church-state relations generally and to indicate what that perspective says about the specific issue of public funding of faith-based health and social service programs. Without such discussion, it is difficult to know how far agreement extends between the Catholic perspective on public policy and the social justice perspective.

Classical Separation Response

Derek H. Davis

Philip Wogaman has written a typically erudite and pithy essay—this time on the topic of how he understands the social justice model practiced by many mainline churches in the United States. I find what he says to be virtually unassailable. That said, since this is a volume that attempts to explain a range of church-state models, I will comment on why I think that social justice advocacy fits within the church-state framework as practiced historically in the United States, since there are many citizens in this country who fail to understand why political advocacy by churches does not violate the separation of church and state. For me, the discussion of social justice advocacy by mainline churches and others is descriptive of what should be advocated within America's church-state framework rather than a model of how the church-state framework should work.

As I tried to say in my own essay in this volume, separation of church and state is indeed important to the American way of life, but it hardly describes all aspects of the interplay between religion and state. This is readily seen in the way that the American system encourages the participation of religious voices in the political process. Were the system one of *complete* separation, it would not countenance the involvement of communities that enter public discourse seeking to persuade government officials of the merits of framing law and public policy to reflect their own distinctive perspectives.

The right of religious communities to engage in political advocacy has been recognized for all of American history. In the years leading up to the American Revolution, for example, the churches assumed a leading role in the political debate on the question of whether the colonies should go to war with the mother country. In the nineteenth century the major causes for political action among the churches and other religious groups were Sunday mail delivery, slavery, temperance and nonsectarian education. In the twentieth century the engagement of religious bodies in the body politic grew to cover a wide range of issues, including social justice, war and peace, homosexuality, abortion, civil rights and poverty. Today more than one hundred religious groups maintain public affairs offices in the nation's capital to organize the lobbying efforts of their constituencies. These groups are highly effective in keeping religion central to the framing of law and public policy. Wogaman's essay is certainly convincing on this point.

Given the time-honored right of religious bodies to be active participants in the American political process, it is not surprising that the United States Supreme Court has not seriously challenged this basic right. For example, in *Walz v. Tax Commission* (1970), the Court held: "Adherents of particular faiths and individual churches frequently take strong positions on public issues, including . . . vigorous advocacy of legal and constitutional positions. Of course, churches as much as secular bodies and private citizens have that right."

Nevertheless, religious groups are subject to losing their tax exemptions for excessive political expenditures or for endorsing political candidates. Otherwise, they enjoy essentially the same rights as secular groups to participate in the political process. Many American citizens complain about the active role that religious groups play in political discourse, even if their advocacy relates to matters that are generally secular—such as poverty, taxation, welfare, race relations, war and peace, and the like. The principles of democracy prevail here, such that the rights of every person or group in American society, religious or secular, that wishes to contribute to democratic governance is free to do so, even encouraged to do so, even though such participation constitutes a technical violation of the principle of church-state separation. *Complete* separation would mean banning the activities of mainline churches and religious lobbies whose sole reason for existence is to influence lawmaking and public policy according to religiously inspired perspectives. Citizens get their values from somewhere, and there is no valid reason to prohibit religious persons from engaging in politics just because their values emanate from religious worldviews. Although many of these lobbies, unfortunately, attempt to issue dictates rather than offer advice, mandates rather than persuasive arguments, the great majority of them have learned to submit their perspectives with some degree of humility, recognizing that America is a democracy shaped by many views, not a theocracy shaped by a few.

Although religious *arguments* are permitted in political discourse, *legislation* that advances a religious purpose generally is not, because of the judicial requirement, pursuant to the *Lemon* test (*Lemon v. Kurtzman* [1970]): that governmental action reflect a secular purpose, that it not have the primary effect of advancing or inhibiting religion, and that it not create an excessive entangle-ment between religion and government.

In terms of political theory the *Lemon* test (although adjustments have been made to it since 1971) reflects the Court's understanding that the nation is es-sentially a *liberal* state rather than a *religious* state. However, according to most scholarly accounts of the liberal state, this designation carries requirements that are in addition to the mandates of the *Lemon* test. Most significantly, par-ticipants' dialogue in public discourse within a liberal democracy must be in-telligible to other participants. Since religious language is unintelligible to many citizens, it should be translated into secular language accessible to everyone. Religious motivation might lie beneath the veneer of certain legisla-tion, but the legislation itself must be couched in essentially secular language. By most accounts this requirement is a logical antecedent to the *Lemon* test, which requires that the final product of public discourse—legislation—carry a secular orientation.

The work of John Rawls, of course, is pivotal for the entire tradition of liberal political thought. In *A Theory of Justice* (1990), he made the basic points just enu-merated in support of a secular basis for the liberal state. Rawls's work has been highly influential in the United States and has widespread support among po-litical theorists, albeit in varying degrees. In recent years, however, liberal po-litical theory has been challenged by a host of communitarian thinkers, all com-plaining essentially that Rawlsian liberal theory unnecessarily undermines the viable contributions to the public good that specifically religious viewpoints can make. Among these critics has been Stephen Carter, who argues in *The Cul-ture of Disbelief* (1994) that religious arguments and even religion-based legisla-tion should be countenanced in a liberal democratic framework.

It is my view, contrary to Rawls and affirming Carter, that religious *argu-ments* in public discourse generally should be permitted. In this regard I have no problem with the mainline churches engaging in political discourse, a po-sition certainly in keeping with Wogaman's chapter. Provided they do not use theological means to achieve political ends, which would be tantamount to at-tempting to erect a religious state, I think mainline churches should have full and complete opportunity to make known their positions on various issues in the give and take of political debate. Common sense may dictate that on many occasions the one advancing a religious argument should translate that argu-ment into secular language in order that it become more intelligible and con-vincing to others, but that should be the decision of the one advancing the ar-gument. Nevertheless, it is suggested here, contrary to Carter and affirming Rawls, that when the public debate on a particular issue is completed and legislation is to be enacted—when the relative free-for-all that is American liberal democracy in which every conceivable viewpoint (religious and secular alike) has been entertained—*the legislation enacted*, consistent with the *Lemon* test, should reflect essentially *secular* aims and effects.

The great weight of evidence is that the Founding Fathers intended, as indicated most demonstrably by their purposeful omission of God's name in the Constitution, to create what is generally referred to today as a liberal state. The decision to break with traditional political theory that placed human government under divine authority was the result of their belief that the power to frame a new government derived not immediately from heaven but from the American people. The Founders created a government that was to be "of the people, by the people, and for the people." This in no way is a denial of their personal religious (mostly Christian) convictions, but the new federal government was to be one in which the people were the responsible parties, not God. The product of public discourse was to be human law, not holy law. This always has been and remains the essence of a liberal state. Advocacy for social justice practiced by mainline churches that recognizes the equal right of other secular and nonsecular groups to make their own contributions to America's political order is essential to the maintenance of American democracy.

I agree with virtually all of what Wogaman wrote; I hope he will find similar agreement with what I have written.

Principled Pluralist Response

Corwin Smidt

Rather than repeating certain preliminary points that I wish to make about each of the Christian perspectives examined in this volume, I would urge the reader to read first my opening paragraph of response to the classical separationist perspective (see p. 117). What was said in that paragraph applies also to the social justice perspective.

Principled pluralists share many theological positions with those who advocate the social justice perspective, but diverge in certain other important matters. Like those who advocate the social justice perspective, principled pluralists hold that the state has a positive role to play (e.g., as stated in the preamble to the Constitution of the United States, "to promote the general welfare" and "to secure the blessings of liberty") beyond that of simply restraining evil (e.g., as noted in the same preamble, "to provide for the common defense" and "to insure domestic tranquility"). Likewise, just as the social justice perspective promotes securing justice as a primary, if not the primary, task of the state, so too does the principled pluralist perspective.

However, the social justice and principled pluralist perspectives differ in some important ways regarding the state's responsibility to secure justice. First, in the final analysis, it would appear that the social justice advocates are more likely than principled pluralists to give greater power and responsibility to the state for enacting legislation to address social problems, as the principled pluralist perspective, through its notion of sphere sovereignty, provides a greater foundation for the role of "civil society" in addressing at least certain kinds of social problems. Civil society is that domain in which people act voluntarily; such action, while conducted within the law, is not compelled by law. It is the realm of social networks, churches, voluntary associations and nonprofit organizations. But it is instructive that the social justice perspective outlined in this volume does not address the role of civil society and its relationship to the role of government. And while the chapter does not reveal where

advocates of the social justice perspective would necessarily stand in relationship to government funding of faith-based initiatives, it is likely that such advocates are, at best, divided in their support of such legislation. It should be
noted that the principled pluralist perspective does not contend that civil society is the realm in which every social problem should be addressed; the state
has a legitimate and important role to play in securing justice. But the principled pluralist perspective recognizes that civil society can and should have a
role to play in addressing social problems, and through its recognition of
sphere sovereignty, it provides a philosophical foundation for its being able to
do so.

Second, the principled pluralist perspective tends to have a broader conception of the state securing justice than does the social justice perspective. According to the social justice perspective, securing justice occurs within a community. Nevertheless, its notion of justice is primarily concerned with each
person being given his or her due (whether in terms of economic resources,
health care or legal rights). Within the principled pluralist perspective, justice
is broader in nature, as it extends beyond such responsibilities for justice simply between and among individuals. In addition, given the presence of different spheres of authority under its notion of sphere sovereignty, principled pluralists hold that one of the tasks of the state in securing justice is to ensure that
each sphere of authority does not exceed its rightful boundaries in terms of
seeking to exercise its authority.

There are also other points of convergence and divergence between the social justice and principled pluralist perspectives. Principled pluralists also reject "scientism," also recognize the role of the empirical sources of knowledge
and also contend that data and human reason should be marshaled in addressing the gulf between what is and what ought to be. However, principled pluralists are likely to be somewhat more skeptical or modest in terms of any resulting conclusions drawn or prescriptions advanced than might advocates of
the social justice perspective.

This is due to two different factors. First, given their Reformed roots, principled pluralists are more likely to emphasize the role that sin continues to
play in shaping our thinking and discernment as well as in human responses
to changing legislation. Thus, while particular reforms and legislation may
help to address certain social problems, we must be cautious in claiming that
such reforms and legislations will solve such problems. Legislative efforts may
alleviate various aspects of the problem, but they likely will not totally eliminate the problem. Moreover, in response to the new legislation, new problems
will likely arise as well.

Second, principled pluralists are pluralists in that they recognize the existence of different worldviews, with the nature of "truth" varying by particular worldview. Thus principled pluralists are likely to be less optimistic than social justice advocates about the likelihood of arriving at some broadly based agreement on matters of root causes of, and likely solutions to eliminate, such social problems.

Anabaptist Response

Ronald J. Sider

I do not find Philip Wogaman's theological discussion of justice very helpful. He seems to want to argue that the biblical teaching about the unmerited grace that God bestows on believers in Christ is important and relevant in answering the question, what is due every person in society? He also thinks the story of the vineyard owner who pays everyone the same wage no matter how long each worked is relevant. (One wonders if Wogaman thinks the carpenter who works on his house for one hour deserves the same payment as the carpenter who works ten hours.)

Wogaman says the biblical material on God's undeserved saving grace means that what is due every person is "to be included in God's intended community of the covenant" (p. 220). This statement is ambiguous. Is the community referred to here the human community or the community of redeemed Christians? It is not clear. Later, however, Wogaman speaks of the "community of humankind," so perhaps he means society in general. But then one must ask whether (and if so, in what precise way) God's gracious, unmerited act of freely giving salvation to those who believe in Christ is really a fundamental clue about what is due each person in the social order.

I think it confuses rather than clarifies to ignore the difference between creation and redemption. The fact that in salvation God freely forgives us without any merit on our part does not mean that justice in society means that goods (salaries, for example) should be distributed in a just society without any attention to the contributions that different members of society make. Normally, the carpenter who works only one hour on my house does not deserve the same pay as the one who works ten hours, and justice demands that I should not pay them the same amount.

As I argued in my chapter, I think there is some analogy between what the church community and the larger society should do. I certainly do not mean to deny any connection (even for the definition of justice) between creation and redemption. But we must state with precision what the connections are. Vague generalization misleads more than enlightens.

Contributors

Clarke E. Cochran is professor of political science and adjunct professor in the Department of Health Organization Management at Texas Tech University, specializing in religion and politics, political philosophy, and health care policy. Dr. Cochran received his B.A. in political science from Brown University and his M.A. and Ph.D. in political science from Duke University. Professor Cochran held the position of Research Fellow in the Erasmus Institute at the University of Notre Dame (1998-1999) and the Shannon Chair in Catholic Studies at Nazareth College (spring 2001). Dr. Cochran is author of several books, including *Character, Community, and Politics* (University of Alabama Press, 1982), *Religion in Public and Private Life* (Routledge, 1990), (coauthor) *American Public Policy: An Introduction* (Wadsworth, 8th ed., 2006), and numerous articles and reviews, including articles in the *American Political Science Review*, *Journal of Politics*, and *Polity*. Dr. Cochran's writing on Catholic healthcare has appeared in the *Journal of Church and State*; *Christian Bioethics*; and *Commonweal*. His most recent book, coauthored with David Carroll Cochran, is *Catholics, Politics, and Public Policy: Beyond Left and Right* (Orbis, 2003). Professor Cochran was ordained a deacon in the Catholic Church in 1981. He serves at St. John Neumann Church in Lubbock and directs the Deacon Formation Program for the Diocese of Lubbock.

Derek H. Davis (B.A., M.A., J.D., Baylor University; Ph.D., University of Texas at Dallas) is dean of the college of humanities and interim dean of the graduate school at University of Mary Hardin-Baylor. He was formerly director of the J. M. Dawson Institute of Church-State Studies and professor of political science, Baylor University, and editor of *Journal of Church and State*. He is the author or editor of sixteen books, including *Original Intent: Chief Justice Rehnquist & the Course of American Church-State Relations* (Prometheus, 1991) and *Religion and the Continental Congress, 1774-1789: Contributions to Original Intent* (Oxford, 2000). He has also published more than 135 articles in various journals and periodicals. He serves numerous organizations given to the protection of religious freedom in American and international contexts.

P. C. Kemeny (Ph.D., Princeton) is professor of religion and humanities at Grove City College. He is the author of *Princeton in the Nation's Service: Reli-*

gious Ideals and Educational Practice, 1868-1928 (Oxford University Press, 1998) and coeditor with Henry Warner Bowden of *American Church History: A Reader* (Abingdon, 1998). He has received research grants from the American Philosophical Society, the American Academy of Religion, Massachusetts Historical Society, Wabash Center for Teaching and Learning in Religion and Theology, and the American Historical Association.

Ronald J. Sider (Ph.D., Yale) is professor of theology, holistic ministry and public policy, and director of the Sider Center on Ministry and Public Policy at Palmer (formerly Eastern Baptist) Theological Seminary, and president of Evangelicals for Social Action. A widely known evangelical speaker and writer, Sider has spoken on six continents, published twenty-nine books and scores of articles. His *Rich Christians in an Age of Hunger* was recognized by *Christianity Today* as one of the one hundred most influential religious books of the twentieth century. His most recent books are *The Scandal of the Evangelical Conscience: Why Are Christians Living Just Like the Rest of the World?* and *Just Generosity: A New Vision for Overcoming Poverty in America* and *Churches That Make a Difference: Reaching Your Community with Good News and Good Works* (with Phil Olson and Heidi Unruh). Sider is the publisher of *PRISM* magazine and a contributing editor of *Christianity Today* and *Sojourners*. He has lectured at scores of colleges and universities around the world, including Yale, Harvard, Princeton and Oxford.

Corwin E. Smidt (Ph.D., Iowa) serves as professor of political science and as director of the Henry Institute for the Study of Christianity and Politics at Calvin College. He is author, editor or coauthor of ten books (including *Pulpit and Politics; Religion as Social Capital* and *Evangelicalism: The Next Generation*) as well as numerous book chapters and articles in refereed journals. Professor Smidt has also served as executive director of the Religion and Politics section of the American Political Science Association and as president of Christians in Political Science.

J. Philip Wogaman (Ph.D., Boston University) is the retired senior minister of Foundry United Methodist Church in Washington, D.C. He is also the former dean of Wesley Theological Seminary where he taught Christian ethics from 1966 to 2002. Dr. Wogaman has served as president of both the Society of Christian Ethics of the United States and Canada and the American Theological Society. He has authored more than thirteen books, including *Christian Ethics: A Historical Introduction*, *A Christian Method of Moral Judgment*, *Christian Moral Judgment*, *Christian Perspectives on Politics, Economics and Ethics: A Christian Inquiry*, *From the Eye of the Storm: A Pastor to the President Speaks Out*. In addition to his contribution to the field of Christian ethics, Dr. Wogaman was a delegate to the United Methodist General Conference, was a member of the World Methodist Council from 1986-1991, and past president of the Interfaith Alliance board of directors.

Index of Names

Abernathy, Ralph, 232

Adam, 129, 130, 228

Adams, John, 95, 100, 101

Aristotle, 47, 218, 221, 238

Asch, Solomon, 228

Assmann, Hugo, 223

Audi, Robert, 34, 35, 36

Augustine, 169

Backus, Isaac, 96, 97

Bacon, Leonard, 17, 18

Barnes, Albert, 18

Barth, Karl, 174, 222, 225, 226

Bellah, Robert, 108

Benedict XVI, 49, 66, 199

Berger, Peter, 32, 141

Berns, Walter, 99, 102, 219

Bhaktivedanta, Swami A. C., 26

Black, Hugo, 11, 25, 63, 84, 119

Bonhoeffer, Dietrich, 226

Bonino, José Miguez, 223, 224

Bradley, Gerard, 89

Bush, George W., 11, 12, 31, 32, 63, 121, 150, 151, 191, 197, 203, 206

Caesar, 112, 143, 158

Calvin, John, 13, 98, 127, 134, 135, 136, 157, 159, 218

Carlson-Theis, Stanley, 150

Carter, Jimmy, 28

Carter, Paul A., 231

Carter, Stephen, 30, 35, 36, 243

Casanova, José, 32, 33, 43, 47

Clinton, William J., 11, 125, 191

Cobb, Sanford, 80

Cochran, Clarke, 13, 14, 39, 40, 47, 49, 52, 62, 67, 74, 75, 76, 77, 78, 79, 114, 154, 198, 238

Cone, James, 223

Constantine, 60, 134, 180

Cotton, John, 98, 99

Cyrus, 188

Davis, Derek, 13, 18, 21, 67, 68, 80, 88, 101, 104, 105, 114, 115, 116, 118, 119, 121, 122, 123, 124, 125, 126, 157, 158, 171, 191, 202, 203, 241

Dawson, J. M., 13, 68, 97, 98, 104, 191

Day, Dorothy, 32, 45

Deutsch, Karl, 185

DiIulio, John, Jr., 12, 191

Dobson, Ed, 31

Durkheim, Émile, 109

Eck, Diana L., 25, 26, 36

Edwards, Jonathan, 18, 147

Elshtain, Jean Bethke, 30, 35

Eve, 16, 129, 130

Falwell, Jerry, 27, 28, 31

Farmer, Paul, 45

Franklin, Benjamin, 40, 43, 105, 124

Friesen, Duane, 174, 185

Frost, Robert, 220

Gandhi, 186, 187, 189, 213

Greenawalt, Kent, 35

Griswold, Stanley, 95

Grounds, Vernon, 28

Handy, Robert T., 16, 19, 20, 21, 22

Hengel, Martin, 177

Henry, Carl F. H., 28

Herod the Great, 176

Hitler, Adolf, 182, 187

Hodge, Charles, 18

Hudson, Winthrop, 12, 13, 22

Hunter, James Davison, 29

Husserl, Edmund, 48

Jackson, Andrew, 30, 101

Jefferson, Thomas, 21, 25, 84, 85, 95, 97, 98, 101, 124

John Paul II, 48, 49, 54, 125, 199

John XXIII, 49, 76, 79

John, the apostle, 133

Jones, Jim, 26

Josephus, 179

Kennedy, John F., 22, 76

King, Martin Luther, Jr., 186, 187, 232

Knox, John, 127

Kraemer, Hendrik, 222

Kuyper, Abraham, 30, 135, 136, 137, 140, 155, 157, 163

Laycock, Douglas, 88

Leland, John, 96, 97, 98

Levy, Leonard, 84, 89, 90, 102

Lincoln, Abraham, 18, 19

Livermore, Samuel, 88

Locke, John, 82, 83, 219

Luther, Martin, 98, 134, 169, 178, 180, 182, 186, 211, 216, 218, 232

Lynn, Barry, 12, 100, 107

Machiavelli, Niccolo, 217

Madison, James, 85, 86, 87, 88, 90, 94, 95, 97, 98, 101

Marcion, 225

Marcos, 186

McGraw, Barbara A., 82

Mecklin, John, 98

Meeter, H. Henry, 132

Melton, J. Gordon, 26

Miller, Timothy, 26

Monsma, Stephen, 68, 127, 140, 144, 146, 147, 150

Moore, G. E. , 102, 227

Murray, John Courtney, 111, 124, 164

Neuhaus, Richard John, 11, 33, 36, 141, 145

Niebuhr, H. Richard, 173

Niebuhr, Reinhold, 171, 180, 210, 222

Noll, Mark A., 18,

19, 21, 86

North, Gary, 140

Nozick, Robert, 219

Paine, Thomas, 94

Paul VI, 49

Paul, the apostle, 133, 143, 172, 183, 188, 211, 220

Perry, Michael J., 33, 34, 36

Peter, 112, 177

Piper, John, 178

Pius XI, 58, 76

Ramsey, Paul, 229

Rand, Ayn, 219

Rauschenbusch, Walter, 23, 24, 79

Rawls, John, 34, 36, 243

Riley, William Bell, 24

Robertson, Pat, 29, 31

Rorty, Richard, 34

Ruether, Rosemary Radford, 223

Rutledge, Wiley, 106

Schweizer, Eduard, 178

Scott, Robert C., 12

Segundo, Juan Luis, 223

Sherman, Amy, 13

Sider, Ronald J., 13, 28, 74, 114, 121,

162, 169, 171, 176, 177, 187, 191, 197, 198, 199, 200, 202, 203, 204, 210, 211, 212, 213, 240, 248

Simons, Menno, 170

Skillen, James, 12, 49, 137, 140, 147, 150

Smidt, Corwin, 13, 72, 117, 127, 146, 154, 155, 156, 157, 159, 160, 162, 163, 164, 165, 166, 168, 200, 207, 245

Smith, Christian, 30, 33

Smith, Timothy L., 16

Stalin, Joseph, 224

Stephen, 220

Theodosius, 110

Thomas Aquinas, 43, 162, 218

Thomas, Cal, 31

Thomas, M. M., 222

Thornwell, James Henley, 18

Turner, John, 99, 100

Wallis, Jim, 28

Walzer, Michael, 16

Washington, George, 100

Weber, Max, 63,

146, 216

Weyrich, Paul, 31

Williams, Abraham, 95

Williams, Peter W., 25

Williams, Roger, 92, 96

Wills, Garry, 32

Wilson, John F., 16, 19, 25, 86, 92

Wogaman, J. Philip, 13, 76, 123, 124, 164, 210, 215, 216, 227, 238, 239, 240, 241, 242, 243, 244, 248

Wolters, Al , 129, 133

Wolterstorff, Nicholas, 15, 35, 36

Wood, James E., Jr., 84, 87, 99

Wuthnow, Robert, 29

Yoder, John Howard, 171, 173, 174, 184, 185, 186, 210

Young, Andrew, 232

Zechariah, 177

Zwingli, Ulrich, 127, 169